J. D Ricards

Catholic Christianity And Modern Unbelief

J. D Ricards

Catholic Christianity And Modern Unbelief

ISBN/EAN: 9783337007294

Printed in Europe, USA, Canada, Australia, Japan

Cover: Foto ©Lupo / pixelio.de

More available books at **www.hansebooks.com**

CATHOLIC CHRISTIANITY
AND
MODERN UNBELIEF.

A PLAIN AND BRIEF STATEMENT
OF
The Real Doctrines of the Roman Catholic Church,

AS OPPOSED

To those falsely attributed to her, by Christians who reject her authority, and by Unbelievers in Revelation; that thus

A CONTRAST

May be easily drawn between the "Faith once delivered to the Saints,"

AND

The Conflicting Theories, and Scientific Guesses of the present Age; and serving as a

REFUTATION

To the assaults of modern Infidelity.

BY THE

RIGHT REV. J. D RICARDS, D.D.
Bishop of Retimo, and Vicar Apostolic of the Eastern Vicariate of the Cape Colony.

SECOND EDITION

New York, Cincinnati, and St. Louis:
BENZIGER BROTHERS,
Printers to the Holy Apostolic See.
1884.

COPYRIGHT, 1884, BY BENZIGER BROTHERS.

❖ DEDICATION. ❖

TO THE CLERGY AND RELIGIOUS
OF

The Vicariate of the Eastern Districts of the Cape Colony, South Africa,

WHO HAVE BORNE PATIENTLY WITH MY MANY SHORT-COMINGS AND IMPERFECTIONS,
AND HAVE FAITHFULLY AND ZEALOUSLY CO-OPERATED WITH ME IN EVERY
UNDERTAKING FOR THE HONOR AND GLORY OF GOD, AND THE PLANT-
ING AND FOSTERING OF CATHOLIC CHRISTIANITY, IN THE PORTION
OF SOUTH AFRICA COMMITTED TO MY PASTORAL CHARGE,

THIS BOOK,

WITH EVERY FEELING OF ESTEEM AND ATTACHMENT, AND WITH A GRATEFUL
REMEMBRANCE OF MANY KINDNESSES RECEIVED,
IS RESPECTFULLY INSCRIBED,
BY

THE AUTHOR.

All I have written I believe to be trustworthy, and in accordance with the constant teaching of the Holy Catholic Church; nevertheless I humbly submit everything contained in this book to the unerring judgment of the same Holy Church.

✢ J. D. RICARDS, Ep. & Vic. Ap.,
Grahamstown, South Africa, June 23d, 1884.

PREFACE.

This work was suggested to me by a man of more than ordinary powers of observation and intelligence, who had travelled over every part of the United States, and through most of the British colonies. His was not superficial travelling; his duties led him to stay for weeks, and months, and even years, in some of the States, and in particular districts; and the same duties gave him an insight into the religious wants of the people he visited. He told me that a book which would treat, in a popular way, the religious theories now so fashionable outside the Catholic Church, and contrast them with orthodox teaching, would be welcome and useful to many. I distrusted exceedingly my powers to accomplish a task, not altogether foreign to my experience; but on consideration that it might help in a small way even to promote the honor and glory of God, I accepted it.

It will be manifest to any one who reads the introduction or glances over the headings of the chapters, that I make no pretensions whatever to scholarship: the life of a missionary Bishop is almost an effectual barrier to careful and prolonged study and to the means of gratifying such tastes. I have, however, been observant of the currents of religious thought outside the Catholic Church in the colony where I have spent thirty-five years of my life as priest or Bishop; and I have occasionally, when I believed it was my duty to check their turbulent course, especially whenever they seemed to assail the ground of Catholic teaching, endeavored to do so to the best of my ability. One cannot travel much, as I have done, over the large area confided to my spiritual care without encountering many un-Catholic notions; and it has been my constant practice to watch attentively these straws of religious opinion, and with the help of such books as I could collect, to examine what was the source of these peculiar views.

It was always a pleasure, not alone in the interests of orthodox teaching, but for the sake of communicating the results of my reading to men remarkable for that outspoken freedom of thought, which marks young countries, to "give reasons for the faith that is in me." It was often highly gratifying to be able thus to remove deep-seated prejudices, and to show those who, by their pleased and grateful attention, invited such explanation, that Catholics were not quite as bad as the teachers of error represented them to be. The frequent remark, "You surprise me," "Is it so, really?" "Can what you say be the real truth?" "How different is what you say from what I have always heard!" often made me hopeful that those with whom I conversed might push their inquiries farther.

This habit of life will explain much that might otherwise be almost unintelligible to readers of the book in Catholic countries. The bold daring of the objections and the answers, so far removed from anything like scholastic precision, would seem to indicate a state of thought and feeling almost unknown to those of the "Household of the Faith." This must be my apology for much that is not found in the pages of ordinary works of a controversial character.

PREFACE. 7

Indeed, this book can scarcely be considered a polemical work at all. There is manifestly a plunge *in medias res*, without any attempt to prepare the way by building up a solid starting-point of sound principles and elaborate arguments. Possibly this absence of formality may cause the book to be more generally read than it otherwise would be. I can assure those who may be thus attracted to examine its contents, that their reading will not be impeded by any show of learning or stiff reasoning derived from treatises on theology and metaphysics.

My object has been throughout to state the difficulties urged by unbelief against Catholic Christianity plainly and even forcibly—much more forcibly than they have been put to me by travelling companions, and men whom I have met, disposed to discuss religious questions. The answers are directed chiefly to common-sense, and are supported by plain matter-of-fact demonstrations carefully selected, on account of their simplicity, from hosts of others more suited to the schools.

The whole plan of the work is conceived on the same principles. I first endeavor to show what Catholic Christianity is as a whole, regarded from the point of view of a believer; how all its doctrines, mysteries, sacraments, worship, and practices spring from a right understanding of the great mystery—God in the flesh, which forms the basis of all revealed religion. I then carefully eliminate this body of doctrine from the misunderstandings and misrepresentations to which it is commonly subjected, distinguish it from the doctrines of Christian sects, and explain fully these differences on the important questions of Justification, Free-will, Grace, and Predestination. If at times this leads me into the path of controversy, I have been careful to turn aside from the well-beaten track as soon as it was possible, satisfying myself with noting, in characters that cannot be mistaken by ordinary intelligence, the essential marks of true Catholic teaching.

When this has been effected, and Catholic Christianity stands forth in its dogmas and practices as I revere and love it, and as I believe it is revered and loved by the two hundred millions of my fellow-Catholics throughout the world, I contrast its sublime grandeur, its venerable antiquity, and its unchanging truth with the fascinations of unbelief.

I do not enter minutely into the analysis of these theories that are the fashion of the hour. It is unnecessary to do so. They are self-conflicting, like their teachers, "tossed to and fro, and carried about with every wind of doctrine," and ever dashing against the sound principles of revealed religion, as established and bound together by the labors of Christian scholars in every age, on the solid foundation laid by Christ Himself.

There is nothing worthy of serious study in any of these ephemeral systems that amuse the fancies of a frivolous and unthinking generation.

"We live," said the late Lord Beaconsfield, "in an age when young men prattle about protoplasm and when young ladies, in golden saloons, unconsciously talk Atheism."

"Positive polity," says another able writer, "is composed of concrete and abstract, positive and metaphysical elements of fact and fiction, of entity and non-entity." It would be a mere loss of time to pick and choose among these glittering toys, sometimes facts, and more often fictions, set before the public by unbelieving scientific writers, and out of these elements to construct something worth battering down by theological argument.

When the scientific teachers themselves understand what they teach, and unite in giving the world something like a system, it will be time enough for the upholders of revealed religion to refute it.

As one of the distinguished lecturers before the Christian Evidence Society says of the grand theory of Development : " Development is in truth as amazing and incomprehensible a mystery as creation. It seems to be but another word for creation. Only they who affect to use it instead of the word *creation* insist upon creation without a creator. The unintelligent and unconscious universe, in their view, is continually creating itself—Professor Huxley's protoplasm breaks it down. All scientific evidence is opposed to the idea that protoplasm was developed out of inorganic matter. The hypothesis of spontaneous life-generation appears to be exploded. Science at any rate, on its own positive principles, has no right whatever to pretend that life has ever been developed out of what was not living."

Just so, at one time in the world's history, we are told by the leaders of progress, everything was inorganic and dead ; then that all was living.

Whence did life come ? It could not be developed. Was it then created ? When scientific men are agreed on this one point—the origin of life—then no doubt there will appear able supporters of revealed religion to demonstrate to an interested public that the source of life is the great, omnipotent, and all-knowing personal God, " by Whom all things were made, and without Whom was made nothing that was made."

In the meantime, and until progress has laid before the world its demonstration of the origin of life, Christians of all denominations can rest securely on the words of the inspired writer, "Thou Thyself O Lord, alone, Thou hast made heaven, and the heaven of heavens, and all the hosts thereof: the earth and all the things that are in it: the seas, and all that are therein; and Thou givest life to all these things, and the host of heaven adoreth Thee" (2 Esdras ix. 6).

CONTENTS.

	PAGE
DEDICATION	3
PREFACE	5
INTRODUCTION	13

CHAPTER

I. Catholic Christianity and its Contrasts............... 35
II. Catholic Christianity and its Mysteries............... 55
III. The Incarnation, the Centre and Soul of Catholic Christianity..................................... 78
IV. Catholic Christianity Developed in the Sacramental Principle....................................... 96
V. Catholic Christianity in some Practical Aspects........ 113
VI. A Glimpse of Catholic Christianity as seen by Faith.... 132
VII. A Further View of Catholic Christianity through its Forms of Worship............................... 150
VIII. Catholic Christianity Misunderstood by Free thinkers.. 171
IX. Catholic Christianity in Relation to Education and Marriage....................................... 191
X. Catholic Christianity as Opposed to Emotional Christianity.. 209
XI. Catholic Christianity, Justification, and Sanctity....... 228
XII. Catholic Christianity untinged by the Gloom of Predestination.................................... 246

CHAPTER	PAGE
XIII. Catholic Christianity and Divine Grace	263
XIV. Catholic Christianity and Material Prosperity	277
XV. Catholic Christianity and Exclusive Salvation	297
XVI. Catholic Christianity and the Alleged Errors of the Sacred Scriptures	316
XVII. Catholic Christianity and some Popular "isms"	337
XVIII. Catholic Christianity and Realism	354
XIX. Catholic Christianity and Spiritism	368
XX. Conclusion	384

INTRODUCTION.

IF one could calmly contemplate the great stream of human life as it rolls on toward the ocean of eternity, and with a keen power of perception, such as is rarely given to finite reason, grasp the aims and projects of the masses as they are swept onward in their rapid course, he would soon be convinced that few among the many millions concern themselves about "the wide, the unbounded prospect" that lies before them after death. It is not simply that "shadows, clouds, and darkness rest upon it," but that they do not care or concern themselves to look forward, and try to penetrate the dark future. Life with its busy cares absorbs the whole attention of the many, and if Death and its immortal consequences roughly obtrude upon their day-dreams, the grim phantom is at once relegated to the land of myths and shadows.

The blighting curse of the present age is the total absence of serious thought about the great hereafter. Well may the words of the prophet be applied to the myriads who are so fascinated with the joys and pursuits of the present short-lived time as to take no precautions whatever against the wreck and ruin of all that should be most dear to beings who "shall never die:"—"With desolation is all the land made desolate; because there is none that considereth in the heart" (Jeremias xii. 11). Men will *talk* occasionally about these all-important subjects, but they will not *think*. They will even jest and trifle about them, if they can in no other way shake off the gloomy vision; and as "the fool hath said"—not thought—"in his heart, there is no God" (Psalm xiii. 1), so will they who "love the world and the things that are in the world" say and affect to believe that there is no future to cause them apprehension.

I believe that no one of ordinary intelligence and observation will deny that unbelief, the offspring of frivolity and thoughtlessness, is rapidly spreading over the whole civilized world. It is not philosophical and reasoning Infidelity that is causing whole nations, in this nineteenth century, to turn away from God and His Christ and the hopes of Faith, but thoughtless and flippant ridicule of the joys and terrors set before us by revelation. It is utter carelessness and indifference about sacred things that is doing this wide-spread mischief.

Voltaire, and the wretched crew who sided with him in the war against Christianity, perverted their splendid abilities in order to fling away the fetters and restraints of conscience and the Divine law. They labored hard, they spared themselves no toil, they shrunk from no sacrifice of honor or truth, to carry out their diabolical purpose, and "*ecraser l'infâme.*"

But the laughing, jeering, mocking infidels of our time have found a shorter way than this to secure what are called "the glorious privileges of Free-thought." They simply caricature revealed religion, picture to themselves an extravagantly ludicrous creation of their irreverent and unrestrained imagination, and, instead of the venerable and beautiful "mother of all the living" that ruled the hearts and guided the steps of her wayward children with infinite patience and love, set up a hateful monster, hideous in its deformity, and destitute of any quality deserving of reverence and affection. They leave all the thinking and reasoning to a few deluded visionaries of science, who, in the pride of their grand discoveries and inventions, have been led to worship themselves, and forget the God who made them; and, borrowing from these prophets and guides some charming but extravagant theories, they amuse their idle hours with fancy sketches of Religion, that convulse themselves with merriment, and which, while they amuse the thoughtless multitude, effectually rob them of every element of reverent and trusting faith.

What do these "blind leaders of the blind" care for patient reasoning and sound argument? They will not give themselves the trouble to entertain a serious thought on such a subject. If they are checked by the thoughtful and the wise, and called upon to explain the principles that are supposed to sustain their crude and whimsical notions of the Deity and the world to come, they at once fall back on the great discovery of the age—Agnosticism. "God," they say, "is the unknown and unknowable."

This great principle of Positivism and modern Freethought being once supposed, there is no going beyond this stronghold. Nay, admit for a moment this crowning bulwark of Infidelity, and the very raw recruits of the movement will dash forth in brilliant charges on the lines of Christian argument. "Who can tell us anything of the unknowable—who hath seen the invisible? Who can say anything with certainty of the dark future? Who will venture to say that we have immortal souls, or speculate on the blank form of eternity of which we can know absolutely nothing?"

Our great leaders in scientific research have settled it to their own satisfaction, that nothing can be established as a fact save through the reason instructed by bodily sense. "This is an axiom, and therefore no one can argue about Heaven, or Hell, or the Immortality of the soul. These things possibly may be; but they are beyond the ken of beings who have their eyes and ears and hands and smell and taste to guide them to rational conclusions. Everything beyond plain and satisfactory results like these is irrational and absurd. And why, therefore, should we concern ourselves about proofs in revelation, and prophecies and mysteries and miracles, when it is manifestly beyond our powers of thought to convince others, or be convinced ourselves, that there is such a thing as a personal God?"

Sophistry like this will of course be readily admitted by the ignorant or unthinking crowd, who care only to drive away from the conscience whatever can put a restraint on their sensual appetites. They have neither the time nor the disposition to confuse their minds with the "musty old questions of the ages of darkness and superstition." *Carpe diem:* "A bird in the hand is worth two in the bush." "Let us eat, drink, and be merry, as we float joyously and swiftly down the stream of life. And if to-morrow we die, why then it will be time enough to think of the future—if indeed there is a future."

This, without exaggeration, is, I believe, the sum and substance of the laughing, gay, and rollicking sort of Infidelity, which is fast dissipating from the minds of the giddy throng even their nebulous and shadowy traditions of the old Faith, that has sustained the world for eighteen hundred years.

It can easily be seen from this that the Infidelity of the latter part of the nineteenth century is much more dan gerous to society than that of any former age. The Voltaireans were wits and scholars. They read a great deal, they were familiar with every passage in the Sacred Scriptures which their leader had applied all his learning to twist and transform into a sense that captivated the polished taste of his admiring votaries. They had learned from him to set a witty or epigrammatic form of expression above all other excellences in writing or in speech; and to esteem the play of fancy most of all whenever it ridiculed what was sacred and venerable in the thoughts and convictions of believers. But the *double-entendres*, and *bon-mots*, and the flashing epigram were above the perceptions of the unread and uneducated, and were the exclusive property of a privileged class. "*Panem et circenses*," cheap food and unrestrained enjoyment, no labor, no taxes—these were the fruits of the new philosophy that charmed the masses. They heeded not the fine sayings and the learned doctrines of the Encyclopædia and the Dictionary of Philosophy, so long as the sovereign will of the people triumphed, and an age of wholesale levelling set in. The gay crowds of the cities of France were delirious with the new spirit of progress. They shouted "*À bas les Aristocrates*," "*À bas les Prêtres*," with the same frenzy as the high-sounding names "*Liberté, Egalité, Fraternité*," and danced like fiends round the tree of liberty. While they had their own way, unrestrained by law and order and the dictates of conscience and the warnings of religion, it mattered little to them how their leaders thought out the political problems of the hour, or what idols were set up for their adoration. They were as brutal as the crowd at the foot of Sinai; and, had a golden calf been placed on the altar instead of a shameless woman, it would have been all the same, provided it symbolized the reign of lawlessness and sensuality.

Things are quite different now. The *brutum fulmen*—the power of the law supported by bayonets—keeps the mob in order. No high-wrought sentimentalism for fellow-citizens will cause men who have money in the funds to fraternize with poverty-stricken wretches who presume to disturb the public order. Simon Tappertits may thunder in dark cellars against government, and the rights of property; trades-unions may now and then show their teeth in public; but if they growl or even bark, they dare not bite. For this reason, the Infidelity that is corrupting the masses of the chief towns of Europe, causes no alarm; and therefore it has advanced unchecked, until now it has reached a point that may well excite the apprehensions of all governments.

It is more than forty years ago that I read of one of the Bradlaugh class, who, in his club-room in London, defied God to strike him dead, if the horrid blasphemies he uttered were untrue, and pointing to the clock, gave his Divine Maker a full five minutes to carry out the imprecation. It is stated, in the respectable publication in which I read the account of the revolting occurrence, that a terror seemed to diffuse itself over the whole assembly as they watched the hands slowly move over the interval, and looked at the sturdy ruffian who had thus dared to outrage and trample out the conscience of his fellow-men stand with folded arms awaiting the result. I venture to state that at the present day, in thousands of working-men's associations in Great Britain, where men speak freely of religion, a sensational scene like this, if attempted, would only provoke a laugh; and that the speaker who would boldly deny the existence of God would be told to pass on to some other point of greater interest and less admitted and understood.

Those who have read in Dickens' "Barnaby Rudge" the account of the Gordon riots (when some fanatics who gloried in the heritage of Free-thought, urged the mob to crush the Roman Catholics of London for daring to petition for something like the free exercise of their religion), may think that nothing could be worse than the condition of the metropolis during these terrible days of riot and confusion. But I feel assured, from what I have read of the secret societies in that great city, and seen of the illustrated printed matter circulated amongst them, that the Gordon riots would afford the faintest idea of the scenes of violence and confusion that would ensue if for any cause the strong arm of the law were paralyzed or suspended. It is a terrible thing to realize to one's self that in these enlightened days, when we are supposed to bask in the enjoyment of that much-lauded Free-thought and independence of Divine authority in religion, there is scarcely such a thing as a conscience in the souls of the most dreaded and dangerous classes; that no sense of right and wrong, and fear of God and His chastisements, would offer the least restraint to the perpetration of deeds, the bare thought of which makes one sick with terror; and that it is only fear of "the powers that be"—cringing, whipt-dog fear—that keeps the mobs of our great cities of Europe in anything like order.

Education without religion is to a great extent the cause of this state of things; but the main cause of all is the absence of Divine Faith, which is the necessary consequence of rebellion against legitimate authority. The Catholic Church, through her divinely instituted teaching body, has never ceased to warn the rulers of this world that the seeds of that wild teaching, scattered at the will of each individual, will infallibly produce its fatal results—"They shall sow wind, and reap a whirlwind" (Osee viii. 7).

Hitherto I have confined the contrast between the Infidelity of the present day and that of the period of the great Revolution of the eighteenth century to the effects on the working-classes, or the uneducated portion of the community. In the higher classes, also, there is much to be noted that makes the Infidelity of the present age more dangerous to society than that of the Voltairean period. The educated Voltaireans prided themselves on an accurate knowledge of the arts and sciences, the facts of history, and the discoveries of the learned, that rendered them, in their opinion, immeasurably superior in learning to the scholars in the service of the Church. This was in truth only a conceit; for the clergy of France at the time had every advantage which could be afforded by colleges and universities, and the long training for the ministry, and the careful study of philosophy, and of "the science of sciences"—theology. This knowledge was practically tested by repeated examinations, and after ordination, by annual conferences which insured competent knowledge in all the clergy. The Voltairean, therefore, to shine in the *salons* and enjoy triumph over his clerical adversary, should necessarily be well-informed, and quick and sharp in argument, on all topics connected with religion.

The Lord Dundrearies of our time and their Ladyships, who have made up their minds to enjoy life and let the future take care of itself, abhor everything like religious controversy. Even amongst the rich and well-to-do commoners such subjects are tabooed; for it is well understood that to raise questions on religion in polite and polished circles is directly opposed to good taste and the *convenances* of society. Lady So-and-so may, through the irresistible instincts of a benevolent disposition, take an interest in certain charitable institutions; or my Lord love to preside at meetings for the benefit of the benighted heathens of Borrioboola-Gha, or Alderman Bull and his amiable lady delight in heading a large subscription-list in the *Times;* but you will scarcely find one of these tranquil and self-satisfied souls who will allow the calm surface of their lives to be rippled by the breath of an earnest discussion about truths that concern the world to come.

There is little to move any of this easy-going class to self-sacrifice or disinterested labor for the honor and glory of God and the good of their neighbor, where the work does not fall in with their notions of what is fashionable and becoming. If the preacher of the church, where they are wont to attend, commends himself to them and their "set" by the suavity of his voice and manner and the æsthetical arrangement of his namby-pamby essays on morality in general, and if the choir sing prettily, they condescend to patronize Divine worship Sunday after Sunday unless they feel indisposed. But woe betide the preacher if he should dare to ruffle their tender sensibilities by allusion to the fact that "the kingdom of heaven suffereth violence, and the violent only bear it away" (Matt. xi. 12), or the necessity of taking up the cross daily, or the judgment, and the wrath to come. He may soon address his appeals to empty benches. These good people are too fond of their own comfort to expose themselves to the danger of having their equanimity disturbed, and they prefer some charming novel, in their own quiet snuggery, to the luxurious ease of the family pew.

It is a well-known fact that there are in fashionable quarters of London whole streets of mansions the Sabbath rest of which is never broken by the sounds of carriages conveying the wealthy proprietors to and from the parochial church on Sundays.

I have been told by an old resident of the great city that the rule of life in these paradisaical retreats, on the Lord's Day, is, within the last fifteen or twenty years, to have a social gathering of kindred spirits on Saturday nights, generally prolonged to the small hours with music and dancing, and a sumptuous supper, to give the greater part of Sunday to indolent repose, and to take a drive in the afternoon to give zest to the late evening meal. When this becomes fashionable and the correct thing, as it seems to be already, how poor are the chances of even a gleam of spiritual life! And when superadded to this the reading of works of a transcendental character, in which a loftier idea of the aims and objects of life is pretended than vulgar Christianity or the Bible suggests, becomes the rage, and these favored children of fortune, reclining on luxurious couches, dream away their existence

> "till human time
> Shall fold its eyelids, and the human sky
> Be gathered like a scroll within the tomb,
> Unread forever,"

what is to become of sturdy, healthy Faith, and walking in the footsteps of "the Man of sorrows"? Well might our Divine Lord, in His luminous vision of these lotus-eaters of the world of fashion in these latter times, exclaim, "When the Son of Man cometh, shall He find, think you, faith on earth?" (Luke xviii. 8.)

It will be readily inferred from this tendency of the age to indifference about religion—life without God, education without God, the poor deprived of the consolations of Faith, and chafing under the sense of cruel wrong, and longing ardently for the day when capital and its possessors shall be dragged down from their earthly paradise, and compelled to share their coveted possessions; the rich wrapped up in the selfish enjoyment and repose that comes of "beauteous order" and the "gladness of the world," that the spread of irreligion and the forgetfulness of God and the future must be far wider than is generally imagined. Yes, and it will continue to diffuse itself with ever-increasing rapidity where it does not encounter the Rock founded by an Almighty hand, and that immovable barrier against which He has assured us even the powers of hell shall never prevail.

If that Rock *could* be upheaved, if that barrier could be swept away, if the "everlasting Church" could crumble into ruins, what then could stem the tide of evil that is rising every day higher and higher, till it fills with alarm every man of mind that watches its progress?

Will Free-thought, and the right of all men to deal as they think fit with the Divine message, stem the surging torrent? Why, this is itself the true source and origin of the growing impiety. If this boasted prerogative of human pride were not sustained by the bond of formularies and creeds, it would long ago have been overwhelmed by the forces it has called into existence.

Will the millions and millions of Bibles that are teeming from the press close the breaches which Pantheism and Socialism, and the other "isms" Free-thought has engendered, are making in its feeble and worthless barrier? Why, it is this senseless scattering of the Word of

God amongst the crowds, who can hardly read, much less understand its pages, that has robbed the Holy Book of that strength and power with which it was endowed while it was carefully guarded by the Church from the touch of profanity, and made it as useless as the dust trodden down on the highways, to oppose the floods of Infidelity.

Will emotional piety, however worked up by stirring appeals to sentiment, dare to sustain itself in the way of the accumulated waters of unbelief, that now assert themselves openly and defiantly, and can already be heard by those "who have ears to hear," threatening the foundations of social order? As well might we hope to dam the furious course of a swollen river with a bundle of weak and perishable reeds.

The only salvation of the world against this ever-increasing danger is, I repeat, the Rock established more than eighteen centuries ago, by our Divine Redeemer. We have His solemn promise that this Rock shall never fail. It has stood the test of perils that seemed overwhelming from within and without. It defied, for three hundred years, the persecution of the greatest power the world ever saw. It has crushed by its ponderous mass the almost immovable heresies that endeavored to sap its deep foundations; and though it stands alone in these latter times, and apart from all human aid to protect it, it seems to smile, with the bright look of unfading youth, on every effort of the powers of earth and hell to upheave it. "Heaven and earth shall pass away, but My word," says the Son of God—the promise to sustain it, "shall never pass away."

It may seem to some that I am a pessimist, and that I exaggerate the dangers to be apprehended from Infidelity.

I mean, therefore, in this work fully to discuss the question, to lay open, with an unsparing hand, the cancerous growth that is gnawing away almost imperceptibly the vitals of our Christian civilization; to tear off the artificial flowers and the frippery tinsel of fine phrases and dazzling figures of speech and polished verses, that cover, like the whited sepulchres described by our Divine Lord (Matthew xxiii. 27), the foul corruption that is poisoning the heart's blood of nations ; to expose the hollowness of those fine-sounding names—" the supremacy of reason," "glorious liberty of free-thought," "universal brotherhood," which for the last few hundred years have lured so many brave and honest and confiding hearts to destruction.

The Catholic Church has been assailed with the most foul abuse, from the very beginning of her warfare with these hateful delusions. Luther was not particularly choice in the language in which he described the "debasing superstitions" and "the abominations of those who bowed the knee to the scarlet woman of the Apocalypse;" and those who praise his contempt and low vituperation of the everlasting spouse of God have, even up to the present hour, not been behindhand with their apostle in heaping up execration and abuse on the Church founded by Jesus Christ. It will not be difficult to show that all these ugly names were as senseless as the cries of "wooden shoes and brass money," so dear to the frenzied mob in the excitement of the Gordon riots.

But do I hope to convince those who shout, with all the fierce zeal of Orangeism, "No Popery" that this zeal is misplaced? No ; but I believe that those who are not maddened with the spirit of party, however bitterly they may, from long-nursed prejudices, hate the Catholic

Church, will, if they venture to read this book, reserve some of their honest indignation and abhorrence for that Infidelity which is striving by every means to annihilate Christianity. They may even learn to understand that the old Church is now, as she was in the beginning, the uncompromising foe of all who say anathema to Jesus Christ, and so may be disposed to allow her in her own way to fight the battles of the Lord, whom they profess to love above all things.

When I read over in the newspapers, the heads and points of the sermons delivered by Protestant ministers in South Africa, on the occasion of the late centenary of Luther, the savage abuse of the Holy Catholic Church and the gushing laudations of Free-thought, I could easily account for the strong feelings of the unthinking and uneducated classes against the Church.

These accept, without doubt or question, what they hear from their teachers. While they fancy they are thinking for themselves, and wondering how "Papists" can be so deluded as to hear and obey the Church, they fail to see that they are themselves led and driven, like a herd of animals who "have no understanding," by fallible men, the slaves of bitter prejudices. If these blind teachers would honestly answer the question, "Are you sure, beyond doubt, that the Roman Catholic Church is the enemy of Christ and His pure doctrine?" they should be bound in truth and conscience to say, "We are not. We may be wrong, and, for all we know with certainty, the old Church may be as right now as she was when she received the commission from our Divine Lord to teach all nations, and treasured the promise of the perpetual guidance of the Holy Spirit in her discharge of this duty."

When men never think of these things, never inquire into the true state of the case as between legitimate and infallible teaching and that which is assumed and irresponsible and doubtful, but are swayed by the mere feeling or passion of the hour, it would be vain to appeal to their reason and judgment. "They know not what they do." They are like the excited crowd who, at the dictation of the Pharisees, yelled aloud for the blood of Christ. He prayed for them because of their ignorance. So does the Catholic Church pray for those who ignorantly persecute her. Our Divine Lord said to His Apostles, that a day would come when men would honestly believe that they were doing God service by persecuting them to death. I have no doubt that many who know nothing of the Catholic Church but what they have heard from fanatical teachers, are in the same position. When I hear such as these cry out "Away with the Church!" and "Down with Popery!" I cannot help liking their expression of strong and earnest feeling. As Dr. Johnson expresses it, "I like strong haters"—that is to say, men who earnestly hate what in their blind prejudice they believe to be vile and contemptible. This is a thousand times preferable to that smile "from the teeth outward," which I sometimes notice on the face of reverend teachers who, while they rave against the Catholic Church from the pulpit and in meeting, profess to be animated with the kindest feelings toward her "misguided children."

There is no hope in my mind that this book will produce any good effect on such as these. They ought from their reading to know better; they should be able to combat their fierce prejudices so far as to acknowledge that the old Church, which is attracting to itself some of the most learned and holy of other communions, cannot be the mass of deformity they love to represent it. It is much to be feared that, with all their rigorous denunciations of Rome, they are sinning against the light; and that therefore they are inexcusable, and not likely to profit by a word in season. I hope better things from their disciples, for I cannot help thinking that, if honest men who really mean to think for themselves and to be fair and just in their estimate of their fellow-men, catch a glimpse of the real facts of the case between legitimate authority and unprincipled rebellion, they will pause in their judgment, and learn to look with some respect upon the old Church, and be disposed to profit by her solemn and repeated warnings against the dangers of Infidelity. I must confess that this thought, and the hope it enkindled, was not the least among the many inducements that urged me to write this book.

If those who imagine that I exaggerate the dangers of Infidelity will obtain information concerning the progress of Free-thought, and its consequences in the United States, they will be convinced that the evils to which I mean to call attention in these pages can scarcely be exaggerated.

The language of Ingersoll in his public lectures, of Dr. Adler in his sermons, and of the Rev. O. B. Frothingham in his lectures and essays, is, to a believer in revelation, of the most daringly blasphemous character that can be imagined. These upholders of Free-thought, especially the first mentioned, assail the Bible and the God of the Bible with an energy that seems almost demoniacal. The old objections, some of them as old as the time of Julian, and Celsus, and Porphyry, are dressed up in the most popular and taking form. Drollery, caricature, anything that will make the large audiences laugh at what Christians hold most sacred, are freely used in this unholy conflict with the inspired writings. The printed lectures are circulated throughout the States, and are eagerly read by young people, who desire to root out of their minds every vestige of reverent faith. Colonel Ingersoll does not hesitate to call the Almighty "revealed to us in the Sacred Scriptures" "a fiend and a monster." He tells the crowds of intelligent men and women who throng to hear him, and greet his sayings with much applause, that "he hates a God of that kind;" and he declares that he will never deliver a lecture in which he will not denounce, in the strongest and plainest terms, "the infamy of the atonement!" He is, he says, a reader of the Bible. "He has wasted a whole year in reading it through," but only "to expose its lies," and "because it is the basis of the infamy of the atonement."

This is simply frightful; but is it not the natural outcome of Free-thought? Private judgment, carried to its legitimate and logical consequences, means nothing more or less than pure Individualism; and Individualism is only another name for Rationalism.

It is not the Word of God, enlightening every individual, as is sentimentally supposed, but every individual giving that meaning to the Word of God that pleases himself, and falls in with the views suggested by his own imagination or his own feelings. This man forms his peculiar notions of sin and of Divine justice as if he fully understood the Infinite Sanctity of the All-pure and Perfect Being who "has made all things well." He finds a mistake in the Bible here, and another there. "It is wrong for the Almighty to bestow free-will upon His rational creatures. It is wrong for God to establish any law that is opposed to man's natural propensities." "Why," he asks, "should not man do as he likes?" Another will, in the exercise of his private judgment, and in the glorious possession of his untrammelled liberty, scoff at authority and creeds and formularies, and rush into Mormonism, or any other 'ism that takes his fancy. By what right will that Protestantism which rebelled against the Church—the only Church then existing, the Church established by Christ, the Church of the promises, the Church which our Divine Saviour commands us to hear and obey under pain of eternal separation from Him—how, I say, will Protestantism, this rebellious child, attempt to check the wayward fancies of her rebellious offspring? What is there to restrain the proud self-sufficiency which, once its whims are gratified, goes on ever wanting more? Must it not end naturally and logically in self-worship, and come practically to the same conclusion as Ingersoll and his fellows—that Humanity is the only real religion? "Why," says this leader of Free-thought, "I could beat the Ten Commandments." And no doubt he might indulge the fancy that he could improve the whole creation, and arrange the world much better, had he been consulted in the work.

There is no limit to human pride. It is the origin of all evil. "I shall be like to the Most High," thought Lucifer; and the first temptation suggested by him to our first parents was, "Ye shall be as gods."

What is the latest outcome of this Rationalism, as it is propounded by the teachers of scientific Positivism in Great Britain? This—that life is not worth living; that the present world, with its varied conditions between excessive wealth on the one hand and squalid poverty on the other, is a huge mistake; that since the strong arm of power, with its ponderous guns and weapons of precision, and inventions for wholesale destruction, is a check on Socialism and Communism and Nihilism, and the other imaginary remedies for human ills, the sooner the whole human race dies out the better for man.

Who does not see the practical consequences of this teaching? Is it not that it is a good thing to compass the ruin of society, and that he deserves well of his fellow-men who will disseminate, by voice and pen, the moral poison that will corrupt and waste away all healthy growth, break asunder the ties that unite the family, check the birth of children, and reduce the civilized nations of the earth to that condition which, years ago, wrung from the eloquent Lacordaire, while deploring the miseries of France, " Show me a *man* among the effete population of our great cities, and I may yet believe in the regeneration of my country."

When, in this once glorious land, Free-thought and Rationalism have brought about such a state of things that it is enacted by law that "citizens are to be reared like cattle and to be broken-in like horses," since, according to the Communistic theory, children are not the children of their fathers and mothers, what may we not expect as these principles are more widely diffused throughout Europe? "The moral unity of France," according to the views of the men now in power, means the extinction of all forms of religious belief, thought, consciousness, or moral life. The French citizen must be taught, trained, fashioned, and drilled by an education, in which the existence of God is a superstition, the name of God an equivocal term, and the moral law a group of conventional usages. What is the obvious and natural consequence of this irreligion and progress of Free-thought?

I answer in the eloquent words of M. Jules Simon: "The miserable and sterile society that such education would produce, would be in France an edition of one man in thirty-six millions of copies—such unity is death." And he adds these significant words: "It is not the loss of a battle or the annihilation of an army that begins the fall of a people: a people dies only by the relaxation of its morals, by abandoning its manly habits, by the effacement of its character, through the invasion of Egoism and Scepticism. It dies of its corruption. It does not die of its wounds."

Men may think that such principles will never be adopted by the English-speaking races. But this is a great mistake. When the Right Honorable Anthony John Mundella, Vice-President of the Committee of Council, recently declared that "these gigantic efforts" in France were worthy of imitation, and that the thoughts and actions of legislatures are constantly tending in the same direction (I quote from a speech of the President of the Board of Trade, reported in the *Daily Post* of the 18th of last January), all thoughtful men who watch the working of the School Boards in England may well be anxious.

But, as I said in the beginning of this Introduction, there are few who *think* in this busy age. Men are so intoxicated with the triumphs of material progress, so wrapt up in the pursuit of wealth, so bent on the "pride of life," that they allow the public prints and newspapers to do all the thinking for them. Their only ambition is to keep *au courant* with the rapid stream that is carrying them on to Eternity, and so they reach it unawares: or, if the distant prospect catches their view, they ridicule its terrors, as they would the hobgoblin stories of childhood.

And what is it that has led to this strange perversion of ideas? Eminently, the frivolity and thoughtlessness of the times in which we live—the logical consequences of revolt against legitimate authority; and finally, the absence of any power to check the headlong course toward Rationalism and Unbelief. The learned Schleirmacher has well said, "Protestantism, in the presence of Rationalism, is like an iceberg gradually melting before the sun."

I have seen the process of its melting in my own experience of fifty years. Critical analysis of the Bible, when the Holy Book stands alone, and unprotected by the shade of "the everlasting Church," is doing its work rapidly and noiselessly. Block by block, it is slipping away into the seething waters of hostile public opinion. Inexorable Rationalism is, with the magnifying-glasses of science, concentrating the rays of its searching examination on every weak point of the helplessly floating structure; mystery after mystery is dissolving. Now it is the sanction of the Divine law. A few years ago it was the sacramental system. Next it will be the Trinity, and probably the whole Athanasian Creed, that will perish under this dissolving power. Then, when the last block of Bible Christianity shall have disappeared, and the great unbounded ocean of Free-thought will have dashed from the world the traditions of the old Faith, there will remain only "the pillar and ground of truth" to preserve the last element of conservatism in society.

If men would only think—if, while they are talking about liberality and freedom of opinion, they would only cast from their eyes the scales of prejudice and bigotry, and really exercise their judgment, how soon would those of good-will be brought to recognize, with wonder and admiration, "the everlasting Church"—the mother of all sound doctrine, and that Catholic Christianity, taught by the Apostles, and which will be taught and explained and developed by their lawful successors to the consummation of the world.

In the first Chapter I purpose to give this ideal of a Christian-teaching Church, as it exists before my mental vision, to show what the Catholic Church really is, and how, although human in its elements, it bravely fulfils its mission under the guidance and inspiration of the Spirit of Truth, which, according to the promise of her Divine Founder, is to abide with her forever. I hope then to dispose of the false notions given of her by her enemies; to show that it is the distortion and the caricaturing of Catholic Christianity that has encouraged the growth and development of the numerous "isms" of the age; to take these one by one, and analyze them and point out their hollowness and corruption; and thus gradually lead those who do not know the Church to look towards her, in the midst of the deluge of evils that are threatening this unfortunate world, as the only ark of safety for future generations.

CATHOLIC CHRISTIANITY

AND

MODERN UNBELIEF.

CHAPTER I.

Catholic Christianity and its Contrasts.

I CAN never forget the impression made upon my mind, many years ago, when, in the course of a long sailing voyage from the colony to England, I was asked by a fellow-passenger to explain what was meant by the Immaculate Conception. Although the person who asked me did not conceal her strong feelings about what she called the "fuss" Catholics made in all that related to the Blessed Virgin—" as if," she said, " there was anything more remarkable in Mary than in any other woman."

I satisfied myself that she wished to have a thorough explanation on the point, and I explained it as clearly as I could. I dwelt particularly on the sanctity of God our Saviour, showing that though He might, for love of us, "annihilate" Himself, He could not part in the smallest degree with His infinite purity; and that, although His chief work in the Atonement was to satisfy for our sins, there could be in Him no actual participation in sin. I then proceeded to show that God the Son had really allied Himself to our human nature, that the flesh of

Christ was the flesh of Mary, and that the Precious Blood wherewith He had washed away the sins of the world actually flowed in the veins of His Virgin Mother. He was truly the son of Mary, as truly as He was the only-begotten of the Father from all eternity—man to suffer and God to save; and from this intimate union with her she must, by an extraordinary privilege, have been not only, as the angel called her, "full of grace," but never, even for a moment of her personal existence, subject to sin in any shape or form. Had she been, like all other human creatures, "conceived in iniquity and born a child of wrath," and consequently, though it were only for a moment, the slave of Satan, there would have been an essential barrier against the perfect alliance of an all-holy Divine nature and the inherent sinfulness of human nature. And I went on to explain that it had ever been the belief of the Fathers and Saints of the Catholic Church that, when her soul was in the first instant united to the germ of her body, she was, through the merits of the Redeemer to be born of her, by a special act of Divine Providence preserved from the consequences of the Fall. She had never been for one single instant the creature and slave of original sin. I further explained to her—for she was a woman of rare intelligence—the cause of the difference of opinion between the leading minds of Catholic schools of divinity on the point, and showed her that in this all were agreed—that the Virgin Mother of Jesus Christ had never been sullied by the stain of even original guilt.

I remember well her answer when I had finished, in which the instincts of a true Christian, believing firmly in the Divinity of Christ, revealed itself: "It must be so—it could not be otherwise. Who could possibly believe that the pure blood of Jesus ever bore the slightest taint of evil?"

I remember too, which is much more to the point, the remark of her husband who was present: "Yes, my dear, it seems all right as Dr. Ricards puts it; but then you should know that Catholic priests [I was not Bishop then] are trained to put their doctrine in any form that is likely to please, and not to be over-particular about the truth, provided they can gain a convert to their creed." It was hard to bear patiently this insult, for it was the first time that the odious charge, "The end justifies the means," was applied to me personally. Alas! I have learned since to know, as every Catholic Bishop and priest knows only too well, that when he ventures to explain the doctrines of his Church to those who are not of her communion, he must be prepared to subject himself, if not to the open charge, at least to the grave suspicion of insincerity and deception.

This thought weighs upon me now, and almost deters me from the task I have set before me. If what I have to say about the Holy Catholic Church will appear reasonable and just to non-Catholics who may read this book, they will in all likelihood say I am not to be believed, I am only faithful to the lessons of deception in which I have been trained, by attempting to give a false notion of the Faith I profess.

I can only protest against so cruel and unjust an insult, and declare before God, who sees the secrets of my heart and will hereafter judge me, that I loathe and detest anything like deception in so grave a matter as declaring "the Faith that is in me;" that I abominate the principle, no matter by whom taught, if it is indeed taught by any reasonable man or body of men, that "the end justifies the means." I hold most firmly that a lie is under all circumstances unlawful in itself; and that no amount of seeming good, or real good, that would be effected by telling a wilful lie could justify the crime.

Though strongly tempted to retort, I will confine myself simply to this solemn declaration, that I have rarely, if ever, seen any doctrine of the Catholic Church truthfully and fairly stated by her enemies. It is this misrepresentation—whether it be wilful, or have its origin in ignorance, I cannot say—that is the chief cause of the success, before the unthinking multitude, of the assaults of Rationalism upon Christianity.

It is hard to conceive how wide-spread is this ignorance. But when we consider that those who are prejudiced against her claims to authoritative teaching, to her intolerance of doctrine opposed to her own, and who hate her honestly on account of the false charges of immorality so often urged against her, cannot take up one of the books of our apologists without feeling all the influence of these prejudices and this hatred; that they are disposed to see evil lurking wherever any particular doctrine or practice commends itself to their judgment; and that there are many of her worst enemies who publicly boast, as I have heard some Protestant ministers boast, that they have never read a Catholic book—the wonder is that those outside her pale know anything of her true character.

A clever writer of the day,—William Hurrell Mallock, —not a Catholic, well says in reference to this ignorance: "In this country [England] the popular conception of Rome has been so distorted by our familiarity with Protestantism, that the true conception of her is something quite strange to us. Our divines have exhibited her to us as though she were a lapsed Protestant sect, and they have attacked her for being false to doctrines that were never really hers. They have failed to see that the first and essential difference which separates her from them lies primarily, not in any special dogma, but in the authority on which all her dogmas rest. Protestants basing their religion on the Bible solely, have conceived that Catholics of course profess to do so likewise, and have covered them with invective for being traitors to their supposed profession. But the Church's primary doctrine is her own perpetual infallibility. She is inspired, she declares, by the same Spirit that inspired the Bible, and her voice is equally with the Bible the voice of God. This theory, however, upon which her whole fabric rests, popular Protestantism either ignores altogether, or treats it as if it were a modern superstition, which, so far from being essential to the Church's system, is, on the contrary, inconsistent with it. Looked at in this way, Rome, to the Protestant's mind, has seemed naturally to be a mass of superstitions and dishonesties; and it is this view of her, strangely enough, which our modern advanced thinkers have accepted without question. Though they have trusted the Protestants in nothing else, they have trusted them here. They have taken the Protestant's word for it, that Protestantism is more reasonable than Romanism; and they think therefore that if they have destroyed the former, *à fortiori* they have destroyed the latter."

This one ground of misconception, so ably put by Mallock, vitiates the whole view of the Church to outsiders. Protestants, laying it down as a matter of fact that cannot be disputed, that the Bible and the Bible only is the sole rule of Faith,—though strange to say this rule is nowhere found in the Sacred Scriptures,—proceed to show with unbounded confidence that such and such Catholic practices and doctrines are unscriptural—that is to say, opposed to their peculiar views of Scripture, and therefore to be condemned.

But the Catholic Church teaches now, as she ever taught, that she was fully established long before a word of the New Testament was written, that she is not the creation of the Bible, and that it belongs to her, as the original guardian entrusted with its keeping, to expound and declare its meaning. Hence, as Mallock sums up the argument, "If we would obtain a true view of the general character of Catholicism, we must begin by making a clean sweep of all the views that, as outsiders, we have been taught to entertain about her. We must in the first place learn to conceive of her as a living spiritual body, as infallible and as authoritative now as she ever was, with her eyes undimmed and her strength not abated, continuing to grow still, as she has continued to grow hitherto; and the growth of the new dogmas that she may from time to time enunciate we must learn to see are, from her own stand-point, signs of life and not signs of corruption."

Such is "the everlasting Church," the Church of the creeds, the Church founded by Jesus Christ, whose life and soul is the Spirit of God, the Spirit of Truth, which, according to the eternal promise of her Founder, must abide with her forever. Such is the Holy Catholic Church as she appears in my eyes, and as she appears to all believers in her Divine institution. I see her include in her vast extent the teaching body and the taught. She offers me the Sacred Scriptures, which she has faithfully preserved from the beginning. She guarantees to me their authenticity and integrity. She declares them to be the inspired Word of God, and offers to explain to me their meaning—often obscure, and hard to be understood. In the discharge of this duty of teaching I know she cannot lead me astray, for does not the Spirit of Truth teach her all truth and abide with her forever? Hence in the Catholic Church I can find rest for my weary soul under the shadow of her wings. There is no need to spend my days in doubting and disputing. From her lips I can know "the truth as it is in Jesus." If there is anything beyond my comprehension in the mysteries which she proposes, I know without doubt that she is telling me what God has told her about Himself. I am not distracted with the thought that He may have meant me to understand this revelation in some other way in which it would be possible for my finite reason to receive it. If the proud feeling that sometimes awakens the primeval temptation, "I shall be like to the Most High," comes to disturb me, and prompts me to rebel against being obliged to believe what I do not comprehend, knowing that God cannot deceive me, I reason with myself and say, "Is it not fitting, is it not natural and right, that I cannot form an adequate idea of the all-perfect Spirit who has made all things? If I clearly saw His Divine attributes, and understood the Divine nature, and the Trinity of Persons, and the Incarnation, and the whole economy of the Atonement, then I might indeed doubt if the religion that was so accommodated to my limited perceptions was really from God."

Hence I see that to receive the message of God concerning these exalted things without the least doubt, as "the evidence of things which appear not," I am paying to God the greatest honor which a rational creature can offer to his Creator. If it be objected that it is degrading to believe, with the full assent of the mind, what is unintelligible, I answer, Yes, it would be degrading to express belief in it if the grounds for this confidence were not in every respect satisfactory.

The blind man believes, on the testimony of his friends, things that are perfectly unintelligible to him, and one might say absolutely contradictory to his limited sense. Place the man born blind before a mirror, and tell him that in a moment a perfect, life-like image of himself is produced, and not only of himself, but of every object around him, you ask him to believe a greater miracle in his regard than we can well imagine. If he test the alleged fact by the sense of touch, he finds evidence to his mind of the absolute falsity of what is proposed to him. It is impossible, he feels, that many objects around him and his own person can be depicted on the flat and uniform surface beneath his hand. But the testimony of this unintelligible fact satisfies his doubts, and he believes reasonably, and without the least blame, the truth that is set before him. Nay, more: he would, in the judgment of all men, though he cannot possibly understand the reasons derived from the laws of reflection of light, judge stupidly and obstinately if he preferred his own opinion in opposition to the positive testimony of those who concur in stating the simple fact. Had we a sixth or seventh sense, whereby we could estimate the real value of supernatural things, we might question the testimony of God, announced by His infallible Church; but being more ignorant than the blind man in the case alleged, it is obstinate folly to resist the testimony. When men clearly comprehend their own dual existence, the nature of the soul, its ubiquity in the material body, what a spirit is, what is life, and a thousand cognate truths, then indeed it would be degrading to believe, in opposition to this supernatural knowledge, whatever was clearly and unmistakably opposed to it. But when the truth of God's teaching, which is immeasurably beyond the testimony of man, affirms the fact of incomprehensible dogmas, it is worse than folly and stupidity to argue against the possibility of their existence.

I remember once a scientific gentleman undertaking to prove to me that the invocation of the saints, as proposed by the Catholic Church, necessarily involved attributing to the saints qualities belonging only to God, and the consequence that we Catholics believed the Blessed Virgin and the saints to be real gods, and offering a wager that he would prove his argument to a perfect demonstration. Though I would not bet on the point, I defied him to his proof. It was no doubt very simple and satisfactory to his own judgment. "There are thousands, perhaps tens of thousands, at this moment," he said, "in different parts of the world, invoking the intercession of the Blessed Virgin. You believe that she can hear them all. Therefore," he concluded, "you manifestly attribute to her omniscience and ubiquity—attributes which all reasonable men confine to the Divine nature." He felt more than humiliated by my answer. I said, "Yes, your argument would be good as regards beings in the present state of existence, where knowledge is derived through the senses. But we are speaking of beings who have 'shuffled off this mortal coil;' who exist in another mode of existence of which we can form no idea; who, really enjoying personal life [for he believed in the immortality of the soul], see without eyes, hear without ears, and stand in no need of matter to communicate with each other. First explain to me," I said, "this mode of existence; describe a spirit to me, and its relations to space. Put all this clearly before me, and then we may talk of demonstration."

Men may be highly scientific, as far as this physical world is concerned, and yet fools compared to the simple humble Catholic who never thinks of questioning the teaching of the Church, which our Divine Lord commands us to hear under pain of eternal separation from Him. The worst of it is, that men learned in science, when an argument of this kind is pressed to its legitimate conclusion, give way to irritation of temper, and forthwith commence abusing the Church, and repudiating her claims to teach us.

"She is," they say, "the enemy of progress; she is behind the age; she is blind to the discoveries of science; she won't move forward with the human family; she teaches now as she did eighteen hundred years ago: how then can any one of common-sense listen patiently to her old-fashioned talk, and be satisfied with her antiquated nonsense? Then she is so perverse and obstinate and intolerant. She condemns every one to eternal fire that will not listen to her stupid mumblings. She persecuted while she dared; but, thanks to Free-thought ['aye there's the rub'], we have through the glorious apostle of liberty, the mighty Luther, flung her authority to the winds. We will judge for ourselves; and if our Divine Lord commanded us to hear her, He did not know how silly and foolish and superstitious and credulous she would become in the course of ages. We are certain that, if He again appeared on earth, He would recognize as His true disciples only those who have learned in the school of progress to believe in positive facts, and what their good practical common-sense accepts. He would care nothing for the senseless and unreasoning crowd who take their religion on trust, and are always pointing out the necessity of simple obedience to legitimate authority, and submission to the Divine will and its ordinances, and taking up the cross daily and bearing it in the spirit of that simple and humble docility which is so opposed to self-respect and the innate spirit of manly independence."

Let me examine for a moment seriously the meaning of these outbursts of ill-tempered and inconsiderate abuse of the venerable Church of ages. Are they really well grounded? Is there at least something sound and sensible on which they rest?

Suppose that I admit that the Catholic Church teaches in this nineteenth century of her existence the same doctrines which our Divine Lord and His Apostles taught, I am met with an outcry on every hand dissenting violently from this proposition. If I say she has toned down the primitive doctrine and adapted it to the spirit of the age, there is the same loud outcry of dissent. It is difficult to determine, in this conflict of contradictory opinions, what is precisely the charge conveyed in this reproach of the Church being in opposition to the progress of society.

"It seems," as Father Oakley so admirably puts it, "that one of the most striking marks of her truth, in the presence of a noisy and frivolous generation, is the fact that she is the inheritor of the reproaches heaped on her Divine Founder. Men do not care nowadays to spend time in considering the marks of Unity, Sanctity, Apostolicity, and Catholicity. They have almost lost the meaning of these terms, but a point like this 'he that runs may read.' Just as our Divine Lord was assailed by

His enemies with the most contradictory charges, so is His Church. His words are literally fulfilled: 'You shall be hated by all men for My name's sake. The disciple is not above his master' (Matt. x. 22, 24). There exists beyond dispute a wide-spread unreasoning hate against the Catholic Church, and the sources of this hatred are as varied as are the conditions of mankind. It is a giant bugbear, which has the faculty of transforming itself into a thousand shapes, as reflected on the retina of a thousand different eyes. It has one side of odiousness to the statesman, another to the civil governor, another to the man of business, another to the men of the world, another to the family man, another to the profligate, another to the rigorist. Some dislike one of its doctrines, some another, while some object to all alike. There is also a large class of persons who have no definite idea about the Catholic Church at all, but abhor it merely because it is unpopular. It must be wrong, they say, or it could not be so generally hated" ("The Church of the Bible," by the Rev. Frederick Oakley, M.A.).

Some say that the Catholic Church is too lax in her morality; others that she is the inhuman tyrant and butcher of conscience. Some maintain that she is the friend of despotism, the extravagant upholder of Right Divine, and others that she is eminently disloyal, and the secret fomenter of anarchy and rebellion. Surely all these contradictory charges cannot be true at the same time. There is one fact and it cannot be doubted, and that is, that the Church, from whatever causes the feeling may arise, is an object of hatred to those who are not of her.

In this respect she stands forth distinct from all other institutions in the world. She is eminently hated alike by unbelievers in Christianity, and by the various and multiform sects that differ from her in their belief. It may be safely said that the one point in which all sects of Christians cordially unite is their hatred of the Roman Catholic Church. This open and avowed hatred is, I maintain, one of the most striking marks that she is the true Church of Christ. The Church of the days of the Apostles was similarly hated. "Wonder not, brethren," says St. John, "if the world hate you" (1 John iii. 13). And the causes and character of this hatred are the same as they were in the time of our Divine Lord: "If the world hate you, know ye that it hated Me before you. If you had been of the world, the world would love its own; but because you are not of the world, but I have chosen you out of the world, therefore the world hateth you" (John xv. 18, 19). Do not these words of our Divine Lord seem exactly to hit the point? For if there be one cause, more than another, the chief source of the world's hatred against the Church it is this—that she is not of the world.

For what does all this ill-tempered abuse, which I noticed above, come to but to this very particular? The Church is old-fashioned, out of time with progress, always in the way of the world. Therefore the world hates her.

Well, let us ask, is the Church quite wrong in teaching the same truths that excited this strong feeling against the Redeemer? Should she change her doctrine with the popular views and fashionable theories of the times? Should she accommodate her principles to the ideas of Free-thought? Should she preach society without God, government without God, education without God, the family without God, sanction divorce, the rule of might without right, and the unprincipled logic of accomplished facts, and all the other wild fancies of unbridled rationalism that are desolating mankind? No, a thousand times, no. "Heaven and earth shall pass away," but the words of Him who is "the way, the truth, and the life" shall never pass away. The morality of the Gospel, as explained by the Catholic Church, is founded on truths that are as fixed and eternal as the God who revealed them, and therefore it can never change. And if the Church is as determined now as she was in the beginning, " when kings of the earth stood up, and the princes assembled together against the Lord and against His Christ;" if to the threats of angry human power she exclaims with the Apostles, "Judge ye if it be just to hear you rather than God," and goes on her steady way, like the wise householder, bringing forth from her treasury " old things and new," as indifferent to the world's censure as to its applause—why should she be charged with stupid obstinacy, and perversity and intolerance? Is not the course she follows the proper one to fulfil her high mission with unshaken fidelity, and, like her Divine Founder, to brave the world's hatred by disdaining to accommodate herself to the world's ever-changing and unstable ways?

Much is made of this cry of intolerance. But is not truth necessarily intolerant? There is no greater enemy to truth than easy and pliant indifference. Old Pagan Rome could afford to offer a home to the false deities of the conquered nations, because she did not possess the true religion herself. But the Catholic Church, possessing the immutable principles of truth, believing that she is guided in her interpretation of this truth by the Holy Spirit abiding with her, can make no sacrifice of this priceless treasure.

"She would therefore persecute," it is objected. "If she had the power she would burn men at the stake if they refused her teaching." The Catholic Church never persecuted, but tried by every means in her power to moderate the spirit of those times that regarded persecution as a necessity against the ravages of error and the levelling principles that sprung from Free-thought. Let men who are forever howling over the abominations of the Inquisition think seriously over these words of Hallam, and they will learn to be silent over the inhuman barbarities of past ages: "Persecution is the deadly original sin of the Reformed churches, that cools every honest soul for the cause in proportion as his reading becomes more extensive" (Hallam's "Constitutional History," vol. i., page 95).

"But," continues the objector, "you cannot deny that she condemns to everlasting fire those who do not receive her teaching." I answer: The Catholic Church condemns no one to hell. She only declares that Faith is a necessary condition to salvation, and that Faith must of its very nature be one, and that Faith includes all the doctrines which our Divine Lord commanded the Apostles to announce to the world; and consequently that they who obstinately refuse to accept this Faith expose themselves, by the ordinance of Christ, to eternal ruin. "He that believeth not shall be condemned" (Matt. xvi. 16). The Church proclaims the terrible law laid down by her Divine Founder, and by every means in her power endeavors to guard all who hear her voice from the dread consequences of its violation. She has not made the law, for it belongs only to the Almighty Lord and Master of all things to determine a law like this involving so severe a sanction. The Church does not condemn any individual, nor judge whether he is " worthy of love or hatred." It is Christ Himself, our merciful Redeemer, who, in His capacity as Judge of the living and the dead, will say to the perversely wicked who had to the end of the time of trial preferred the conceits of Free-thought to the immutable law of God, " Depart, ye accursed, into everlasting fire." "Who is he that shall condemn? Christ Jesus who died, yea who rose again, who is at the right hand of God, who also maketh intercession for us" (Rom. viii. 34).

These are some of the charges which are, in angry moments, hurled at the venerable Church of God when she mildly remonstrates with Christians who prefer toying with the creations of Free-thought to what they call her old-fashioned teaching. There are of course many others—indeed, their name is legion; but it would be worse than useless to notice them here.

The main point, the question of questions for all who hope for life eternal through the merits of Jesus Christ, is to determine whether the Church founded by our Divine Lord, which could never fail in her office of teaching and expounding His doctrine, has a right divine to teach us, and if we are bound to receive her teaching. The right to teach with authority, and the duty of simple and docile obedience to the teaching body, are principles which jar with the restless spirit of the age. I have hitherto tried to reconcile them to the prejudices of believers.

To go further would be to enter into the mazes of historical and polemical argument, which makes the whole life of Christians who "will not hear the Church" a weary, endless round of doubting and disputing and protesting. As regards Unbelievers, Rationalists, Agnostics, Positivists, Pantheists, and Atheists, I would say to any such as may care to look through this book—

Be sure you set before your eyes as the object of your Free-thinking assaults not some peculiar form of Christianity, but Catholic Christianity. Don't set up some monstrosity or caricature of Christianity tinged with the sombre shades of predestination, or decked out with the meretricious ornaments of sentimentalism and the glaring colors of emotional fervor. It will be easy to bear down with your lance of common-sense such lifeless scarecrows as these. You may poke them out of the field with the lath of ridicule or the light weapon of wit. If you are in earnest in supporting the claims of natural religion against such travesties of revealed truth as private judgment independent of Church authority has developed, you can hardly feel comfort for your inward consciousness in such poor triumphs. It will be only loss of time, a mere sham-fight with shadowy nothings, from which can come no solid, practical advantage.

Mark well the position of the Catholic Church, and you will soon find that you have an adversary worthy of your steel. Her ground in the contest is clear and unmistakable. She claims to be the old Church founded by Jesus Christ and His Apostles. She claims to be the Church of the unfailing promises. She proves her right to explain the written Word of God with infallible authority. Any teaching bodies that dare not make these claims can evidently be no teachers or defenders of dogmatic supernatural Revelation. "Any supernatural religion that renounces its claim to absolute infallibility it is clear can profess to be a semi-revelation only." I quote again from Mallock: "It is a hybrid thing, partly natural and partly supernatural, and it thus practically has all the qualities of a religion that is wholly natural. In so far as it professes to be revealed, it of course professes to be infallible; but if the revealed part be, in the first place, hard to distinguish, and, in the second place, hard to understand—it may mean many things, and many of these things contradictory—it might just as well have been never made at all. To make it in any sense an infallible revelation, or in other words a revelation *to us*, we need a power to interpret the testament that shall have equal authority with the testament itself."

This is putting the truth plainly and fairly, and it is so clearly taught by an example that there can be no longer any mistake about it. "That example," continues this writer, "is Protestant Christianity, and the condition to which after three centuries, it is now visibly bringing itself. It is at last beginning to exhibit to us the true result of the denial of infallibility to a religion that professes to be supernatural. We are at last beginning to see in it neither the purifier of a corrupted revelation nor the corruption of a pure revelation, but the practical denier of all revelation whatsoever."

It will not do for the unbeliever to say with Ingersoll, "That God of the Bible is a fiend; I will have none of Him—a God who created hell to punish His creatures for faults they could not help, who has taken away from human nature all liberty of action, who takes infinite pleasure in the tortures of His helpless children," etc., etc. This may be the God of Calvinism, but it is not the God set before us by Catholic Christianity—far different. "The Lord God, merciful and gracious, patient and of much compassion, and true; who keepest mercy unto thousands; who takest away iniquity, and wickedness, and sin" (Exodus xxxiv. 6, 7).

These writers who lead the van in natural religion are loud in their praises of free-will, natural goodness, and natural virtue, as if these qualities of fallen human nature were ignored by the religion of the Bible. They are no doubt disregarded by the heresies that, in their blind zeal against Pelagianism, destroy the power of the human will, and deny it any ability of co-operation with Divine grace. Man, according to the stupid upholders of these opinions, is like a brute or a tree as far as free-will is concerned, and is the helpless victim of necessity, cursed and lost eternally by the dread fiat of His creator. But man, in the fixed belief of Catholic Christianity, is endowed with free-will, inclined no doubt to evil by the loss of sanctifying grace, but though disinherited, perfectly free in the full possession of his natural faculties, and able, through the grace purchased for us all by the death of Christ, to regain his lost inheritance, and reign forever with God in Heaven.

I never read anything in the shape of stories of the imagination that gave me more heartfelt pleasure than those charming pages of Charles Dickens which excite our sympathies for the most fallen and uncared-for of the human family. There is a germ of good in poor creatures like "Joe" in "Bleak House" and "Nancy" in "Oliver Twist" that ordinary Christian charity might develop into bright flowers fit for paradise. Many of the religious orders of the Catholic Church prove by their successful labors that this is no sentimental belief, but is in fact their *raison d'être*. The Rationalists hate and execrate cant and hypocrisy and its accompanying vices; and Catholic instincts, if they are guided by Christian charity, naturally abominate such characters as are represented under the Heaps, and Pecksniffs, and shepherds, of a false and deluded Christianity.

If Catholic Christianity were only understood by the brilliant and gifted leaders of modern Free-thought, and studied apart from the wretched and grovelling imitations of it founded on animal feeling and gushing sentimentalism, they would fall down and worship it. I can conceive nothing more pure and beautiful, more worthy of God, as far as we can know of His loving mercy, and more consoling to poor fallen humanity, than the practical teaching of the Catholic Church as it is developed in her whole system of belief and morality; but more bright and glorious still, breathing of Heaven and angelic purity, meek and humble of heart like the lowly Jesus, self-sacrificing like the Redeemer, as it is eminently exemplified in the ecclesiastical state and in the religious orders of both sexes. It will be my purpose to bring this truth before the reader in the chapters immediately following.

CHAPTER II.

Catholic Christianity and its Mysteries.

THOSE who take a real interest in the education and training of children find a positive delight in meeting occasionally with a bright specimen of unaffected candor and simplicity, who, looking into the eyes of the teacher with that expression which seems to impart intelligence to the faithful hound, timidly yet trustingly unfolds the germ of some original thought. If the very clever writer who has told us such charming stories about "Alice" and her childish dreams would concentrate his marvellous powers of observation on the religious notions of gifted children, and set them before the public in his attractive style, he would confer a positive blessing on the age. I have heard myself such pertinent questions put me by a young boy or girl in the catechism class that I felt myself for a moment unable to answer, carried away as I was by the wistful look of the little questioner and the thoughtful words, to analyze the process of mental working that had evolved this budding flower of fancy.

What was the deep meaning of the words of our Divine Lord, "out of the mouths of infants and sucklings thou hast perfected praise" (Matt. xxi. 16), or what was the vision before the mind of the inspired Psalmist when he penned them? Who shall say for certain when the most learned interpreters and commentators differ? It strikes me however, in relation to the subject of mysteries, which I am to treat of in this chapter, that these words of our Lord have an intimate connection with those addressed to the Apostles fascinated by ambitious dreams of future glory—"unless you become as little children, you shall not enter into the kingdom of Heaven" (Matt. xviii. 3). He was reproving the proud indignation of the chief priests and scribes when He declared that the little ones crying out "Hosanna" in the Temple had offered to Him "the most perfect praise." It would appear from the whole connection that simple, humble, child-like Faith is more precious in the sight of God than the grandest speculations of proud reason about the Divine nature and its attributes.

The mother-superior of one of our convents told me that while she was explaining the mystery of the Trinity to a class of youngsters, a bright-eyed, intelligent-looking girl said to her, "Mother, how can the three Divine persons be one person? There is father, and mother, and my big brother at home, and they all love each other so fondly, and they all say the same thing to us little ones, and they never dispute; but they are not one." She first told the child that the catechism did not say the three Persons are one Person, or that three Gods are one God, because that would be saying what was manifestly impossible. "It tells us," she went on, "that the three Persons have all the one Divine nature. What that nature is we cannot clearly understand. It is too great, too vast, too immense, for our little minds to grasp it. Look around you: it is the great God who has made everything you see—this huge earth with all its creatures, the heavens above you, the sun and moon and stars, and His presence fills all space. If we could comprehend what the great God is, He would then cease to be God. He would no longer be the Infinite Being He is." While the good nun thus explained the mystery to the wondering child, it required no effort of the imagination to mark the effect of this simple teaching on the soul sanctified by Baptism, and sweetly disposed by this sacrament to supernatural Faith. I could well understand that the teacher was awed and impressed by the reverent expression, and the uplifted eyes, and the clasped hands, and that she could scarcely restrain her tears as she saw the moist eyes and quivering lip of her interesting little pupil, who was no doubt praising God with that perfect praise so dear and precious in His sight.

What a contrast to this simple, docile, reverent Faith is the cynical and blasphemous effrontery of one of the leaders of modern thought, who says in the presence of a large audience, who have led one another to believe that it is the correct thing to laugh and be amused at the wit of the lecturer, "If we had been born in India we would have believed in a God with three heads. Now we believe in three Gods with one head"! This is one of the effects of Free-thought: it has led clever men to fling Faith and reverence to the winds, and set them on to misuse the talents God gave them to caricature Himself and misrepresent His Divine message.

Suppose some one were to point out to this genius of modern progress, "You are misrepresenting Catholic Christianity. Nowhere does the Catholic Church teach that there are three Gods. She teaches, on the contrary, that there is but one God, and that there cannot by any possibility be more Gods than one. The very idea of God involves a Being infinitely perfect, and supreme

Lord and Master of all things, and therefore necessarily excludes another being equal to Himself in these Divine perfections. He would probably shrug his shoulders, and say, with the flippant tone of our fashionable Agnostics, "Have it your own way—you may of course be right, but the fact is we can know nothing about the ' unknowable.' And if there really exists such a Being as you describe, one of the clearest arguments against His perfections would be His asking reasonable beings to believe what they do not understand."

Let us briefly examine this argument—God has no right to require of us to believe incomprehensible mysteries.

My readers may not fear that I am attempting to lead them into abstract, learned, metaphysical reasoning on the point. What I have to say will be very briefly put, and will appeal rather to common-sense than to profound learning. I know it would be a great mistake on my part to stuff this book, meant for the general public, with the dry elements of scholastic teaching. I want the public to read what I have written, and to think a little as they read on. I can scarcely hope that the majority of readers will do more than this. Serious reflection on anything that does not fall under the scope of sense would be a marvel in the busy world "of facts and figures." Let us then ask ourselves the simple question, Has our Creator a right to require us to believe the incomprehensible information He has given us about the Divine nature? Is it fair to ask us to receive into our finite minds what is beyond our powers of mental conception? What is the use of this knowledge which we can never apply to any practical purposes? Is a religion that proposes mysteries to the belief of its adherents a sensible religion, or a religion such as a man of sound, practical, common-sense should accept?

Instead of one question I have put several; but they all help to bring out the Rationalistic notion—What in the name of common-sense have reasonable beings to do with what is beyond the reach of reason? Now in reply to all these matter-of-fact questions, I say, It is quite clear that, though we may from the visible creation rise to the conception of the existence of a supreme necessarily existing Being, and that this Being must be endowed with infinite perfections, we can know nothing adequately of the nature of this Being except what He condescends to tell us about Himself. We may, by the study of His works, be brought to bow down and adore His infinite power and wisdom and goodness. But, if I wish to penetrate farther into the perfections of this great Being, I plunge into a fathomless abyss, a mighty, boundless ocean, in which the finite mind wanders hopelessly and is lost. If God, taking pity on our mental weakness, is pleased to enlighten us by a supernatural light, if He condescends to give us a glimpse of His real nature, ought we not to accept with gratitude the Divine light which is shed upon us, and reverently venerate and adore the sacred shadows which this light reflects? Christians believe that God has actually given us this Revelation of Himself. Catholic Christianity maintains that this Revelation, partly written, partly given by word of mouth through our Divine Redeemer, has been intrusted to the Church's teaching till the end of time; and that the teaching Church is helped and enlightened in preserving and explaining this Revelation by the Holy Ghost constantly abiding with her. In this way Catholic Christians know with certainty what God has taught;

they know beyond doubt whether a plain, intelligible fact or truth is proposed to them, or whether they are called on by Divine authority to accept and believe a mystery.

When Rationalists assail the Christian mysteries they do not as a rule keep this point clearly before them. Their arguments are mainly directed against Bible Christianity; and there, it must be confessed, they are eminently successful. If there is no infallible authority to assure us by its living, speaking voice that the truth proposed for belief has been certainly revealed by God, and that it has been revealed in a sense which admits of only one interpretation, and that in this interpretation is involved some dogma which our minds cannot grasp, there can be no such thing as belief in mysteries.

The fact that Bible Christianity cannot fairly and logically insist on belief in mysteries is clearly shown by the constantly growing disposition on the part of the adherents of this form of Christianity to do away with all mysteries, to abolish the Athanasian Creed, and to explain everything of a mysterious character as merely figurative and symbolical language. Now, taking our stand on this solid rock of Catholic Christianity, we Catholics argue thus: 1st. Do any truths incomprehensible to man exist? 2d. Has God a right to require that man should believe truths which he does not comprehend? We can afterward demonstrate the practical value of such truths.

With regard to the first point, there can be no doubt that we all believe in truths which we do not comprehend. As the celebrated Abbé McCarthy puts this point in the clearest light, I quote his eloquent words: "On whatever side you turn your eyes, whether you fix them upon yourself or upon the objects which surround you, whether you turn them to the heavens above or cast them down to the earth upon which you tread, do you not everywhere encounter limits to retard you, or depths and obscurities to confound you? In the first place, you find them within yourself. What is that substance which constitutes the principle of volition, of thought, of deliberation and action within you, the source of sensation, of motion, and life—in a word, your soul? Nothing is more present, nothing more interwoven with your existence. It is, as it were, the groundwork of your being; it is your very self. What is this substance? Endeavor to grasp it within your thoughts, to examine it, to analyze it—you cannot. There is no fact which you feel so intimately, as that you live. But what is your life?"

It is well known that the vital principle in all creatures, as well as in man, is the very point where the most scientific analysis of being is checked. We may talk about protoplasm and cells and molecules, and build up the creature according to our fancy; but what is that life which sets the minute organization in motion, and the loss of which in a moment reduces the most elaborate mechanism to decomposition and ruin? We know not; it is all a mystery. No one doubts, while he is in active health, that he has absolute power over his limbs, but who understands the manner in which this power of thought and will is exercised? Men may, by patient study, bring out before them the elaborate structure of the organs of sense; they see how admirably the eye is adapted for seeing and the ear for hearing; but who will tell us the shape or color or form of the immaterial substance that receives the impressions of sight or sound, or how the image painted on the retina is conveyed to the spiritual substance which, from the very nature of its operations, must be without parts; not presenting in its simple nature one point of contrast with the material image that affects it.

It is needless to pile up the argument with illustrations from outside. Take the most ordinary phenomena of nature—the growth of a blade of grass, the sprouting of a grain of corn. You may with the microscope watch these operations in the very first instant of their external action. You can see, as any amateur familiar with the use of the instrument understands, the action of fertilization in the common duck-weed, or any other species of the Lemna that grow in our pools or ditches.

But what is it that in the first instant of this apparent life has quickened the seemingly lifeless sphere into activity? No one can tell. It is a mystery to the most experienced savant as to the ignorant rustic. The profound ignorance of man who, in the exaltation of his pride, when he chances to stumble over some new isolated fact in the physical world, fancies he knows everything, is well expressed in the words of Ecclesiastes: "And I understood that man can find no reason of all these works of God that are done under the sun: and the more he shall labor to seek, so much the less shall he find: yea, though the wise man should say that he knoweth it, he shall not be able to find it" (Ecclesiastes viii. 17).

There is not a single truth, even in the natural and physical order, which is not incomprehensible in some respect or other. Even in that science which may be said to be the growth of man's own thought, pure mathematics, there are mysteries where the keenest mind must stop and declare that it has reached a limit which it cannot pass. How ridiculous, is it not, before the face of these clouds and shadows, in the midst of which we walk in this material world, to complain that religion should ask us to believe incomprehensible truths regarding the Infinite God and "the depths of His knowledge and wisdom"?

How many a poor ignorant scoffer at revealed religion and its mysteries, who boasts that he is a man of common practical sense, who believes nothing but what he sees, is altogether ignorant that there is not an hour of his waking life in which he is not virtually giving the lie to this Free-thinking theory! If he did not believe, on the testimony of others, the ordinary natural phenomena with which his life is intimately blended, and of the true nature of which he knows as little as a child, he should miserably perish. He scarcely knows the first rudiments of common physiology—how his body is nourished, and what are the constituents of his food, and how his blood circulates. If he waited first of all to understand all these complicated arrangements, and their causes and effects, before he attended to his bodily wants, in case he did not die of hunger, he would soon be eminently qualified for a lunatic asylum. There can be no doubt, then, that incomprehensible truths exist. Let us now see if God has not a perfect right to ask us to believe truths about Himself which we do not comprehend.

I have already shown that it was to be expected, from the very nature of the case, that if God actually condescended to tell us some of the secrets of His being, these secrets, quite beyond the reach of our finite gropings, should necessarily be incomprehensible—that is, above the powers of our mind to understand them, but not in any way opposed to the natural lights of our reason.

The chief argument of the Rationalists on this point is: "God is a God of light. He is Omniscient. Whatever emanates from Him should be clear, luminous, and intelligible. In proportion as the intellect of man is clear and well developed, so are his teachings on the subject of his studies. While the vain pedant mystifies his audience with bits and scraps of sensational information, illogically put together and out of order, full of contradictions and extravagances, the really learned man can adapt himself to the capacity of children. Should it not be so eminently when God speaks to us? Ought not all His teachings to be luminous as the sun itself?"

I thought it well to give this argument the full force with which it appeals to the judgment of the unthinking multitude. But how very silly is its sophistry! I have already shown that nature, science, and every grand truth connected with our existence in this world, are full of mysteries, surrounded by shadows which our intellect cannot penetrate. And from whom do all these emanate? Is it not from the great first and supreme Cause of all that exists? Is it not from this omniscient, luminous God?

If men, by careful study and preparation, are able in proportion to their learning and industry and care, to adapt themselves to the intelligence of their audience, to make what is clear to themselves clear to others also; if they can teach others to understand whatever is intelligible, and quite within the scope of the ordinary perception of individuals—does it follow that when the Omniscient God deigns to draw aside a little the veil that hides His Infinite nature from our sight, the supernatural light should not dazzle and bewilder us? Must God give us lights equal to His own? If He lifts the veil a little for our good, and to let us know something about Himself that will make us love Him with a more reverential love, fear His justice, and adore His sanctity, as we are thus attracted to Him by the clearer knowledge of His goodness and patience and infinite mercy, is He bound to display all His infinite perfections to gratify our pride?

Pressed in this way, the objectors will reply: "No, no. We must admit that the finite cannot take into itself the Infinite; as well might we hope to hold the vast ocean in the hollow of our hand. But God cannot oblige us to believe what we cannot understand. This would be to require the sacrifice of our reason, and that would be in the last degree absurd!"

It is easy to pierce through the flimsy covering of this specious reasoning. But that the age is eminently an unreasoning one, the prophets and leaders of modern Free-thought would not dare so impudently to abuse the public confidence. The men who reason thus will require their children to receive their teaching on matters that are perfectly incomprehensible to them. They will require the ignorant, on the authority of the learned, to believe things which seem contrary to the evidence of sense—to believe, for instance, that this earth constantly revolves with wonderful velocity; that the sun, which seems to their untrained eyes to rise and set, is stationary. They will require the blind man to believe all the phenomena of light. In this they are acting quite conformably to right reason and common-sense. And they go farther still, they will dogmatize on the exaggeration of these sound principles, and grow mad with passion if their pet theories and systems of evolution or spontaneous generation are called into question. "Why," they say, "should the ignorant herd who have never gone fully into these subjects, dare to doubt our superior knowledge, and the accuracy of that process of induction which has led us from fact to fact, till we have reached that height whence, like gods, we can with a glance take in the vast field stretched out before us, create system upon system, and pronounce it all 'to be very good,' and satisfactory to ourselves and the whole world."

But I reply, How can they consistently require this acceptance of their teaching and entire submission to their authority, when they deny that men ought to exhibit the same deference and the same docility to the sovereign and infallible intelligence of God?

I will conclude the argument with the eloquent words of the illustrious preacher already quoted. He is addressing Rationalists on this very point. "When you refuse to admit that in science and enlightenment the Infinite Being has a far greater superiority over any mortal, even the most enlightened, than the full-grown man possesses over the child, or the man who sees over the blind man, or the philosopher over the ignorant man, I must confess that your blindness and your inconsistency seem to me the greatest of all mysteries; and if this be what you dignify with the appellation of philosophy and wisdom, it is what I term not only inexcusable audacity and impiety, but incomprehensible stupidity and folly."

The only question that can reasonably be urged is this: Has God spoken? Do we know, can we know, with certainty what He has revealed? Is there no chance that we may be deceived, either concerning the fact of the Divine message, or the incomprehensible mystery that this message sets before us? If the revelation comes from Him it must be true, whatever may be the difficulties or obscurities which it may present to us. All our arguments to the contrary are as senseless as the argument of a blind man against colors, or those of a deaf man against sound and speech.

How absurd then, is the whole of this reasoning of Free-thought. Why will it not fix on what is fairly within its province and argue upon the question of fact, Has God really made a Revelation? But this would require time and trouble and serious thought; and so the leaders of modern Free-thought, in direct opposition to the practical inductive philosophy so much applauded by them, talk of the "unknowable," shrug their shoulders, and say—"This Religion cannot be true, because it teaches things that are beyond our comprehension." In all other matters of learned inquiry the mode of procedure is quite the opposite of this.

I quite agree with the system of inductive philosophy, now so much in vogue, as regards physical science, and also to a certain extent as regards revealed Religion. By all means let us have facts before we theorize or speculate. The facts collected by Darwin are unquestionably of immense value to the scientific world; so are the facts fairly tested and demonstrated by Huxley.

Every one knows what in these days would be called the "sell" of the merry monarch. "Why," said Charles to his learned courtiers, "does a dead fish out of water weigh heavier than a living fish in water?" There was any amount of theorizing over the assumed fact, till a shrewd philosopher raised the point, Is it positively a fact that the dead fish weighs heavier? He showed by actual experiment that there was no such fact on which to speculate, and so solved the humorous riddle.

Now, in the matter of Revelation, there are certain facts to be established; and, thanks to the labors of learned

Christians of all denominations, the great fact that there has been a Revelation is demonstrated beyond possibility of doubt. I have in the diocesan library here a valuable work in seventeen quarto volumes, collected from the works of over one hundred most distinguished writers on the subject. It is called *Démonstrations Évangéliques* and includes extracts from the learned Fathers of the Church, from the celebrated French and English historians, theologians and preachers, Protestant as well as Catholic, infidel as well as believers. When I say that the names of Bacon, Grotius, Descartes, Pascal, Boyle, Locke, Leibnitz, Bayle, Tillotson, Jean Jacques Rousseau, Leharpe, Poynter, Paley, Buckland, etc., figure amongst them, an idea may be formed of the vast accumulation of evidence which the learned Abbé Migne, the editor of the work, has brought to bear on the sensible and striking facts demonstrating the truth of revealed Religion. Prophecies and their fulfilment, miracles, the testimony of so many thousand martyrs, the conversion of the whole civilized world, the preservation of the Church, summed up in the eloquent passage of Macaulay on "The Everlasting Church," offer ample scope for the keen scrutiny of Freethinkers.

But this accumulation of evidence alarms them, and so, departing from the sound principles of inductive reasoning, they rush into the boundless and obscure field of doctrine, and involve themselves in stupid arguments, regarding the possibility or probability of matters which are altogether beyond the reach of their reasoning powers. Facts are disregarded, although they are the only accessible and palpable part of it, in order that, behind the leaden barrier of Agnosticism, they may amuse themselves with caricaturing God's truth, and losing themselves in the mazes of silly speculations and unmeaning evasions and distortions of the sacred Word of God.

When I read that thousands of intelligent people in America attend the lectures of Ingersoll, and applaud the fun and humor that would have no enlivening point but because it is directed to subjects that were once venerable and sacred in their eyes, I am confirmed in the profound conviction which has forced itself on my mind, that the blighting curse of the age, which threatens all social order and real progress, is this flippancy and silly love of variety and change and piquancy, that the luxury and the love of wealth has made necessary to relieve the monotony of material enjoyment.

I saw a picture, some years ago, in the gallery of the Louvre reserved for modern artists. It presented a view of the state of society in the luxurious days of the effete Roman empire. It is before my mental vision now—not gross and revolting to Christian eyes, but telling its tale of desolation in the dress and attitudes and expression of a set of Bacchanalian revellers tired of enjoyment and weary of life. It seemed as if the ordinary gratifications of sensuality had become repulsive to them from satiety, and that they had neither hope nor spirit even to dream of new pleasures.

We have not yet come to this pass, but any one who thinks seriously may mark the unmistakable signs of its near approach, in the perverted literature of these evil days, in the degradation of the stage, in the decline of classic art in music and painting, in the indifference to anything that can raise the soul above the earthly things of earth. We may note it too in the dress and fashions of the time, concentrated on low and depraved tastes that seem to ape the sensualism of our African savagery.

There are unmistakable signs of the utter hollowness and want of solid Catholic Christianity in the masses of nations that once were thoroughly Christian, in their habits and modes of thought. A generation or two hence, if the lotus-eaters, who are insensibly and lazily drifting down the stream of dreamland, yield themselves entirely to this seductive influence, that stupor may come on the world which invariably precedes the upheaving of anarchical revolution.

The languid Romans of the declining days of the Empire could scarcely rouse themselves to the realization of the terrible fact that the tide of savage barbarism was at their gates, when they were swept away helplessly in the mighty deluge. The voluptuous courtiers of the age of Louis XV. mocked and derided the sullen growlings of the coming storm, and so miserably perished.

It may be said that in this nineteenth century we are free from those striking inequalities between the favored upper classes and the trampled-down poor, which were among the chief causes of the great Revolution. But there are crying evils of the kind even now. What will happen when the hitherto uneducated classes come fully to understand the fact that in Great Britain about eight thousand of the privileged idle class hold in their hands 46,500,000 acres of the land of the nation, and that, though these lands represent a value of between three and five thousand million pounds, or an annual value, for the three kingdoms of England, Ireland, and Scotland, of one hundred and eight millions sterling, the taxes borne by the privileged few amount to only four and a half millions?

It is no wonder that Mr. Kaye, one of the foremost political economists of the time, has said—" The classes who are deprived of the natural means of improving their social condition, will rise more and more fiercely against the obstacles that beset them, the more clearly they perceive these obstacles. If it is necessary or expedient that the present landed system should be continued, it would be wiser to get rid of every school in the country. To give the people intelligence and yet to tie their hands, is more dangerous than to give fire to a madman."

Some years ago Mr. Fawcett wrote: " Production has increased quite beyond the most sanguine hopes, and yet the day when the workman shall obtain a larger share of the increase seems as far distant as ever; and in his miserable abode the struggle against want and misery is as hard as ever it was. The result of this is to create a profound hostility to the fundamental principles upon which society is based." Well has a distinguished writer portrayed in a few pithy words the economy of social life at the present time: " It is a philosophy of despair, resting upon an arithmetic of ruin."

It is very easy for those who ought to preserve themselves from the *laissez-aller* disposition of this frivolous age, to say, as did the French noblesse on the eve of the cataclysm, "*Après nous le déluge.*" But statesmen should ponder in time on the signs of the growing whirlwind of conviction that is rising in the public mind, and open their eyes to the proximate dangers which Freethought, education without God, and the other liberal views, so fashionable now, are rapidly generating. Let any unexpected cause relax the firm arm of physical force, and who can form an idea of the immensity of the desolation that is even now threatening the social fabric!

I had almost forgotten to point out the use and value

of incomprehensible truths of Revelation. The thoughts to which I have just given expression suggest them.

Mysteries in Religion check the evil of pride—the source of all the miseries of our fallen race; they clearly indicate to man that there are limits to his curiosity. "Thus far shalt thou go, and no farther," is the plain lesson of every mystery. And, while they check our pride, they irresistibly transport our thoughts to another life, where all that is mysterious now, will form in its ample development and in the unbounded prospect it will open to the emancipated soul, the infinite source of joys without end, ever varying and ever delightful. Were our thoughts of future bliss confined to visions of earthly pleasure, we might picture to ourselves the satiety of happiness. We know that the sweetest music will weary with monotony, and in time, if continued, become a real torture; a bed of roses will soon lose its fragrance. Such thoughts help us to realize to ourselves the force of that objection of Rationalism conveyed in the "damp clouds" and "give him a harp" of Ingersoll. But when, in connection with the incomprehensible mysteries of Religion, we know that delights are in store for us hereafter, of which in the flesh we can have no conception, we are helped to feel the force of the consoling words of the Apostle—" Eye hath not seen, nor ear heard, nor hath it entered into the heart of men, what things God hath prepared for them that love Him" (1 Cor. ii. 9).

If now we view Catholic Christianity in its mysteries, how beautiful, how consoling! How far beyond any ideal of the human imagination is the view with which it gladdens us! There is no question of dreams or fancies, but "the evidence of things that appear not."

The soul seems to expand with the vastness of the prospect presented to it. It sees "dimly" of course, and "as it were through a glass," the happy state "prepared for it from the beginning of the world." God Himself, the centre of all things desirable, who alone can satisfy the longings of the heart, will be "its reward exceeding great."

There is something in the very fact that it cannot conceive the immensity of the Divine perfections, that fills it with a foretaste of bliss. If the joys we hope for in the better land were clearly defined, though they might gleam and glisten with the brightest flashes of human eloquence, and appear before us adorned with all the flowers and graceful imagery of the poet, we would soon learn to strip them of these adventitious charms, and viewing them in their naked poverty and emptiness, come to despise them as the perishable and unsatisfactory joys of earth. Who would care "to fight the good fight," to battle bravely with the world, the demon, and the flesh, to take up the cross daily and follow after Christ, if the crown prepared for him hereafter were one such as we might covet in this world—a gilded toy to amuse the eye for a season, but dim, tarnished, and worthless under the first breath of eternity.

Mahommedans, whose souls have never been invigorated with the pure atmosphere of a Heaven, "where nothing defiled can enter," may sacrifice life and the fleeting joys of earthly pleasure for an eternity of sensual repose. But the Christian, who has learned to fix his affections on the all-holy and perfect treasure prepared for him in the kingdom of God, must ever spurn with contempt pleasures and delights that derive their charm from anything that is of the earth, earthly.

It is only when we associate bliss hereafter with the purest intellectual satisfaction we can conceive, that the soul seems lifted above the weaknesses of the frail body, and impelled to do and dare great things for the possession of that unbounded knowledge to be found in God. Religion may set this glorious prize before us, but no revelation that our souls can bear in this prison of the flesh, could possibly afford us more than a faint gleam of the exquisite delight with which we shall be inebriated when, seeing God "face to face," we shall behold "the secret things" of all knowledge in the brightness of His glory.

"No man can see God and live;" and so, whatever God tells us of His own nature and perfections, and the future prepared for those who love Him, must be tempered and toned down to suit our finite perceptions; and we must be not only content but grateful that He has only dimly revealed these incomprehensible mysteries. Here we are as children, speaking of things we do not understand, lisping as it were the language of Heaven, but reminded constantly by these unintelligible accents of our true country, towards which during life we were always hastening.

When Rationalists say that our mysteries are not only incomprehensible, but actually contradictory to reason, absurd, and ridiculous, they go rather too far for the common-sense of their hearers. They imitate those fanatical Christians who fancy they are demonstrating the truth of their religious views by overwhelming the old Church with a heap of the vilest names they can put together. The greater the heap and the more high-sounding the vituperations the better—"idolatrous," "blasphemous," "monstrous," "diabolical," "absurd,"

CATHOLIC CHRISTIANITY AND ITS MYSTERIES. 75

and "ridiculous." This class of reasoners, whether Christian or non-Christian, forget an axiom which, if not known in precise terms by the general public, is well understood : "*Quod nimis probat, nihil probat,*"— "What proves too much, proves nothing." If the mysteries of revealed Religion are absurd and contradictory, then all the great and learned men who for the last eighteen hundred years have adorned the Christian name by their talents, and genius, and profound wisdom, were simply besotted idiots. There were millions and millions of such men, giants of literature, many of whom are regarded by the learned of to-day as the benefactors and most distinguished ornaments of humanity: and they were Catholics, who heard the Church, and learned their religion from her lips. The conceited and impudent Rationalist, who with jaunty air points at these great men the finger of scorn, and calls them "blind fools, leaders of the blind," is likely to establish his own character for senseless vanity in the minds of a discerning public.

When the definitions of the Church that declare the revealed mysteries are read with ordinary attention there is no ground whatever for the charge of contradiction. If some other form of expression, that has its origin in stupid ignorance or ingenious malice, is attributed to the Church, and the true doctrine is misrepresented, all the specious reasoning of her adversaries is directed, not against the dogma, but against a mere misapprehension or distortion of the true doctrine.

If a Rationalist says that the Church requires and forces her hearers to believe the palpable absurdity, that three Gods are one God, that three persons are one person, he is only stating what is absolutely false; and, though he may indulge in sparkling wit and ridicule in tearing the monstrous proposition to rags, he is only imitating the infuriated bull that tramples and gores and tosses the senseless object flung in his face to deceive him.

All the shocking irreverence applied to the Blessed Eucharist, "The wafer God," "The priests' God," etc., have their origin in the same culpable ignorance or the same malicious misrepresentation.

If earnest men, who pride themselves on their superiority to blind prejudice, and their honesty of purpose, would only take a little pains to know what Catholic Christianity really is, if, instead of learning this from the bitter enemies of the Church, they went to the fountain source, and disregarded altogether these turbid and muddy waters, what a glorious spectacle would they behold in the mysteries proposed by the Catholic Church! They would see then at a glance the wonderful unity and admirable connection there is between these revealed truths, and that one almost necessarily grew out of the other. They would not of course comprehend how three persons really distinct can exist in a single nature; but they would be helped, by the study of their own unity of person in a twofold nature, to conceive of the Divine nature something infinitely superior and more incomprehensible. They would see at once that without this distinction of persons the Incarnation would have been impossible, and that there could be no Atonement. Believing firmly that the Uncreated Word, " by Whom all things were made," became man, that Christ was as truly God as He was man, and that in Him there is but one Person, and consequently that all His actions are those of a God; that consequently Mary is the Mother of God; that the Blessed Eucharist is the means invented by

Almighty love to bring home to every individual of the Christian family, as long as the world lasts, the fruits of Redemption; similarly they would perceive that the Sacramental system almost naturally grew from the same stem; that the doctrine of the Immaculate Conception and the Devotion to the Sacred Heart are the gradual unfolding of the blossoms of Faith on the Tree of Life.

This one view of the intimate connection and harmony of revealed truths would of itself be sufficient to fill them with reverence and admiration for that tree planted by a Divine hand, which has stood the storms of ages, and is now, in the midst of the wreck and ruin of Impiety and Heresy, as vigorous and flourishing as in its palmiest days; offering, in its ample shade, calm and quiet rest to the weary and distracted nations of the whole world.

CHAPTER III.

The Incarnation, the Centre and Soul of Catholic Christianity.

I HAVE always felt that the practical life of an earnest Catholic must be of a supernatural character. He cannot realize to himself what his religion teaches, without feeling that he is moving in the midst of spiritual influences that mould and fashion and determine every impulse of his being.

Some of the weird traditions of my native country—the stories I have heard in earliest years of the "good people," "the whispering of the angels" when the infant smiles in its happy slumbers, the wail of the benshee, all these pretty harmless legends which live in the glowing imagination of the Irish peasant, are not after all stupid superstitions, but outcomes of revealed truth embalmed in the poetry of nature. They tell of the fervent piety of a people who in the ages of Faith "walked with God," when "the Emerald Isle" was the only safe home of Religion, and an "Island of Saints." It is probably this natural tendency of the imagination to rise above the stern realities of material life, to see and feel the kind Providence of our Heavenly Father directing the crosses and afflictions of cruel suffering, in bad seasons, and persecution more cruel still, and the miseries of poverty, hardly known in other lands, that renders many a poor uneducated Irish mother, who knows no learning but her beads and the rudiments of her catechism, a perfect heroine in that most exalted of virtues, the nighest to angelic perfection—entire submission to the blessed will of God.

It is the same inherent instinct of a lively Faith, that enables them to ward off the assaults of polemical intrusion, and to overcome with ready wit the arguments of Biblical learning. My memory teems with amusing instances of pharisaical pride brought low, and sanctimonious cant balked and baffled by happy retorts and flashes of pleasantry that overwhelmed the assailant with "the inextinguishable laughter" of an appreciative audience. Humorous as they are, they spring from the earnestness of religious conviction, and from the almost perfect realization of some revealed truth, long the subject of serious meditation.

I am almost tempted to set one or two anecdotes of the kind before my readers, but I feel "*nunc non erat his locus.*"

One thing is quite certain, though even learned Protestant Divines affect to mourn over the superstitions and blank ignorance of the poor in Ireland, they might learn wisdom from the ingrained and intense piety developed in the school of adversity. Devotion most tender and affectionate to the Mother of the Saviour is strikingly characteristic of this piety. The gentle Virgin, "with the boy-God upon her knee," or Mary standing at the foot of the cross, is constantly before the eyes of the poor beadsman, or the fixed internal gaze of the mother and her children, as they repeat the "Our Father" or the Angelical salutation. They hope, in the deep sense of their own unworthiness, that they may pray with unbounded confidence when their humble petitions are offered in the presence and with the approval and recommendation of the Holy Mother of God.

It is a remarkable thing that in this land of the old Faith the Catholics of high and low degree never salute Mary, as they do in England and other lands, with the title of " Our Blessed Lady," but speak of Her and to Her, invariably, as the " Mother of God." It may be that our good Father in Heaven, in consideration of the many trials that in Ireland beset the Faith of the people, filled their souls with the comforting and sustaining belief that lies under this tender appellation, which comprises in itself all the riches of His infinite condescension and mercy.

The point suggested by these thoughts is so admirably put by Cardinal Newman, and falls in so entirely with the object of this chapter, which means to show that the great mystery of the Incarnation is the chief ground of Catholic Christianity, that I give it almost *in extenso* from that admirable sermon, " The Glories of Mary for the Sake of her Son :" " When the Eternal Word decreed to come on earth, He did not purpose, He did not work, by halves; but He came to be a man like any of us, to take a human soul and body, and to make them His own. He did not come in a mere apparent or accidental form, as Angels appear to men ; nor did He merely overshadow an existing man, as He overshadowed His Saints, and call Him by the name of God; but He ' was made flesh.' He attached to Himself a manhood, and became as really and truly man as He was God, so that henceforth He was both God and man, or, in other words, He was one Person in two natures, Divine and human. This is a mystery so marvellous, so difficult, that Faith alone firmly receives it; the natural man may receive it for a while, may think he receives it, but never really receives it; begins, as soon as he has professed it, secretly to rebel against it, evades it, or revolts from it. This he has done from the first; even in the lifetime of the beloved disciple men arose, who said that our Lord had no body at all, or a body framed in the heavens, or that He did not suffer, but another suffered in His stead, or that He was but for a time in the human form which was born and which suffered, coming on it at its baptism, and leaving it before its crucifixion, or that He was a mere man. That 'In the beginning was the Word, and the Word was with God, and the Word was God,' and 'the Word was made flesh and dwelt among us,' was too hard a thing for the unregenerate reason.

" The case is the same at this day; mere Protestants have seldom any real perception of the doctrine of God and man in one Person. They speak in a dreamy, shadowy way of Christ's divinity; but, when their meaning is sifted, you will find them very slow to express the Catholic dogma. . . . Now, if you would witness against these unchristian opinions, if you would bring out distinctly and beyond mistake and evasion, the simple idea of the Catholic Church that God is man, could you do it better than by laying down in St. John's words that 'God *became* man'? and again could you express this more emphatically and unequivocally than by declaring that He was *born* a man or that He had a *Mother?* The world allows that God *is* man; the admission costs it little, for God is everywhere, and (as it may say) is everything; but it shrinks from confessing that God is the Son of Mary. It shrinks, for it is at once confronted with a severe fact, which violates and shatters its own unbelieving view of things; the revealed doctrine forthwith takes its true shape, and receives an historical reality; and the Almighty is introduced into His own world at a certain time and in a definite way. Dreams are broken and shadows depart; the Divine truth is no longer a poetical expression, or a devotional exaggeration, or a mystical economy, or a mythical representation. . . . By witnessing to the *process* of the union, it secures the reality of the two *subjects* of the union, of the divinity and of the manhood. If Mary is the Mother of God, Christ is understood to be the Emmanuel, God with us."

This passage, which I have somewhat abridged, seems to me to bring out with peculiar force and power the fundamental mystery of revealed Religion. Once this mystery is believed in all its fulness, there can be no difficulty in believing in all its consequences. The Child adored in the crib at Bethelehem is the God by whom all things were made. Those little hands stretched out towards the Virgin Mother in infantine helplessness, are the hands of God; these eyes dimmed with the tears of dawning human life are the eyes of God; that voice, as yet inarticulate and murmuring of unintelligible babyish sorrow, is the voice which once awoke creation into being. What is there that the great God has not given us in this mystery? What gift can be imagined larger or more bountiful on His part to fallen man? When we believe, with all the assent of our minds, the joyful tidings that He has thus given us His Son to be our real brother, flesh of our flesh and bone of our bone, His loving condescension is complete.

It would be almost impossible, in the limits of one chapter, to set forth the extravagant notions entertained by Christians outside the Church, concerning this great mystery. They all more or less converge to one point—" to dissolve Jesus Christ," as St. John expresses it—" and every spirit that dissolveth Jesus is not of God." They would by some figment or other try to break the Hypostatic or Personal union of the Divine and human nature in our Divine Redeemer. They picture to themselves a double personality in Jesus Christ, a man-Christ and a God-Christ—a being partly man and partly God. This is the most distinctive character of the heresies of the present time in reference to the Incarnation. Christians who are not Catholics do not care to speak about this mystery. They affect so great a reverence for it, that, in their idea, the union of God and man in the Redeemer is to be respected as was the word "Jehovah" by the Jews. If they are pressed to explain what they believe exactly, it will be found that, if they commit themselves at all to any distinct formulary of belief, this belief will incline first of all to that form of Appolinarism which supposed that in Christ the Divinity took the place of a soul; and when it is pointed out to them that this belief would necessarily involve the suffering of the Deity in the Divine nature, they either fall back on Arianism pure and simple, by denying that Christ is God, or, which is more likely, as being less directly in opposition to the traditions of Catholic Faith, they will stand as firmly as they can on the ground that there was a man-Christ and a God-Christ, and that, somehow or other, the two individuals were blended into one. It was, they assert, the man-Christ that was born of Mary; it was the man-Christ that suffered and died and came to life again.

That this is no imaginary or fanciful notion of Bible Christians' belief in Christ will be made clear if the argument is pressed: for then they who hold this view will become violently dogmatic, and exclaim, "How could God suffer?" "How could God die?" "How by any possibility could the Creator become the child of His own creature?" Here we see clearly, as Cardinal Newman says, the Divine maternity of Mary becomes the real test of orthodoxy. God really suffered in His human nature. God really died in the same nature. God was buried in the tomb, and God was truly the Son of Mary. For says the Athanasian Creed, not yet I believe abrogated from the formularies of belief of all Bible Christians, " The right faith is that we believe and confess that our Lord Jesus Christ, the Son of God, is both God and man, perfect God and perfect man: yet not two but one Christ—one altogether, not by the confusion of substance, but by the unity of person."

Protestants seldom realize to themselves what is involved in " obedience to the faith"—that to believe what God reveals often requires self-sacrifice and bowing down in all simplicity and humility to the truth of His holy Word. They do not like to subject themselves to this ordeal, and therefore they would much prefer to receive the mysteries of revealed Religion without questioning too particularly what is the dogma to which we must assent under pain of eternal ruin, for "without Faith it is impossible to please God" (Heb. xi. 6).

The very opposite is the habit and disposition of Catholics: they require to know exactly, without doubt or evasion, what mysteries God proposes to them by the voice of His Church. They love to meditate upon these words of life, to analyze them, and to see their intimate connection with other revealed truths, and to draw from them sound practical principles for their guidance. If Faith, or entire assent of the mind without doubt, to everything God has revealed, be essential to salvation, it cannot be right and safe to follow our own fancies about these tremendous truths. We are bound to know, as far as we can, what they mean, and to be most careful not to put some notion of our own in place of what the God of all truth has revealed.

Thus as regards this primary mystery of the Incarnation, men who desire to please God should say—Must I believe that God really suffered and died in His human nature, and that Jesus Christ, God the Son from all eternity, was truly the Son of Mary? No matter what the consequences of this profession of Faith may be on other articles of his creed, he must not heed these consequences. "If we have Faith," says Cardinal Newman, "to admit the Incarnation itself, we must admit it in its fulness; why then should we start at the gracious appointments which arise out of it, or are necessary to it, or are included in it?"

I think the consequences are so obvious, in one respect at least, of professing true Catholic Faith in the Incarnation, that they cannot escape the perception of any reader who glances even hurriedly over these pages. He will see that if God our Redeemer is truly the Son of Mary, or in other words that if "Mary is really the Mother of God," the whole aspect of Protestant thought and teaching as regards the Virgin Mary is completely wrong.

But there can be no doubt upon this point. If our Divine Redeemer were not perfect man to suffer and perfect God to save, if the two natures were not united in the one Person, united so intimately in this firm bond of personality that they can never for all eternity be severed, there would be no such thing as the Atonement, and every fragment of Christian truth would be dissolved, "as a cloud is consumed and passeth away" (Job vii. 9). See how clear and distinct is the teaching of the Catholic

Church on this point! When God the Son became man He did not take the germ of a body and unite it to His divinity, but He took a perfect human nature—a body and a soul. At the very moment the soul was united to the germ of a human body, in the chaste womb of the Virgin, before that soul and body had a personality of its own, He took it to Himself and made that perfect human nature His own forever. There was no personality to be displaced. There could be no such thing as a mere man-Christ, there was no individual existence even for a moment, but the individual second person of the Blessed Trinity.

From this it follows that the Catholic sees at once the high position to which the Virgin is exalted in the economy of salvation. She is not only "full of grace" and every perfection that finite human nature is capable of receiving, but she is the connecting link between the great God and His sinful creatures. It is the flesh and blood received from her that enabled the second Divine Person to offer up the sacrifice of expiation. Through her is communicated to us the Divine life. She is the mother of all the living; and through this common maternity we are made children of God and heirs to the kingdom of heaven. If God truly became her son, then we see at once that she never could have borne the least taint of sin. The Immaculate Conception is no longer "a shadowy mysticism" or "a new article added to an overgrown creed," but the natural expansion and growth and development of a truth that existed in the body of revealed doctrine from the beginning.

Let this mystery be thus clearly understood, and then every other truth of Christianity springs as it were spontaneously from the living stem. One of the greatest mistakes made by the enemies of the Catholic Church, whether they are Christians or Infidels, is that the Church is the guardian of a fossilized creed that stands in the way of healthy progress. She is, on the contrary, the faithful guardian of the light of Faith, that lives and burns within her bosom, kindling the ardor of piety in the hearts of her children by exhibiting to them the glowing pile of the traditions of past triumphs and the accumulated heap of innumerable records of immortal hope, in her many contests with the powers of this world. The Church is a living organization; and the breath of her life is the Spirit of Truth abiding with her forever. She lives now with the life breathed into her at Pentecost, and this life manifests its vigor in proportion to the violence of the assaults to which she is subjected. When lately she defined the doctrine of the Immaculate Conception, the savants of this unthinking age beheld in her action only the affectation and trifling of senile vanity. But to those who have received her Founder with all the fulness of His revelation, and to whom He has, in consequence of this generous Faith, given power "to be made the sons of God," there is evidence, in this most remarkable act, of her supernatural vitality and unfailing vigor.

The main effort of this age of unbelieving progress is to trample out the supernatural character of Jesus Christ. Jesus is indeed in its eyes the most distinguished of human sages, an admirable philosopher, the best of moral teachers. It will admit, with the unbelieving Pharisees and Sadducees, that " no man ever spoke like Him," but it ridicules the idea that He was " the Word made flesh." This is the brilliant discovery which science has made in the field of theology, so long neglected by it, and it rejoices exceedingly. With one bold stroke it has, it fancies, laid bare the vain subtleties and scholastic absurdities of past ages, and its Renans and Strausses and the herd of Positivists and Agnostics clap their hands because they have shown the world how to get rid of the mystery "that tormented them." But in the midst of their unholy triumph, lo! the old Church, which they would make believe was dead of inanition, speaks out with a voice that makes itself heard and felt throughout the whole world, and proclaims the Immaculate Conception. She brings forth Mary—" the high and strong defence of the Holy One of Israel," and by whom "all the heresies of the past have been destroyed." She points to the ever-faithful guardian of the mystery of the Incarnation, and because she believes her to be "the Mother of God," as firmly as did the Fathers in the Council at Ephesus, she crowns the Holy Virgin with the bright diadem of spotless and immaculate perfection.

This is precisely the answer one trained in the ways of Catholic Christianity would expect to be given by the venerable Church of ages to the blatant ravings of modern impiety—not a direct answer, for the frivolous and thoughtless crowd are unworthy of this attention, but a sign set up on high that cannot be gainsaid or mistaken, a light to them that sit in darkness, and a beacon to guide men of good-will safely through the chaos and desolation of modern society, its upheavals and its ruins, wrought by the secret and persevering action of the elements of unbelief.

Once the Incarnation is accepted in all its plenitude, there is no reasonable ground for unbelief in any of the mysteries. Take the Blessed Eucharist, for instance, in which we Catholics firmly believe that the Body and Blood of Christ are verily and indeed received, and are therefore present, in some wonderful way that we do not understand, under the outward appearances of bread and wine.

There are, no doubt, difficulties in the way of entire belief. "It is a hard saying" still to the unregenerate, who have either never received the grace of Faith, or, having received it in Baptism, have come wilfully to reject it. Just as the unbelieving multitude forgot the Almighty Power which fed them in the wilderness with a few loaves and fishes; as they forgot how He ruled the storm, and was omnipotent over all the forces of nature, and said to one another, "How can this man give us His flesh to eat?" as they obstinately shut their eyes to the proofs of His Divinity, and closed their ears to any teaching, even from Heaven, that seemed to conflict with their own notions of things—so do unbelievers now cry out that, no matter what God may say, however clearly and emphatically He may express Himself, either by His own words or the teaching of His Church, they will not believe the Catholic doctrine of the Real Presence. "How," they argue, " can I contradict the testimony of my senses?" "I see bread and wine, I taste bread and wine, I touch bread and wine, I smell these elements: how can I then, as a rational creature believe that flesh and blood are present before me?"

Here again there is the usual misrepresentation of the doctrine of Catholic Christianity. You are not asked to reject the testimony of the senses. The senses testify only to the outward appearances of things, and in the Blessed Eucharist the outward appearances of bread and wine remain unaltered. You only correct the ordinary judgment that is founded on the evidence of sense, and do not pronounce that the invisible substance is there, because in this particular instance you are warned by the voice of God to suspend your judgment. If God had not spoken and told you that the invisible substance, whose existence is known not by sense but by an act of the mind, is His Body and Blood, you would be quite right in judging that bread and wine only are really present. The presence of the Body and Blood of the Lord is perceived only by Faith; and Faith, as the Apostle tells us, "comes from hearing the Word of God."

"But," continues the objector, "it is monstrous to believe that a material substance can by any power be changed into the spiritual substance of God, that a creature can create the creator."

Here again is the same sort of misrepresentation. The Catholic Church has never taught that a material substance is changed into God. It has taught from the very beginning to the present day that God cannot deceive us, and that when our Divine Lord says a certain thing which He presents to us is His Body, we are bound to believe Him. When Christ offered what seemed to the Apostles to be Bread, He said, as plainly as words could express the truth, "This is my Body." He did not say This Bread is my Body, but clearly and distinctly, as the Evangelists give his words—"This," that I offer you. Had He said This Bread—He would have announced a proposition which could no more be true than the absurd doctrine, put in the mouth of the Church by unbelievers, "One God is three Gods."

No doubt the Apostles believed the words of their Divine Master. They saw at once that in this wonderful way the promise which had once so startled them and drew so strongly on their faith was fulfilled. We can easily picture to ourselves the joy and consolation which filled their simple and trusting hearts at the last supper, when they were made one with Jesus in the Holy Communion. What Christ did then, He gave power to His Apostles to do in like manner, and commanded them to do it.

And what, after this brief explanation of the Catholic doctrine, becomes of the objection changing Bread into God, and the creature creating his creator? By the power of God, and by the order of God man speaks, and the substance of Bread is changed into the Body of the Lord. "But," our objector will say, "this doctrine is inconceivable. How could Christ hold in His own hands His Body?" It is inconceivable to our ways of thought, but it is in some way possible to the great God—and we know that Christ was God.

But how can we possibly believe that the Body of the Lord is present in ten thousand places at the same time— that it is in Heaven at the right hand of the Father, and yet really present in innumerable places upon earth? We must believe Him who has the words of eternal life, for we believe and confess that "He is Christ, the Son of God." "But is it not contrary to common-sense to believe that the same body can be present in different places at the same time?" Yes, it is impossible to conceive this of a mortal body, subject, as our bodies are, to the laws of space and the other laws of material substances. But who shall tell us, in a way that is intelligible to our senses, what is "a spiritual body"? (1 Cor. xv. 44.) Who will explain how the few loaves and fishes were, by the blessing of our Lord, in many mouths at the same time? How was it brought about that the fragments of the feast exceeded the original loaves and fishes, since it is clear, from the words of the sacred text, that there was no addition as we should understand it—"twelve baskets were filled with the fragments of the five barley loaves" (John vi. 13). There is as much of an apparent contradiction here, as we, according to our way of conceiving things, see in the body of the Lord held in the hands of the Lord. How did the body of Christ walk upon the waters? How did it penetrate the closed doors of the room where the disciples were assembled, and yet be palpable, visible, and subject to the ordinary laws of matter? How did that body, mangled and torn with many wounds, that lay dead in the sepulchre, pierce the solid rock at the moment of the Resurrection?

There are many things not imagined in human philosophy which have to be cleared up and fully explained before we can apply the laws of our limited experience to fetter the powers of the Omnipotent God. " You believe in the Incarnation," we say to the caviller: " do you receive this mystery as it is defined by Catholic Christianity? Do you bow down your reason, and put aside all the objections which your proud thoughts might excite within you at this marvel of omniscient and omnipotent love? Then cease to ask, 'How can this man give us His flesh to eat?'" Having given up His life to save us, though as God and in His Divine nature He was incapable of suffering and of death; having reduced Himself to the condition of a helpless babe; nay more, having stooped, God as He was, to be less than man—" a worm, and no man "—what limits shall we set, according to our poor views, to the excess of Divine love shown so prodigally in the whole economy of Redemption?

Suppose a learned Jew were to enter the stable of Bethlehem, and to hear from the lips of a Catholic, that the weeping infant was the God who made all things, on what conceivable principle of philosophy such as we can understand, could this Jew receive the glad tidings? He would be bound by every principle of sound reason and common-sense, unenlightened by revelation, to laugh contemptuously at the senseless idea. But men who set no bounds to their joy and gratitude for the manifestation of love shown in the birth of Christ, turn short in their acceptance of the traditions of the Faith, and presume to blaspheme that other mystery which, to a well-ordered Christian mind, is the natural outcome and complement of the Incarnation.

There is only one drawback which I see to the consoling Faith of the Catholic Christian, and that is the consciousness of our want of appreciation of this great mystery. We do not value, as we ought, the Infinite condescension displayed in the adorable Sacrament of the Blessed Eucharist.

What shall tepid and indifferent Catholics say at the awful judgment, when those, who knew nothing, or had but a most imperfect idea of this priceless treasure, will charge them, as well they may, with a want of reverence and love for the Blessed Eucharist? " Had we known," they will say, " what was meant by the abiding presence of the man-God, had we observed in the piety and fervor of Catholics the outward signs of a real and lively faith, and thus been attracted to inquire into its mysterious meaning, how easy it would have been to have loved God above all things, to have borne the heat and burden of the day, to have struggled bravely on through the many tribulations of life, and, fortified by the Bread of Life, to have reached the kingdom of Heaven!"

Thoughts like these naturally crowd upon us as we realize, as far as our poor finite minds can realize, in this great Sacrament, the breadth and depth of the love of the Sacred Heart. But we are weak in all things, most weak in Faith. We seem not to feel the greatness of the gift; as we disregard the terrors of His justice, so we seem to forget the patience and long-suffering of His Infinite mercy. And thus outsiders to the plenitude of Catholic Faith, who make no allowance for our manifold imperfections and our narrow conceptions of the Infinite, behold in our tepidity and indifference towards the Blessed Eucharist, an unmistakable proof of the hollowness of our professions. No wonder that Infidels, noticing the bad lives of many Catholics, who neither practise the duties of their religion, nor are restrained by its threats of the Divine vengeance, conclude that we have no real belief in the mysteries which should challenge all our gratitude, or excite our liveliest apprehensions.

A clever writer has thus recently combated the Christian Faith in the eternity of torments. If we believed it, he says, we could not rest; the horrible thought that some one dear to us might be enduring in hell the inconceivable miseries of the "worm that dieth not and the inextinguishable fire," would rob us of anything like happiness. There could not, he argues, be any possible pleasure for the true believer, who really set before his mind the bare possibility of ever coming to "that place of torment." And as it is a fact that men who profess to believe in the eternity of woe are happy, and "marry and think of marrying," and spend their lives in the enjoyment of good things, there is, he triumphantly concludes, proof positive that Faith is only a sham, and that we feed our belief on mere fancies and words without meaning.

How little do such reasoners reflect on the selfishness of humanity, and how natural it is for the best of us to live almost entirely in the present, and forget the hopes and terrors of eternity! There is One alone who perfectly gauges the depths of human feeling, and who fully understands the many weaknesses and imperfections of our nature, for He is not only omniscient, but has made actual trial of our infirmities; "tempted in all things —save sin—even as we are tempted." He has made us free, and He knows that the primeval fall has in a manner "bewitched" our liberty. He will not deprive us however of the plenitude of that gift, which, notwithstanding all its wild excesses, is the glory of humanity. He constantly bestows upon us the supernatural gifts of grace, that sweetly incline this wayward will of ours to good— but He will not force its compliance with these gentle impulses that warn us to provide for "the one thing necessary." He has wisely provided for our want of co-operation with these precious gifts of Infinite mercy.

Later on we shall see how this kind Providence is manifested in the organization and direction of His Church. In the next chapter, we shall consider how He has provided for our wants and miseries, for our coldness and indifference, for our thoughtlessness and frivolity, for our weakness and infidelities, in the sacramental system of Catholic Christianity.

CHAPTER IV.

Catholic Christianity Developed in the Sacramental Principle.

MONSEIGNEUR DEVEREUX, the first Bishop and Vicar Apostolic of the Eastern Districts of the Cape Colony, often described to me the want experienced by souls, who, though not Catholics, were distinguished by a pious disposition to have something sensible as the object of their adoration. In his large experience, he had met with many Protestants of both sexes, people of education and position, who expressed to him this feeling of a void and emptiness in their devotions, and of a craving after something real and clearly defined to their minds, before which they could pray with earnestness and attention. They could not, they said, form to themselves any notion of the great God; and they felt, as it were, lost in dreamy speculations about the nature of the Infinite, when they wanted most of all to solicit His blessings and invoke His help and protection. They dreaded, they said, anything like an anthropomorphic or human conception of the Deity; it would seem so like Idolatry; and from their vague and misty ideas of the Incarnation, they shrank from appealing directly to the Saviour as their God.

No doubt the same sentiment led to the material visions of Paganism, and to the peopling the *amœna loca* of this world with imaginary deities. It may account also for the worship of what is called Nature, which is the result of Rationalism, and finds so many votaries amongst the æsthetic writers and thinkers of the present day.

To the Catholic properly instructed, and understanding the spirit of his religion, such thoughts and fancies are impossible. He clearly understands that God our Saviour has fully experienced in our nature all its weaknesses, and all its longings for direct communication with the Author of its being. In the prayers of the daily Mass, he is reminded of the stooping down of the Great Being who has made all things, that we might be enabled to rise through Him to the full appreciation of the tie that binds us to "Our Father" in heaven. Thus in the Offertory, we have this beautiful prayer used by the priest, when he pours a few drops of water into the wine in the chalice: "O God, who didst wonderfully create the dignity of human nature, and more wonderfully still renew it, grant us by this mystery of this wine and water, to become sharers of His Divinity who deigned to become a portion of our humanity." And again in the Preface of Christmas Day: "That while we recognize God in a visible form, we may by Him be caught up into the love of the invisible."

He is taught also, in the popular devotion of the Rosary, to meditate on every striking fact of the life and humiliations and sufferings and death of "the Word made flesh." In the Holy Eucharist, with the instinct of a lively faith, he almost feels the touch of the God-man abiding within him. In the Benediction of the Blessed Sacrament, the most ordinary evening devotion in Catholic churches, he receives the blessing of the Emmanuel. In the processions on solemn occasions he is taught to realize the fact that the Saviour is ever abiding with us, "passing along amongst us," as He did once visibly on earth, "doing good." In the Sacrament of Penance, he recognizes in the voice of the priest, the voice of Him who said to Magdalen, "Go in peace, thy sins are forgiven." When the soul is fluttering on the brink of eternity, and the vanity of all earthly things is revealed in the glimmering of the dawn of eternity, and he shrinks back affrighted at the threshold of the dread passage which he must face alone, and sees in spirit the powers of darkness banding together to hinder him on his way, it is not, he knows well, the words of an earthly comforter that whisper courage, it is the voice and the hand of God Himself, who, by the ministry of His priests anoints his body for the last struggle, and reminds him that he must not fear, for Christ has conquered death, and in His person has enabled us all to share His triumph. Through the great sacrament of the Incarnation, he realizes to the full, the efficacy of the other sacraments which are its complement; and so, while yet on this earth of shadows and darkness, he sees the object of his Faith, it may be dimly, but yet clearly enough to put to flight the earthly thoughts that might rise between him and the object of his devotion.

There is not in the whole world a Catholic, however lowly his position among men, who has not learned at his mother's knee to feel these august privileges, and to place himself in close communion with the supernatural. If he be a man of "good-will," he can walk and converse with God here below and, through the instincts of Divine Faith, share in the privilege our first parents enjoyed while they were yet innocent, and hear the very voice of God speaking to his heart.

This is the wonderful blessing which Catholic Christianity offers in the sacramental system to all her children. It is worth while to dwell upon it for a few moments, and endeavor to catch another glimpse of the loveliness of this pure Faith, so little known and understood outside the Church.

I have already said that Protestants are afraid to analyze the mysteries of revealed truth. They consider it irreverent to inquire deeply into their meaning, and they regard it as an unmistakable sign of fitting respect for the Lord and Master of all things to cultivate this feeling. No doubt in a certain sense they are right.

There is such a thing as sinful curiosity and an irreverent attempt to pry into the unfathomable secrets of Infinite Being. If a man in the pride of his intellect will give way to the dangerous temptation that it is in his power to sound these depths, and by the aid of science accurately discriminate how much for example of the Divine nature could be assimilated in the human soul, or to determine how far the human brain could bear the tension of omniscience, or the human heart the vast and boundless love which is in God, or to calculate by algebraical formulas the relations of the three Divine persons to each other, this subtle speculation would deservedly bring its own punishment. "He that is a searcher of majesty shall be overwhelmed by glory" (Prov. xxv. 27). We are warned in the Sacred Scriptures against this highmindedness. "Seek not the things that are too high for thee, and search not into things above thy ability" (Ecclesiasticus iii. 22). "Be not high-minded, but fear" (Rom. xi. 20).

But when I say that Protestants fear to study the incomprehensible truths of Revelation, I do not allude to lofty speculations such as these. They fear to set before them, as far as reason can conceive them, the wonderful ways of God in His dealings with us, and shrink from meditating on the depths to which He has humbled Himself to make us happy. They go farther than this in their misplaced reverence, and like the Jansenists, form to themselves notions of what is becoming to the Deity in His relations with His creatures, and lay down precise and rigid laws of respect and decorum, which, no matter how they may be contradicted by Revelation, are never to be transgressed.

This is altogether opposed to the first principles of Catholic Christianity. Far from encouraging the exaggerated feelings of awe which would only fill us with terror of approaching God and sever our affections from Him, the Catholic Church endeavors, throughout her whole liturgy and by her explanation of the sacramental system, to teach us to cultivate hopefully the closest relations with God, that can be derived from anything that He has been graciously pleased to tell us of His Infinite Condescension. Hence these devotions to every shred of the history of the Passion of our Saviour, the sacred wounds in the hands and feet and side, the Precious Blood, the crown of thorns, the lance and nails, the Sacred Heart. All these in endless variety rise before the mental vision of the devout Catholic in his daily prayers, and touchingly invite him to approach in spirit and venerate and adore the Sacred Humanity of our Divine Lord.

But here it will be asked by those who are not Catholics, "Can we really adore the Body of our Divine Lord? Can we, fixing the eyes of the soul on the Sacred Hands and Feet, embrace them in spirit, as though they formed part of the Divinity? Can we, contemplating the beatings of the Sacred Heart, as it throbbed with convulsive agony in the Garden of Gethsemani, or was broken on the cross, bow down and worship this material object as the seat of Divine love?

I answer at once, undoubtedly we can; and more, we ought to adore and worship the Sacred Humanity of our Divine Redeemer in whatever way it appeals to our devotion. And the reason is because the main object of this devotion is the Divine Person, and because this Divine Personality cannot be considered as something separate and apart from the Sacred Humanity.

It is of the utmost importance to make this point clear; for Protestants constantly accuse the Catholic Church of a coarse and material worship, and pointing to the explanation given in our prayer-books of the Devotion to the Sacred Heart or Precious Blood, exclaim, "This worship of the Roman Catholic Church is evidently a carnal worship; and Roman Catholics cannot possibly, with such materialistic conceptions, worship 'in spirit and in truth.'"

Those who reason thus show unmistakably that they do not understand the doctrine of the Incarnation, as it is defined and has ever been explained by the Catholic Church. Their ideas only reach the old heresy of Nestorius, or, to go back farther still, owe their existence to that spirit of error which, even in the time of the Beloved Disciple, attempted to "dissolve Christ," or to divide the honor due to our Divine Saviour into two distinct acts— adoration to the Divine Person and inferior honor to the Humanity sanctified by His Divine presence. Nestorius, when it became evident that the Council of Ephesus would proclaim Mary to be the Mother of God, was heard to exclaim, "As for me, I can never make up my mind to say that a child of two or three months is God, nor to adore an infant at its mother's breast."

Modern unorthodox Christianity, when it does attempt to define its views and opinions on the Incarnation, is forced to approve of the views of the old heresiarch of Constantinople; for with Nestorius, it should say, by the very fact of condemning the adoration of the Humanity of our Lord, that the Sacred Humanity might indeed be adored with the Godhead, that is, like a separate being by its side, but by a different act. This view, plausible as it seems, is condemned as a heresy by the Fifth General Council, which pronounces Anathema upon all who do not adore the Manhood with one and the same adoration as that which is paid to the Everlasting Word. "If any one says that Christ is to be adored in the two natures (where two adorations are introduced), but that God the Word Incarnate with His own flesh is not to be adored with one adoration, as was always handed down by tradition in the Church, let him be anathema" (Fifth General Council, Second of Constantinople, col. 8, 9).

To make the matter clearer. Suppose we abstract the notion of the Divine Personality from the Body of Christ, and we regard the Heart by itself, or the Head crowned with thorns, or the wounded Hands and Feet, fixing our eyes only on the image of our Lord, as it is represented by painters, would it not in this case be a sort of material idolatry to adore these portions of the Sacred Humanity?

The answer given to this question by our Divines is simply this—In the matter of adoration it is unlawful to make such an abstraction. If you suppose that a separation did take place between the Human nature of Jesus Christ and the Divinity, then of course the Body or any part of it could not be adored. But this separation cannot take place. The two natures united by the bond of Personality are united forever and ever, and cannot be separated even in imagination.

To make this plainer still. Suppose we regard the Body of our Divine Lord when it was separated from the soul, when it lay dead in the lap of the Mother of Sorrows, or while it lay in the tomb cold and stiff, was it to be adored then? Undoubtedly it was, because the Body was united to the Divinity as well as the soul. The Divine Word did not allow the soul to form a barrier to His union with the Body. He made the Personal union extend to each; and this union was not broken for a moment, even in death. The Sacred Heart of Jesus cold in death was intimately united with the Divinity, and as such was deserving of the honor and adoration due to the second Divine Person of the Blessed Trinity.

Here there is no uncertain sound, not even the whisper of a doubt, to distract the devout thoughts concentrated on the image of our Divine Lord. We can picture Him to ourselves as we please, the Child in the manger of Bethlehem; the Child in the arms of the young Mother, and watched over by St. Joseph in the flight into Egypt; the Child disputing with the learned doctors in the Temple; or the Man of Sorrows, sorrowful even unto death, crowned with thorns, scourged, or sinking under the weight of the heavy cross, or dying on Calvary. If we prefer to contemplate Him in another form and to refresh our Faith by the glorious Mysteries, we may in company with the Apostles and the Holy Virgin behold Him newly risen, see Him mounting up into heaven, or hear the rushing of the Holy Spirit, as they heard it on the day of Pentecost.

There is no limit to the pious imagination. We may call in the help of genius and art, to enable us to picture to our fancy brighter, clearer and more enrapturing visions of the birth, life and sufferings, humiliations, death, and the glorious triumphs after death. In whatever form the Sacred Humanity most touchingly awakens our sympathy, or excites our reverence, we may by every means in our power call up the vision, to fix our wayward thoughts, and satisfy this craving for something, that, through the senses, may appeal most effectually to our souls; and fall down in spirit and adore and love without one misgiving that we are trespassing on the Divine Condescension, or offending the great God by endeavoring to communicate with Him, in the only way that satisfies the infirmities of weak human nature.

When the true teaching of Catholic Christianity is understood, who for a moment would think of finding fault with simple-minded Catholics and children gathered round the humble crib, constructed rudely by themselves, and communicating to each other by their reverent looks and bearing, and the chanting of the touching Christmas hymns, something of the feelings which animated the poor shepherds on Christmas morning? Surely no one but a blind Pharisee would protest against a devotion so simple and so natural as this, particularly when it has the high sanction of Him, who loved to gather round Him the little children, and to hear their expression of praise and love—the most perfect praise ever accorded to Him openly in this world. To Catholic Faith, whatever chills devotion founded on the teaching and practice of the Church, must be contrary to the best instincts of our nature, when they are enlivened and exalted by Grace. The earnest Catholic cannot help shuddering, when he hears the whining cant of pity deploring piety of this kind, for it seems to him as if men, in their spiritual pride and the obstinacy which results from, it were rudely thrusting themselves between the good God and His children, and attempting to rob Him of what is dearest to Him in this world, the expression of their unaffected love and heartfelt devotion.

There is certainly such a thing as over-reverence, and gloomy severity in the worship of God; for it was this spirit which was one of the chief causes that separated France from God in the period of the great Revolution. There were of course other causes, the spirit of licentiousness, and covetousness the offspring of Free-thought; but even temptations like these could scarcely have torn away the hearts of the children of the eldest daughter of the Church from their good mother, if these hearts had not been first estranged from her, by the cold and rigid spirit infused into her by unnatural and morbid Jansenism. The Church of France, half poisoned by Gallicanism, and robbed of her generous and benevolent nature by the withering influence of this most insidious of all heresies, was regarded as a sort of step-mother by the children who once revered and loved her. She denounced the consoling and healthy practices of genuine Catholicity, and rose up, in her rigid austerity, like a hideous nightmare between the good God and His trusting children. They dared not receive the Divine Saviour in the Holy Communion without a laborious preparation of wearying weeks and months. They were cut off from the usual evening Benediction. Confession was made something like what Protestants mainly regard it—" a cruel butchery of the soul." The Rosary and the popular forms of devotion, which the faithful were accustomed to recite with the confidence and artless and unaffected ways of children addressing a loved father or mother, were to be drawled forth in measured accents, involving tedious rests and pauses for the renewal of attention and the fixing of the thoughts, all determined by fanciful rules opposed to the natural flow of pious feelings. No wonder that the service of God in the family and confraternity became gradually hateful from this prim Puritanism, and that the many who had been taught by pious parents, brought up themselves in the wholesome traditions of the Faith, to see a kind and indulgent Providence in every event of their daily lives, shrunk within themselves at the new ideas of a God indifferent to individual piety, and gloomily meting out to the predestined elect, the rewards determined by Him irrespective of personal merit or demerit, and the punishments allotted by invincible fatality from all eternity.

Every one acquainted with the history of this unfortunate country well knows that habits of thought, like these I have just mentioned, found the middle classes and peasantry of France destitute of spiritual aid, when the deluge of Free-thought, and the upheavings of Communism, and whirlwinds of hatred to aristocracy and kingly power and all their associations, burst upon society. Prayer had fallen into disuse, the sacraments had been long neglected, the churches were deserted. There was no anchor of hope, no shelter for the poor victims carried about by every blast of the new opinions, and driven hither and thither by the leaders of the countless clubs. The consequence naturally was that unbelief soon led to social destruction.

"History repeats itself;" and if a social revolution one of these days startle Europe, there will be no vestiges of Faith outside the Catholic Church to stem the flood of evils that are already invading society. If the sacramental system were something merely human, then it would be silly to attach to its disuse, consequences so serious and appalling; but when we consider that it is Divinely instituted as a help to human weakness, we cannot wonder that its voluntary rejection by human pride should bring with it effects so disastrous.

The Catholic Church has taught from the beginning that our Divine Lord, even during His stay visibly in this world and while His followers were sustained in their Faith by His sensible presence, made use of plain outward means to confer His blessings on those who needed them. He did this to prepare future generations for this palpable method of bestowing His favors. It manifestly needed on His part no material ceremonies to heal the afflicted who had recourse to Him. He who, when it pleased Him, had changed the whole face of chaos, brought forth by His sovereign will from original nothing, and formed it into the beautiful world of creation, who had said "Let light be," and forthwith light beamed on the heaving mass of being external to Himself, was in no way obliged to have recourse to external agency, for the accomplishment of His many acts of beneficence.

He had merely to will interiorly the desired change, and at once the blind should see, the lame walk, the deaf hear, and the dead arise. But we know that while He walked about on this earth, "as many as touched Him were made whole" (Mark vi. 56). He seemed to make it a necessary condition to the effect of His healing power, that He should "touch" those who applied to Him for relief. He, who could easily have produced all the effects of Infinite power by His mere word, or rather by His will alone (for even words are sacramental means), yet was pleased to act upon His creatures by the intervening agency of matter.

In healing the sick, He was accustomed, as we read in St. Mark, to "lay His hands upon them;" and they were evidently aware of His sacramental action. He confirmed their ideas in a most remarkable manner; for, as the sacred text tells us, "He took the deaf and dumb man apart, and putting His fingers into his ears, and spitting touched his tongue, and looking up to heaven, He groaned, and said to him Ephpheta, which is Be thou opened" (Mark vii. 33). And in a still more striking manner He brought out this sacramental way of action in the cure of the blind man recorded by St. John. For "He spat upon the ground, and made clay of the spittle, and spread the clay upon his eyes, and said, Go wash in the pool of Siloë" (John ix. 6, 7).

Surely there must have been some meaning attached to this constant mode of action. It would be worse than blasphemous to assert that He acted in this way through mere caprice, or influenced by the feeling of a common juggler, to delude the senses of those "who watched Him." And what other cause can reasonably be assigned than to train His disciples to mark the Divine plan on which the Incarnation rests, of leading men, the creatures of sense, to receive with child-like faith the manifestations of Infinite Condescension.

No teaching can be conceived more in harmony with this idea, than that of the Catholic Church, as expressed by the Council of Trent. "A sacrament," according to the Catechism of the Council, "is an outward sign, which, in virtue of the Divine institution, not only typifies, but actually works holiness and justice." Our

Divine Lord wrought cures not only on the afflicted body by means of touch and other sensible acts, but taught His disciples, that the ills of the soul were to be healed by the same external agency. I need not enter into the proofs of this position further than to call attention to the instruction given by Him to Nicodemus, on the curative effects of Baptism: " Amen, Amen I say to thee," are His words to the learned Jewish doctor, " except a man be born again, he cannot see the kingdom of God " (John iii. 5). Nicodemus understood these words in a carnal sense, and asked for an explanation. Our Lord gives it as follows: " Amen, Amen I say to thee, unless any one be born again of *water* and the Holy Ghost, he cannot enter into the kingdom of God." No one can read this passage without marking the connection which our Saviour establishes between the " weak and needy element" of water, and the omnipotent Spirit of God; water not the sign only, but the efficient cause, as well as the Holy Ghost, of effecting the " new birth," or this cleansing the soul from sin.

If it occurs to any one to challenge this doctrine, and to endeavor to explain it in some metaphorical sense, he can no more succeed, than if he attempted to rob the external action in the cure of the blind man, of its power in effecting the cure. If he asserts that it is absurd to unite the material instrument of water with the gift of God, he is met at once by the action of the Apostolic Church, which evidently connected with the use of water the cleansing of the soul from sin. " See," said the Ethiopian convert to Philip the Deacon, " here is water; what doth hinder me from being baptized?" In the tenth chapter of the Acts, when the unmistakable signs of the descent of the Holy Ghost on the converted Gentiles were clearly noticed by all present, St. Peter says—" Can any man forbid water that these should not be baptized who have received the Holy Ghost as well as we?" (Acts x. 47.) Ananias says to St. Paul, " Rise up, and be baptized, and wash away thy sins" (Acts xxii. 16).

There are many other texts bearing upon the same point, but in a work like this, meant for the general public, it would be out of place to pile up quotations. He " who runs may read " that there is abundant proof from what I have said, that our Divine Lord connected not only the healing of bodily ills, but those of the soul also, with the use of material instruments.

This is, the sacramental principle, which, I say, flows almost naturally and directly from the proper understanding of the mystery of the Incarnation. We, by means of these " beggarly elements" of nature, "become sharers of His Divinity who deigned to become a partaker of our Humanity."

The great mistake of the so-called Reformers consisted in this, that they yielded to the notions of that false spiritualism which, about the period of the uprising against the teaching of the Church, affected so many minds. They could not see, or rather they would not see, that the obvious principle of the sacramental system, as taught by our Divine Lord, was to humble human arrogance and pride, and to inculcate the humiliating lesson that, as man had ignominiously delivered himself over to the domain of the baser world, so he needs the mediation of this earth, to rise above it. Hence, according to them, the sacraments are only pledges of the truth of the Divine promises for the forgiveness of sins. It was too humiliating to believe that the elements of matter could have, even by the Divine institution, the power to effect this transformation. But, if we mark the use made by our Divine Lord of these elements, in the regeneration of a fallen world, we shall see, with a force that bears down all the resistance of proud reason, that this was actually an essential part of the economy of salvation.

The following eloquent words of Father Oakley bring this truth so powerfully before us, that I prefer to quote them, than to develop the point myself:

"Three out of the four great elements of nature are thus directly named in Scripture, as having been reclaimed from the power of the evil one, and consecrated to Divine uses. The *water*, once employed as the terrible minister of God's avenging power for the destruction of the world, is now converted into the instrument of His saving grace; the *air*, that treacherous material of the 'wind and storm,' when collected and condensed into which it 'fulfils His word' and desolates the smiling face of the earth, enters within the sacred portals of that holiest of material temples, the Human Body of our Incarnate Lord, and reissues from it in the Divine Breath, which imparts to the first priests of the Church the power to forgive sin: the *earth*, doomed by the voice of God, at the Fall to yield the baneful fruit of the primeval curse, is moulded by the plastic hand which made it into a compost of sweet medicinal virtue. The fourth great element of nature received its consecration, too, on the Day of Pentecost; and when the Christian beholds that most awful of all the scourges of sin and weapons of chastisement, the material fire, he can contemplate it, not as the agent which swept from the earth they polluted, the cities of the plain, or which is to burn up this beautiful but devoted world, and itself to be gifted with immortality, to the end that it may accomplish God's purposes upon the wicked, but as the substance which embodied the great Pentecostal gift—the symbol, not of wrath, but of the zeal of God, which then heralded the conversion of the world, and now burns with bright innocuous light as the watch-fire of His love before the Tabernacle of the Blessed Sacrament. Animated and invigorated with this plentiful benediction vouchsafed to us in the sacraments, it is no wonder that the life of the Catholic Church should be as vigorous now as it was in the beginning."

I will endeavor to trace, in the following chapter, the undying influence of the sacraments in sustaining the spirited energy of those to whom in a special manner has been committed her activity in this world—the clergy and religious orders.

CHAPTER V.

Catholic Christianity in Some Practical Aspects.

IT is chiefly in times of great social cataclysms, when law and order are for a while overpowered, and men are whirled hither and thither by the wild fury of revolution, that the calm enduring spirit and determined courage of Catholic Christianity most strikingly displays itself. No one can read the history of the late reign of terror in Paris, without meeting with many episodes in which the majestic character of true religion shines forth as brilliantly as it did when the infant Church was struggling against the persecutions of the Roman Empire. The Rev. Father Pérraud, priest of the Oratory, at the close of his magnificent sermon on the martyred Archbishop Darboy, exclaims, " Christianity! verily and indeed it shows itself here as it was wont to do in the early days of its history. The world has waned old, but Christianity has not altered. It still brings forth the same faith, the same spirit of forbearance, the same serenity, the same peaceable and humble fortitude. Throughout every age, our martyrs walk forth hand in hand and maintain the same tradition." Whilst we read the account given of the slaughter of the Archbishop and his five companions, at the prison of La Roquette, we are carried back in spirit to the days of the Catacombs.

Often it happened, in the times of the persecution of the early Church, that the Catacombs, the ordinary refuge of the Christians, were rudely broken into, and there in the dark passages, the Christians, unseen by any eyes but those of God and His angels, were cruelly murdered. The infuriated soldiery found the object of their search often, as in the case of Pope Stephen the First, either engaged in offering up the Holy Sacrifice, or assisting at this sacred rite.

There is an old inscription, belonging to the time of Antoninus Pius, who began to reign in 138 A.D., which brings all this vividly before us. It records in a very beautiful and feeling manner, the death of one Alexander, who was slain as he knelt at the altar about to sacrifice, and it deplores the wretched times, when there was no security for the persecuted even in the caverns of the earth, and when their bodies were deprived of decent burial.

How like is all this to the secret communion of the hostages in their prison, the Blessed Sacrament having been conveyed to them in such a way as not to attract the notice of their guards; and then the secret death, in the dark corner of the winding alley between the prison and the outer rampart, and the mutilated bodies flung into a common grave!

When in the June of 1875 I visited the present Archbishop of Paris I could not help realizing to myself, as I ascended the staircase of the palace, the scene enacted in that very spot, when the good and amiable Monseigneur Darboy was dragged away a prisoner by a fiendish mob. What a worthy follower of his Divine Master! No resistance, no reproach, as calmly dignified then, as when, arm in arm with his friend the President Bonjean, amidst the grossest insults, he proceeded with dauntless courage to the place of execution.

It is easy for natural courage to face death bravely in the battlefield, or when one's friends are near to sustain, by their sympathy, the fortitude of the sufferers. But it is real religion alone that enables its children to go forth serenely, calmly, and with humble fortitude, and even with a holy joy, when there is no accusation, no shadow of any crime, and death, violent and ignominious as men can make it, is robbed of every gleam of earthly consolation. So died the brave Archbishop and his brave priests in the prison of La Roquette.

And so, if God requires it, are ready to die for the honor and glory of His name thousands and tens of thousands of pious men and women, who deem it their greatest happiness to have left all things for the sake of Jesus Christ, and who are full of hope that if they were further called to die like their Divine Master amidst mockery and insults, that He would give them the courage and resolution to follow Him, bearing His cross to the very end.

When the Jesuit Fathers left Grahamstown, in the April of 1879, for the Valley of the Zambesi many Protestant gentlemen who had made their acquaintance, and had learned to appreciate their splendid gifts of education and training, wondered how such men could go forth with joy and gladness into the wilderness to die for savages, who could never appreciate their worth, and would never be grateful for sacrifices so great. The world calls this enthusiasm, or fanaticism, or superstitious piety; but such is not the estimate of Catholic Christianity.

The Catholic Church regards those "to whom it is given" to accept so glorious a vocation, and to be faithful to it to the end, as the chosen followers of the Crucified, to whom will be secured for all eternity a bright crown of glory, infinitely surpassing all that this world could give them. There is no such thing as pious sentimentalism in the men and women whom our Divine Lord calls to follow Him, in the path of perfect renunciation. There may be a generous enthusiasm or a spirit of heroic devotion in the soul of the young ecclesiastic or the young religious, who at first feels the whisperings of Divine grace and the interior call, "If thou wilt be perfect, go, sell what thou hast, and come, follow me" (Matt. xix. 21). But this ardent feeling soon settles down into a firm purpose. Humility, obedience, the renunciation of self, also strongly insisted on in the training of those who desire to serve God in the spirit of a true vocation, leave no place, after a time, for the natural suggestions of unbridled self-direction.

This is one of the grand secrets of Catholic Christianity, not made a secret by the Church, or because she in any way conceals her doctrine, but hidden from the eyes of the frivolous and unbelieving world. If the novice persists in nursing a mere sentimental piety, is good only by fits and starts, according as the natural feelings are swayed by motions congenial to them, is hurt by trials of obedience and humiliations, is always cherishing the pseudo-martyr spirit, and grieving, and "looking back," the trial of earnestness will in time manifest the absence of the right spirit. Sooner or later, the Superior will, in the discharge of a most important duty, rendered imperative by the strict discipline of the Church, have to say, "'No man putting his hand to the plough, and looking back, is fit for the kingdom of God' [Luke ix. 62]. In the name of God, return to the world, you may serve Him there with fidelity, He has not called you to follow Him in the state of religious perfection."

It is the absolute ignorance which prevails outside the Catholic Church, and amongst uninstructed and worldly-minded Catholics of the nature and obligations of a real vocation, that creates such false impressions about the manner in which Superiors deal with young people who believe they are called to leave all things and follow Christ. They will say for example, that it is wrong in those, who ought to understand the rash impulses of youth to encourage such an impression. Parents will feel aggrieved that their "hope and pride" and comfort in this world have abandoned them. And there will be any amount of real or affected sympathy amongst friends for the young person, who promised to be so great an ornament to society, and who is now " shut up" in a convent or a seminary. But if the vocation prove a real one, if the true gold manifests itself in the crucible of the Novitiate, how misplaced is all this false sympathy, and how serious is the position before God of those, who have presumed to stand between Him and the object of His fondest love! No wonder that the Church, while she warns under pain of her severest censures all Superiors to prove and test with the greatest care the reality of a vocation, excommunicates whoever will dare knowingly and wilfully to interfere with the firm purpose of those who believe, with the approval of their spiritual director, that they have been really invited by God to leave the world and to enter into His service.

It is the same ignorance of the spirit and hidden life of a good priest or fervent religious, which disposes the public at once to take up any tale of scandal that is propagated by the enemies of the Church. Sensational stories of the "Maria Monk" style will be read with avidity by thousands, who would regard it, as an intolerable bore, to hear or read anything that Catholicity has to say about the excellence of the religious life, or the sublime character of the priesthood. They have made up their minds that the state of those whose "solicitude," as St. Paul expresses it, is only "for the things that belong to the Lord, how they may please God" (1 Cor. vii. 32), is an unnatural state, and that the life of nuns and priests who do not marry is something too exalted for ordinary mortals. So when one of these base publications, issued by persons, who rely for their gain on the credulity and vitiated and prurient taste of the ignorant and fanatical rabble, comes within their reach, they eagerly devour the sickening details, not perhaps for the gratification of sensual curiosity so much as to prove the correctness of their estimate of humanity. And never doubting of the truth of the narrative, or questioning its credibility, they at once congratulate themselves on the soundness of their judgment. "It is only," they say, "what might be expected; human nature is human nature all the world over, and people who aim at heights beyond their fellows must expect sooner or later an ignominious fall." How little do they, who think, or speak thus, know of the ways of God! How completely ignorant are they of the very elements of a life really and wholly devoted to God, who entertain seriously these ignoble, low, and vulgar sentiments!

They who are really called to follow their Divine Model in the way of genuine self-renunciation, understand better than any one else that "the kingdom of Heaven suffers violence, and that the violent only attain to it." They know that "to make their calling and election sure," they must "work out their salvation with fear and trembling;" they must "watch and pray," and "be never weary." They feel that their very profession exposes them, more than ordinary Christians, to the assaults of temptation; and so they constantly "strive" to be found worthy to enter the narrow way that leads to life. This thorough conviction of their own natural weakness and unworthiness of the Divine predilection is the very groundwork of the whole spiritual life. Without this real and practical belief, that it is God alone who can make that possible, which is beyond the powers of nature, and who " will perfect the good work which He has begun" in them, they would be building their spiritual edifice on sand, or something as frothy and unstable as mere emotional sentimentalism.

Worldly people are apt to think that the religious dress, and the open profession to live for God alone, must carry with it a sense of pharisaical pride; but never was there so great a mistake. Priests and religious know well that they are not better than others, by the fact of having been called to a more perfect state. This gratuitous grace of a vocation has been bestowed upon them, not on account of any merits of their own, but through God's pure mercy; and they clearly understand that "to whom much is given, from them much will be expected." In taking on them the yoke of religion and the livery of Christ, they have in reality only taken up the cross, and the aim of their lives must be to follow humbly in His footsteps, who bore it in the midst of ignominy and insult. The doctrine of the Catholic Church on the much misunderstood subject of "vocation" is so clearly and beautifully expressed by Father Oakley, in his admirable little book, "The Church of the Bible," that I cannot forbear giving an extract:

"All Christians are 'called to be saints' (1 Cor. i. 2).

All are called to a state of perfection (Matt. v. 48), but not all to the same state. There are divers 'mansions' in the earthly as in the heavenly kingdom of God; various grades of merit in the one as of glory in the other; different stages or elevations of spiritual and moral responsibility, opportunity, and desert. Each of these states has its own proper 'element,' which to such as are created for it, is congenial; and to such as are not, is oppressive if too high—meagre and unsatisfactory, if too low. If those who are called to a lower level of perfection, find themselves perchance in a higher, they are like creatures of earth, when suddenly brought into the highly rarefied atmosphere of some lofty mountain. They are distressed, and at length they droop and drop. Souls cannot rise above their proper spiritual level. They whose place is the more elevated region of responsibility can live indeed, in the lower; but their powers of action are cramped, and the true end of their being is thwarted, if not frustrated. It is in the body spiritual as in the body social and political. One has his gift after this manner, and another after that. Some are, as we say, 'born to great things,' manifesting even in childhood, the germ of their future proficiency. The Christian warfare, like the battlefield of nations, has its heroes, and when such as are born to heroic distinction, are employed in a limited sphere of action, we say that they are 'out of their place.' Thus in the Church: the vocation of some is to marry, of others to remain unmarried; of some to quit the world, of others to mix with it for its advantage; of some to give the superfluity of their wealth to God and the poor, of others 'to leave all that they possess' for the higher departments of the Christian service; of some to cultivate the temper of obedience with a proper reserve in favor of their own judgment, of others to resign their conscience into another's keeping in all that is not manifest sin. This is the Church's doctrine; and it is most obviously and unquestionably borne out by the very letter of the Bible."

If this doctrine were clearly understood, it would explain much that is marvellous in the ordinary life of Catholic Christianity. "How," it is constantly said in this colony, as it is said elsewhere,—" how do priests get on with their churches and institutions? How are nuns able to build their convents and develop their schools? Their people are generally poor, and yet they invariably succeed."

The answer is plain to any one of ordinary penetration. They succeed, because it is their special work, the work to which they believe they have been called; and their hearts and souls are, as a rule, concentrated in this work. They are thoroughly in earnest, just as much as worldly people are to make a fortune, and be successful in life. If the work which they set before them is within their means, if it has been prudently and wisely undertaken, it is bound to go through. If not within the lifetime of this priest or that superior, it will be accomplished by some one else who will take it up in the same spirit and carry it through as a matter of course.

"How is it," again it will be said, " with this Religious order; it is always in trouble, always persecuted, always abused and hated by the world, and yet it flourishes?" In fact we may put those expressions of wonderment in the very words of the Apostle—"As dying and behold we live; as chastised and not killed; as sorrowful, yet always rejoicing: as needy, yet enriching many; as having nothing and possessing all things" (2 Cor. vi. 9,

10). That one answer, already given, explains everything. They seriously and deliberately believe with entire conviction, that they have been called to this particular state, and that nothing happens to them, while they are endeavoring to fulfil its duties and obligations, but by the Divine appointment. Therefore such as these can say with the Apostle, " In all things we suffer tribulation, but are not distressed; we are straitened, but are not destitute; we suffer persecution, but we are not forsaken; we are cast down, but we perish not" (2 Cor. iv. 8, 9).

Here lies the secret of the vigorous life of the Catholic Church. If for a moment we do not attend to the supernatural inner life of God's Holy Spirit animating the entire body of the Church, we shall see that all her priests and Religious are individually called to do God's own work in God's own way.

There is no sentimental straining after this idea. It is a settled and sure conviction in the inmost soul of every one, who has received the grace of a Vocation to the sacred ministry, or to serve God alone in the Religious life; and therefore in whatever is undertaken purely and simply for God, they believe they must be successful, not indeed successful in the sense in which this word is understood generally, not that the work will be carried through so as to gain the applause of men, or fully and fairly accomplished by energy and perseverance; but that it will be done in the manner God wills it to be done, and with that amount of satisfactory results which He is pleased to accord to it.

This is one reason why the Church must ever and always be victorious in her struggle with the world. The spirit never dies in those to whom her interests are chiefly committed. During the three hundred years, the Church battled with the power of Imperial Rome, and throughout all the fearful persecutions of the Pagan Cæsars, though swept from the face of the earth, and compelled to hide its head in the caverns of the dead, its spirit was irrepressible. The successors of St. Peter, from the depths of the Catacombs, ruled the Faithful spread throughout the vast provinces of the empire, sent forth Bishops and devoted Missionaries, who contrived to fulfil their arduous duties in the very palaces and courts of their persecutors; so that, when peace came at last, it was found that baffled and discomfited paganism preserved only the mere external signs of a worthless and hollow existence.

I would call special attention to this persistent and unyielding spirit of Catholic Christianity. It is always the same. Persecution may for a time retard its progress. Generation after generation may see it as if thrown back, defeated and powerless, and notice that its sphere of action is growing narrower and more circumscribed; but it lives all the time with the immortal life and spirit infused into it by its Founder; and, when the pressure is removed, it bursts forth again in all its vigor.

Look at Ireland, when Catholic Emancipation broke the chains of the most oppressive penal code that ever fettered religious liberty. Notwithstanding her poverty, and the crushing weight of debt and taxation heaped upon her by the " Union," in less than half a century, the whole land was covered with beautiful churches, and convents, and Catholic Institutions of every kind, that excite the wonder and admiration of every stranger who visits her shores. There was nothing violent or spasmodic in all this. It was a steady healthy growth, that showed itself throughout the whole island, as soon as the restrictions were removed.

I believe that every honest man, who is not the unconscious slave of tyrannical prejudices, and whose perceptions are not hopelessly dimmed and overshadowed by bigoted misrepresentation, must see in this constant growth and development, when circumstances are even in the least degree favorable, a power that manifests its Divine origin. It is not in ordinary nature to sustain itself thus for long centuries of cruel oppression, and to live with unfailing vigor, while every evil influence that could, humanly speaking, blight and poison its existence, was at work to destroy it; and then, at the first appearance of a fair season, to rise up as it were with giant growth, and push forth its branches and flowers and fruits, with an energy that seems all the greater from being restrained and crushed down for such a length of time.

If we ask ourselves why is there this marked difference between "the everlasting Church," and all other Institutions in the world—that, whereas the latter soon perish and become extinct under long-continued adversity, the Catholic Church acquires new life and strength from the worst forms of persecution, we can only answer that the life and soul and spirit of the Church is the immortal Spirit of God Himself. This constant indwelling of the Spirit of Truth is a "fountain of water springing up into everlasting life;" and when the invigorating waters, meant in Divine mercy to be poured out upon the nations, are dammed up by the perverse ingenuity of man, and the powers of hell, they naturally fertilize the Church herself, and gather strength for the day of deliverance.

But, if considering further that the Church is a society composed of individual human beings, we ask ourselves how is the Divine life communicated to every member; how are Catholics sustained in the varied conflicts often so painful and trying to weak human nature, we then behold, in all its beauty, the plan contrived by Infinite Wisdom and Love to preserve even the weakest of her children, who will obey her voice and look up to her with confidence and respect. It was not enough to satisfy the care of our Divine Redeemer, that all who "believe in Him and keep His word" should be comforted and sustained by the "rock" and "pillar and ground of truth," it did not satisfy His compassionate love to unfold, in the beautiful and touching parables of the Gospel, how "the good Shepherd" cared for the weak and little ones of the fold. These consoling proofs of the largeness of His paternal heart might seem too vague and indefinite; and therefore He gave us all a sensible pledge and assurance of an intimate union with Himself in the Holy Communion. He Himself would abide forever with each of us who desired it, under the appearance of our ordinary food, to be our helper in the hour of trial, and to make us feel and know beyond all doubt, that we were individually sharers in His Divinity, and therefore able to encounter all the evils and dangers with which earth and hell could threaten us.

I know it must be difficult for those who are not Catholics to realize to themselves anything like this Catholic Christianity, so strikingly brought forth in the abiding presence of our Saviour in the Blessed Sacrament. They have been taught to regard it as something absurd, impossible, and contradictory. But, if, with their eyes fixed on the mystery of the Incarnation, contemplating God made manifest in the flesh, receiving at it were the Child Jesus from the hands of the Virgin-

Mother, and like the happy Simeon, holding in their arms " their salvation," they tried to picture to themselves the Catholic doctrine, they would, I believe, be forced, in spite of themselves and their prejudices, to exclaim— " How beautiful ! How Divine ! Oh that such a Faith could be a reality ! If Catholics do indeed believe with a firm and undoubting faith, that they actually embrace their Saviour, and are made one with Him, then indeed it is no wonder that the Saints and Martyrs had courage and strength to suffer all torments and persecutions for the sake of Christ; and that they, who receive a special call to follow Him, are able effectually to renounce all things—and attach themselves entirely to Him."

It is easy for the greatest stranger to Catholic truth, the moment he has caught a glimpse of this mystery, to understand that the good priest must be ever ready to give his life for the flock; that he heeds not the dread plague, nor the danger of infection from deadly fever or pestilence, in the discharge of his duty. It is only natural, he will admit, that the earnest Religious, and the fervent nun, must, with a firm belief in the Blessed Sacrament, enjoy a Paradise on earth. How delightful to be able at any time to go before the Tabernacle, and with the eyes of Faith to behold Jesus Himself watching and waiting and welcoming those who come to visit Him. If I might venture to lift a little the veil that hides the interior life not only of the fervent priest or nun, but of the good pious Catholic, who tries, in the midst of a busy world, and many pressing cares and solicitudes, to live and walk in God's Holy Presence, how wonderful it would all seem to those, who have been taught to regard Our Holy Religion as a mass of silly superstitions ! The morning meditation, the Colloquy of the Soul with God, the pious affections and desires, the practical resolutions; then the Holy Mass, and the transports of loving confidence, as the inward cry goes up—" Look on the face of Thy Christ, and for His sake have mercy"—all these thoughts should, if he once allowed the possibility of their truth to come near him, fill his soul with reverent admiration.

With what a new meaning the "*Kyrie eleison*" and the "*Agnus Dei*," and the "*Gloria in excelsis*," known before only perhaps in their musical associations, flash upon the soul of a stranger to our Faith, as, helped by the Incarnation, bearing, as I have imagined it, the Divine Infant in his arms, he catches just a passing vision of the sublime grandeur of Catholic Christianity. With what awe would not such a one, while under these impressions enter into a Catholic Church, where, by the light burning before the altar, he knows the Blessed Sacrament is preserved. Do not the words of Holy Writ occur to him— " How terrible is this place! This is no other but the house of God and the gate of Heaven " (Gen. xxviii. 17) ?

How different are the ceremonies, and the Vestments, and so many things about the Sanctuary, that once perhaps excited only feelings of pity and contempt for Catholics, when they are seen by the light of even one ray of Faith in the Real Presence ! I can well imagine the sense of shame and confusion, that must overwhelm a well-ordered mind and an honest nature, as it allows the dread thought to enter—" What if this Religion, which I once fancied to be so silly and puerile, should be the only true Religion! Certainly it was once the only Faith of the whole Christian world."

There cannot be a reasonable doubt, from the construction of the chapels in the Catacombs, and the inscriptions to be found there, that the Mass was celebrated in these vaults: and that men and women knelt around an altar, " whence," as St. Augustine expresses it, "was dispensed that Holy Victim, Who has cancelled the handwriting that stood against us."

In the subterranean Church of St. Clement's, may be seen, represented in the old frescos, unmistakable by the inscriptions, Clement himself, who conversed with St. Peter, clad in the same shaped Vestments worn now by priests at Mass, and standing at an altar, with his face turned towards it, and away from the people. It is not therefore, as non-Catholics represent it, a new rite unknown in Apostolic times. It is certainly, as shown by these venerable monuments, which speak for themselves, more than seventeen hundred years ago, when the Mass was celebrated with lamps and lights and other symbols of Faith and piety. How overpowering too is the testimony of the ancient Liturgies, still preserved in all their integrity, scarcely committed to writing during the three hundred years of persecution, when the "Discipline of the secret" was in force, and everything connected with the Divine worship was carefully concealed from the prying eyes of irreverent Pagans, and in consequence differing in form for each great Church, yet when compared agreeing perfectly in substance, and all testifying to the fact, that, in the days of Constantine, Christians worshipped as Catholics do now. When by the edict of the first Christian emperor, the Church was allowed to come forth from its hiding-places, and to erect Basilicas and large buildings for the assembly of the Faithful, they assisted at a sacrifice, which they believed to be the very same as that of Calvary; in which, as in the Holy Mass of the present time, the real Body and Blood of Jesus Christ were offered up, to apply the merits of Christ's death for the benefit of the worshippers and their deceased relatives and friends, and then communicated, by the hands of the priest, to those who desired to receive the Heavenly Gift.

These are I believe the considerations that must pass through the mind of a fairly educated non-Catholic, who is tolerably acquainted with the history of the early Christian times. And, if, as I suppose, he endeavors while he reads, to keep before his eyes the great mystery of the Incarnation, as it was brought before the shepherds in the stable of Bethlehem, he cannot help but see, in the worship of the Catholic Church and her sacraments, the almost necessary complement of this fundamental article of Christian Belief.

Slight and imperfect as this brief glance may be, at the real nature of Catholic Christianity in its outward worship, and external ceremonial, it is enough to indicate the undying energy and the sound vitality which must animate the children of the Church, while they receive with docility and respect the teaching of their venerable mother.

It would only encumber this chapter if I were to point out more clearly how the seven sacraments are intimately connected with the one great sacrament of the New Law—the Incarnation. If it be once understood, that the Incarnation is a reality; in other words, that the Eternal Word "by Whom all things were made," at a certain definite time, nearly nineteen hundred years ago, was born into this world, had a mother who gave to Him her flesh and blood, and nursed and suckled Him, and watched over Him in the years of helpless infancy, and brought Him up to manhood; if it be firmly believed that Jesus Christ, the Son of Mary, is one individual person with

God the Son, as truly and as perfectly God as He is man; that this Person suffered in His soul and Body, and died upon the cross, then I maintain that there cannot be a shadow of reasonable difficulty in believing what the Church has ever taught concerning the Blessed Eucharist. The real presence of the Body and Blood of Christ in the Mass and Holy Communion is nothing more or less than the wonderful means by which the fruits of the Atonement have been, from the night of the Last Supper, are now, and will be to the end of time, brought home to the hearts of believers who will only "prove themselves," and worthily partake of these Heavenly favors.

This short sketch in bare outline of Catholic Belief, in its most essential attributes, provided it be calmly and seriously examined, will satisfy any reasonable non-Catholic, that there is reason for the hope, that burns brightly in the soul of every faithful member of this great body, that as the Church has triumphed over the heresies and errors of past ages, so will it, in God's own good time, prevail over the wild theories of present Unbelief. Men who firmly believe that God Incarnate is with them in all their ways, ever near them, ready to be made one with them whenever they desire it, "*Christipheroi*" or Christ-bearers, as St. Cyril loved to call his people, must be invincible forever. Ridicule, blasphemy, outspoken contempt of God and Holy things, will only kindle more and more the Faith of those who, in obedience to our Divine Lord, "hear the Church," and learn from her lips what they are to believe about every tittle of the Divine Message. Every insult and injury offered by Unbelievers to Christ and His work in this world, can have no other effect than to make us love Him more and more, Who, for us men and our salvation, came down from Heaven and dwelt among us once in the visible flesh: and now is seen, by the eye of Faith, abiding with us, walking in our midst, and touching us with His healing hand in all the sacraments.

In the next chapter, I mean to show that, with all its supernatural helps, the Church is composed of men, and not of angels; and that we must always, in considering its action and progress, regard this human element, as God regards it, with patience and compassion.

CHAPTER VI.

A Glimpse of Catholic Christianity as seen by Faith.

I HAVE already in Chapter III. noticed in passing, a clever *ad hominem* argument against the eternity of punishment, and it may be as well to develop it in connection with the imperfections of practical Faith in the consoling mysteries of Catholic Christianity, which will form the subject of the present chapter.

Men who combat the eternal and awful sanction of the Divine Law, say this dogma, that the wicked will burn forever and ever, cannot be true, because no one actually and really believes it. Just picture to yourselves, they say to the public, what it is to suffer in a roasting fire, even for the few moments that life could endure so horrible a torment, imagine that in some extraordinary way, life is sustained for hours, and days, and years, and ages, and millions of ages, and you will find that the mind breaks down in the attempt to conceive so terrible an evil. Suppose that you prolong the torture only for some limited period—for a year or two, and that it is not a human being, but some brute animal that suffers, why the heart sickens and the brain reels at the horrible idea. Surely, they conclude, it has never entered into your mind to conceive the possibility of a fate so terrible being actually endured by some one dear to you. The bare thought of anything so dreadful would destroy every germ of earthly comfort and happiness. You would have constantly before your imagination, day and night, the shrieks of the unfortunate victim. You could not sleep, you could not take your meals, you would go mad. But none of these effects are noticeable even in pious Christians. There is no case on record where belief in the eternity of punishment has produced these effects, and consequently people only *say* that they hold this belief; it is impossible that it could be a settled conviction.

I have put the argument as forcibly as I could, because it is dangerously insidious particularly to weak, and unenlightened, and unreflecting Faith. The answer to it will involve the answer to the objection which I mean to meet in this chapter.

In the first place then, this application of the properties of a material fire, this "roasting," etc., to the fire of hell, is not sanctioned by any definition of the Church. The Church does not anywhere teach in precise terms that there is an eternal fire in the sense in which infidel writers make it the object of their abuse and denunciation. She teaches indeed that there is an eternal pain of "sense," as well as an eternal pain of "loss" for those who, by their own most grievous fault, and by the voluntary and deliberate abuse of their free-will, have obstinately renounced God and the future glory which He so freely offers us. Whenever she speaks of the sad fate of the reprobate, she uses the terrible words of the Sacred Scriptures—"Depart ye accursed into everlasting fire" (Matt. xxv. 41). But she has never declared that we are to understand this "fire" as meaning a fire like that to which we are accustomed in this world. Holy writers treating on the subject tell us, that the fire in hell is created only for torment, and not for any of the purposes to which we are accustomed to apply it in this world. And we know that it must possess peculiar properties incompatible with the fire that cooks our food, or ministers to our comfort, because it must affect the spiritual essence in torturing the souls of the perversely wicked.

If it be urged that the language of the Sacred Scriptures is explicit on the point, in the case of Dives, Catholic Christianity teaches us that every circumstance of a parable is not to be pressed to its strict meaning, and may be corrected by other teaching with which it does not accord. So that all the stress that is laid on "roasting" and "frizzing," etc., is not applicable to the idea of the punishment of "sense" in the region of the damned.

But the main point of the argument contains a notable fallacy. Though the torments of the reprobate are inconceivably great, it does not follow that we can, while in this mortal state, so realize the truth that it should necessarily check and "turn awry" the whole current of our ordinary lives. The Apostle tells us that "the sensual man perceiveth not the things that are of the Spirit of God; for it is foolishness to him and he cannot understand" (1 Cor. 11. 14). "We see now through a glass in an obscure manner" (2 Cor. xiii. 12). Even when our Divine Lord was teaching His disciples, "They understood not the word, and it was hid from them, so that they perceived it not" (Luke ix. 45).

It is only the Saints whose minds are elevated above the suggestions of sense, through fasting and mortification, and thus disposed to co-operate with the grace of God, and profit by its lights, and who devote all the energies of their souls "to perceive the things of God," that have so keen an insight into the spiritual world, that it moulds and fashions the thoughts, words, and actions of their daily lives. They, by constant self-command, have so curbed and restrained the natural tendency to mental dissipation and distraction, that they are more like angels than men, and are ever in the Divine presence, and thus, like St. Paul, see and know "hidden things" connected with the life to come, which it is not given to other men to understand.

We read in the lives of the Solitaries, that some amongst them were so impressed with the visions, vouchsafed them of the future judgment and punishment, that they could not forget, even for a short time, the dread convictions which had impressed themselves on their minds. St. Jerome in his quiet cell at Bethlehem, living only for God, and working indefatigably with all his powerful mind and abundant learning, to promote His honor and glory, often imagined that he heard the fearful clang of the last trumpet summoning him to judgment.

But these are very exceptional cases; and it is therefore a complete fallacy to infer that, because Faith does not constantly keep before us, in the midst of the distractions and cares of life, even its tremendous truths—it is therefore only a sham belief or Faith of the lips only, and not of the heart.

This answer applies perfectly to the matter before us— "Yes," will say those who catch a glimpse of the beauty of Catholic Christianity, "no doubt it *is* beautiful in its mysteries, and in the admirable connection of its doctrines, and in the comfort and consolation afforded by its sacramental system. Beautiful beyond anything that can be conceived in its teaching concerning the Blessed Eucharist; for what can raise man more above the things of earth, and fill him with Divine life more perfectly, than the conviction that he may, whenever he pleases, visit his Saviour, and commune with Him "as it were face to face," and be made one with Him in the Holy Communion? Yes, all this is true—but it proves too much. It is too beautiful to accord with the lives of ordinary Catholics. They cannot possibly believe in these delighful and consoling doctrines; for if they did, they should be Saints." " Why," continues the objector, "if I could believe this, I would already be raised above this earth—I would live and walk with God. Oh! the bliss to fold Him, as it were in my embrace, to fall at His sacred feet, to feel with Thomas the place of the nails, to place my hand within the opened side, and feel the beatings of the Sacred Heart!"

Those who might be disposed to reason thus, or to attach importance to imaginary feelings of this kind, would show at once that they have a poor knowledge of themselves, and a poorer knowledge still of human nature. There may be, in this weary world of temptation and trial, some few privileged souls, who thus live continually in the presence of our Saviour. They have schooled themselves by persevering habits of prayer and meditation, and above all of simple obedience and docility to prudent direction, to receive these higher gifts of God, vouchsafed to very few, of being caught up into ecstasies, in which every distraction from without is cut off by the physical insensibility to these impressions, and the whole soul is so fixed on God, as to forget for a while all its little cares, and conceits, and vanities.

When I visited Bois d'Haine, and saw the girl Louise Lateau, and spoke with her, and marked her simplicity of character, and watched her, after I had given her the Holy Communion, fall into an ecstasy, I could understand, that one so good, and so sorely tried, who had made it from childhood the constant habit of her daily life, to meditate as continually as possible on the Passion of our Lord, should, as she described her visions to me, see Him bending beneath the heavy cross, in the crowded streets of Jerusalem, and hear the shouts and yells of His tormentors. She told me that this was what she saw, whenever she seemed dead to the perception of external objects. "Do you see our Divine Lord?"—"Yes."—"Does He appear ever to see you? Do you catch His eye as He passes along?"—"No, never."

It was not difficult to believe that a Catholic like this peasant-girl, who seemed to be leading a supernatural life, might, on receiving our Divine Lord in the Holy Communion, have enjoyed the exalted gift of feeling herself in the visible presence. But those who fancy that Catholics generally should enjoy these blissful visions, and feel all the interior comfort that ought to spring from a lively Faith, can know very little of the spiritual life and its experiences. They expect far too much, they imagine to themselves a state of mind and feeling that is altogether beyond the power of ordinary humanity.

It is not anything of this kind we learn from the teaching of our Saviour. He, who, "for us men and our salvation," came down and dwelt amongst us, and shared our infirmities and sorrows, knows what is good for us. He has compassion on our miseries, for He shared them abundantly. He knows by this experience, which we can appreciate, how far we need comfort and support, and what may, through our vanity and self-love, be changed from real consolation into a temptation to spiritual pride. He is therefore sparing in the distribution of these higher gifts.

What a world of meaning there is in that reproach addressed by Him to the three Apostles in the garden of

Gethsemani! "What! could you not watch one hour with me?" One hour! and that hour the very one when He needed, actually God as He was, *needed* human sympathy! When He had put away the strong defences of His Divinity, and dismissed the Blessed Angels, who ever waited upon Him, and subjected Himself to the most overwhelming feelings that can sway the soul, and He was "sorrowful even unto death," and He knelt quite alone, with the blood gushing through the pores of His trembling body, and He had become "a worm and no man," had parted even with manly courage, and was thrown flat upon the ground by the irresistible force of blank fear and desolation, it was only then, under these extraordinary circumstances of supreme helplessness, that He said, as if grieved and disappointed, "Could you not watch one hour with me." He did not expect much in the way of comfort, who, once only in His life on earth, complained of the unkindness of His friends. On the cross, when His heart was breaking, a cry of similar complaint to His heavenly Father was wrung from Him by the intensity of His agony. Surely this example of patient endurance through a whole life, darkened throughout by the shadow of the cross, should teach us, whose lives must be made conformable to His, that we are not to expect in this world to enjoy the full consolations and the bright visions of Faith.

Although the Church is a Divine institution, Divine in its Founder, Divine also in its Mysteries, and means of grace, it is a society of men, who are commissioned by Jesus Christ to carry out His work. Those who are called to be teachers and rulers in the Church, no doubt, receive special gifts, to enable them to discharge faithfully their important functions. But they, like all God's intelligent creatures in this world of sin, bear the responsibilities of free-will. They may, or may not, make a proper use of the supernatural graces bestowed upon them. God will not force them to do what He earnestly desires. No more will He force those who form the main body of His Church. They may, or may not, make a proper use of their august privileges as Catholics. They may trifle with the gift of Faith, and expose it to irreparable danger, by toying with liberalism and infidelity; they may neglect the sacraments, and leave untouched the Bread of life. If they wilfully persevere in this course, a time will surely come when the gift of God will be taken away from them, and given to others more likely to profit by it.

But God is patient and long-suffering, and it is consoling for Catholics to know, that there is no sin however grievous, that necessarily destroys and uproots Faith, save only that sin against the Holy Ghost, which consists in the wilful rejection of Faith itself. "It is impossible," as St. Paul says, "It is impossible for those who were once enlightened, have tasted also the heavenly gift, and were made partakers of the Holy Ghost, have moreover tasted the good word of God, and the powers of the world to come, and are fallen away, to be renewed again unto penance" (Heb. vi. 4, 5, 6).

There is no priest, who has been many years on the Mission, who has not had personal experience of both these modes of dealing on the part of God with bad Catholics. It is wonderful how long Faith may survive a course of sin, and even scandalous sin. I have before my mind, now, striking instances of this mercy. I have known men who, plunged into grievous excesses, have for years despised warnings, and paid no attention to pressing exhortations, and yet, in some wonderful way they have clung to certain practices of their religion, and have said, even in the excess of their debaucheries, the prayers taught them by a good mother. Such as these, when it was least expected from them, have renounced sin effectually, turned to God with all their hearts, become real penitents, ever maintaining a deep sense of their wretched ingratitude to God, and have thus been preserved from even the temptation of self-justification.

I have before my mind cases too, where there was no public sin or scandalous immorality, but only a yielding to the spirit of worldliness, followed sooner or later by a positive renunciation of the Faith, and I cannot remember one case where Faith thus lost was ever recovered again. There have been instances in my experience where those unfortunate Catholics were brought to see the greatness of their loss, and the utter hollowness of the fashionable theories, which they had preferred to the teaching of the Church, and where there was real regret for this folly, and those who had erred, longed with all their hearts to win back the precious treasure they had lost. But, as far as human eyes could judge, they wept and sighed in vain. They could not believe again. "The things of God were foolishness to them and they could not understand."

There is no more dangerous mistake on the part of converts to the true Church, than to imagine that they shall find perfection in Catholics, that every priest will be an Apostle, and every nun a St. Teresa. Through the gift of God, they see in a moment revealed to them, in all their lustrous beauty, the doctrines of the Church. After they have spent perhaps years in inquiring and reading, and satisfying doubts, and attempting to clear up difficulties, earnestly trying, by the best efforts of their intelligence, to grope their way to God through the midst of darkness, the light has suddenly burst upon them, as it did on St. Paul near Damascus. The scales of prejudice drop from their eyes, they drink in the lessons of the Catholic religion, with an avidity that tells of their long hunger and thirst, and at once they seem to rise to the third heaven, in the joy and consolation afforded by the practices of the Faith. They cannot go to Holy Communion often enough; they would wish to receive the Most Holy, twenty times a day, if it were possible, they are all aglow with the happy excitement of having found the rich treasure—"the pearl beyond all price." They desire to mount the rugged way to Heaven with giant strides, for, can they not "do all things," they say, "in Him who strengthens them" in the sacraments, and above all in the Most Holy Sacrament of the Altar. And when they are counselled to be moderate, and simple, and obedient, and told that God does not require extraordinary things, but that they should do well the little of which they are capable even with His helping grace, and to "watch and pray" and guard against self-confidence, they are chilled by such prudent counsel. Then after a time, they begin to look around them, and to notice that their fellow-Catholics do not share their ardor, that most of them are toiling slowly and steadily onward, often slipping and falling, and it may be settling down into sloth and tepidity.

This excites their surprise, and their wonder is increased, when they discover that priests are not angels, but men "compassed about with infirmity"—sons of Adam, sons of sinners, who have their own sins to offer for, their own temptations to encounter; that Religious too have their imperfections. When they see all this, they are apt to be distressed, and it may be disenchanted and disappointed with the Religion they have embraced, and tempted to believe that it is not in reality the beauteous Heavenly thing they once thought it was.

They were with these views, simply forgetting that the fairest works of God are always marred and spoiled by our imperfections: and that God Himself, respecting our free will, cannot give the brightness and purity of Heaven to what is only human after all.

Our Divine Lord has prepared us for these disappointments in the beautiful parables, in which He has described "the Kingdom of Heaven," or His Church on earth. In the thirteenth chapter of St. Matthew, there is a series of these parables, and we have only to combine them, when we see at once how admirably they describe that strange mixture of good and evil, of piety and lukewarmness, of earnest zeal, and cold indifference, that marks the different members of the one true fold. This is so strikingly put by Cardinal Wiseman, in his essay on the " Parables of the New Testament," that my readers will, I am sure, thank me for giving an extract from that polished writer, and profound thinker.

After speaking of the parable of the sower, as the preliminary or introductory parable of the whole series, in as much as it lays down the necessary dispositions for receiving with profit the words of Christ, he goes on,—
" The seed then sown by Christ in this field of the world, that portion of it even, which fell upon well-prepared ground, was soon to be disturbed by the enemy. A spurious seed would soon be scattered among it, and would spring up side by side with the blade of genuine grain; that is, even in the Church itself, and among the

faithful, there would arise corruption, vices, and scandals; the parable of the cockle."

So it must be with all things human. "There must be scandals;" it would be folly to expect anything else. It is only the founders of false sects, whether deceived by fanaticism, or maliciously deceiving others, that have pretended to form a society where all would be perfect. No careful watching, no plucking up the weeds, will preserve the field of the Church from this mixture of good and bad: and so our Divine Lord who "fully understood what was in man," ordained that the separation was to be effected only when the time of the great harvest shall come. The sorting of the fish is to take place on the shore of eternity, when the angels of God, assisting in the great judgment, will be the sorters of good and bad. Wickliffe, and Huss, by declaring that sin put an end to all rights, aimed at a society of the immaculate.

Every heresy is tainted with the same foolish notion of a perfect community. It was the grand characteristic of Donatism. "The basis of that heresy and schism," says Cardinal Wiseman, "was that the Church could only consist of incorrupt members, and that every portion of it which tolerated or forgave those guilty of a grievous crime, had forfeited its claims. Protestantism is essentially Donatist, whether in its High-Church theory of branch separation from the trunk, or in its lowest evangelical idea of an invisible elect Church."

Hence those who admire Catholic Christianity, as all must admire it who once discover it clear of the mists and shadows of prejudice, and distinct from the misrepresentations of its enemies, should understand, that this beauty, and grace, and supernatural and divinely conceived harmony and order, is only the ideal before the mind of the

Saviour. He manifested this truly Divine conception when, on the night before He suffered, He prayed that all who believed in Him might be made so perfect in unity and love, that the world would be converted at the charming spectacle. In that prayer, our Divine Lord exhibits to us His fond desire, and shows us what He would actually accomplish, if we would only freely give Him our hearts, and suffer Him to mould them as He willed. The reality is very different from the ideal; human infirmity, human weakness, imperfections, even among the just, continual falling away from fervor, not to speak of scandals of a grave kind, are ever soiling and disfiguring the glorious work of God.

This view of the Church as it really is, a society of men, believing all, as if with one mind, the same mysteries, confessing, as if with one mouth, the same doctrine, partaking of the same sacraments, nourished by the one saving Bread of life, bound together under the one visible head, the Vicar and Representative of Christ; yet all differing in degrees of piety or wickedness, a heterogeneous collection well figured by the "crowd of bad and good gathered to the wedding feast" (Matt. xxii. 10) explains away at once the difficulties urged against the sanctity of the Catholic Church.

"Can she," it is argued, "be a Holy Church, where there is so much immorality, where there are so many scandals, where, even amongst those who ought to be patterns of every virtue, there is so much weakness? Can we call that Church a holy and perfect Church, where even the very head and representative of Christ has been, as in the case of some Popes, a notorious sinner?"

Yes; I reply she can be Holy, perfectly Holy in her teaching, Holy in her sacraments, Holy in everything that can help to make men saints; and yet exhibit all these blemishes, because she is composed of men, who may resist grace, and profane sacraments, and do whatever their evil nature suggests, and they are determined to carry out. Admitting even for a moment the grossly exaggerated stories of immorality in her rulers, one answer to all this is readily found in the fact, that, even amongst the chosen twelve, there was one who sinned so grievously, that our Divine Lord said of him, "it were better for him that he had never been born." Further, as to the objection that there were bad Popes, I reply that, even if this were established as a fact by historians above suspicion, it would not affect the sanctity of the Church, as regards her holy teaching, and the means of grace; it would only prove that, in spite of the weakness of human nature, the glorious work of the Son of God would produce, in men of good-will, the sanctifying effects intended by its Divine Founder. The Scribes and Pharisees, though they were "whited sepulchres," were approved, in their office of teaching the people, by our Divine Lord: "All things whatsoever they shall say to you, observe and do" (Matt. xxiii. 3). Neither they who sat "in the chair of Moses" nor those who were, by Divine appointment of the Saviour, to fulfil the work committed specially to St. Peter, of "confirming the faith," were guaranteed, by any promise, from personal weakness or actual sin. They might therefore sin, and sin grievously, yet the Faithful should obey their commands, and observe their doctrine.

I do not deny that grave charges of ambition and immorality have been made by many Protestant writers, and even Catholic historians of the Gallican school, against some of the successors of St. Peter; but there is no doubt that these charges rest on weak foundation, and that they have been grossly exaggerated by the enemies of the Holy See. Much of this accumulated rubbish is fast disappearing from the pages of genuine history. The disinterested labors of learned men, superior to vulgar prejudice, such as Frederic Hurter, Professor Voight, Doctor Hock, Roscoe, and I might add the writings of Leopold Ranke, are establishing more and more clearly and satisfactorily, the truth of the words of a celebrated writer—that "History," especially in all that relates to the Catholic Church, is "a vast conspiracy against truth."

But even admitting that, amongst the 260 Popes, there were a few whose lives were tainted by "the pride of life" and even immorality, what would follow? Should we then believe that the solemn promises of the Divine Founder of the Church had been made void? No, this could never be. "Heaven and earth shall pass away, but His words shall not pass away" (Mark xiii. 31). This only could be reasonably deduced from such scandals—a truth not understood perhaps when our Divine Lord described His Kingdom on earth in the parables, that this Kingdom, the Church, was constituted, as well in its teaching body as in all its members, of weak human elements, and should consequently exhibit more or less, even in those in the highest position, the taint of their personal weakness and infirmity. There was no promise—there could be none consistent with free-will, that engaged our Lord, from the beginning to the end of His work, to provide sinless successors to His first Vicar on earth. The promise of supernatural aid was to secure "the Faith once delivered to the saints" from corruption. Men who occupied the chair of Peter, and became by their office the "mouthpiece" of the Spirit of Truth, might fall into sin, but, "for the sake of the elect," they would still be guided in the ways of sound doctrine, as were Caiphas and the exponents of prophecy and the law in the Jewish Church, and would not be allowed to lead the flock into the noxious and poisonous pastures of heresy and immorality.

How beautifully is not this truth expressed by the Apostle! "God who commanded the light to shine out of darkness, He hath shined in our hearts, to give the light of the knowledge of the glory of God in the face of Christ Jesus: but we hold this treasure in earthen vessels, that the excellency may be of the power of God, and not of us" (2. Cor. iv. 6, 7). How stupidly Protestants mix up together inerrancy of teaching and impeccability of life! They will not believe it possible that Holy and sound doctrine can come to men through the lips of weak and sinful mortals; as if our Divine Lord had made angels and not men the ministers of His gospel.

There is another view of the subject which forces itself upon me here. Non-Catholics will not believe that Priests and nuns can be faithful to the grace of their vocation, because they look only to the weakly earthen vessel. They know very clearly how weak human nature is in their own persons, how prone to evil, how easily overcome; but they seem not to recognize the power of supernatural grace. As Cardinal Newman expresses it, "Men of the world know the power of nature; they know not, experience not, believe not the power of God's grace; and since they are not themselves acquainted with any power that can overcome nature, they think that none exists, and therefore, consistently, they believe that every one, Priest or not, remains to the end such as nature made him, and they will not believe it possible that any one can lead a supernatural life. And when they hear of the life which a Priest must lead by his profession from youth to age, they will not credit what he professes to be. They know nothing of the presence of God, the merits of Christ, the intercession of the Blessed Virgin; the virtue of recurring prayers, of frequent confession, of daily Masses; they are strangers to the transforming power of the Most Holy Sacrament, the Bread of Angels; they do not contemplate the efficacy of salutary rules, of holy companions, of long enduring habit, of ready spontaneous vigilance, of abhorrence of sin and indignation at the tempter, to secure the soul from evil."

If those who rant and rave against the Holiness of the Church could catch only a glimpse of the interior life of a good priest, or a fervent Religious, what a marvel that would be to them! How completely would their ideas be changed! The daily meditation, the examination of conscience, the constant thought of the presence of God, the pious ejaculations, the frequent lifting up of the heart to God, all this carried on in the busy thoroughfares of life, unrevealed exteriorly by a look or any outward sign, would seem to them almost incredible. If it were given them, like the servants of the prophet, to have their eyes opened, so that they could see the angels of God ascending and descending, to mark the bright gleam of happiness on the face of the guardian spirit, so proud of the purity of his charge, and the flashes of beauteous light from Heaven, as grace after grace and blessing after blessing descends on the soul of God's faithful servant, then would they behold with admiration what is meant by the supernatural life in Catholic Christianity, and what a blissful thing it is to walk with God in this world, and to minister to Him in the spiritual and corporal necessities of His children.

This is no imaginary sketch, it must be something like the reality of a Holy life in "the city of God" on earth. And, if the stranger to our creed went farther, and pursued the same train of thought and vision, as regards the service at the Altar—surely it would not require any efforts to realize to his mind that blissful sight described by St. John Chrysostom, when he tells us, that, as he performed the sacred rites, he saw the angels around him, bowing down and worshipping "the lamb that was slain from the beginning of the world," and supplementing by their ardent fervor the coldness and insensibility which must ever accompany even the best efforts of the soul, while it is enclosed in the prison of the body, to rise to the perception of things supernatural

In the next chapter, I mean to summarize the view of the Holy Catholic Church, as it appears to the eyes of enlightened Faith. It will then be seen more clearly what is this creation of God on earth, that is assailed so fiercely by the arms of Christian error, and daring infidelity, and how widely different is Catholic Christianity, from the miserably distorted object which is held up by its enemies to the ridicule, and scorn, and hatred of an unbelieving world.

CHAPTER VII.

A Further View of Catholic Christianity Through its Forms of Worship.

A GREAT deal has been written to show how preferable is the simplicity of Protestant worship, to the gorgeous ceremonial of the Roman Catholic Church. Very learned men, who probably were so full of this notion of the fitness of simple prayer, that they never troubled themselves to study the symbolic character of our ceremonies, have denounced them as unmeaning "mummery." In their view, the solemn, and stately, and well emphasized reading of approved prayers, and the chanting of popular hymns, and antiphons, and the polished essay on some moral subject, are immeasurably superior to a grand High Mass, with a full choral service, embellished by strains of the highest artistic music, and an eloquent exposition by the preacher of some great mystery of Revealed Religion with its practical consequences, and a touching exhortation to generous resolutions.

Putting aside for a moment the all-important consideration, what does the Almighty prefer, as far as we can know of His good pleasure, let us view the disputed point in its purely human aspects.

I believe that any one who takes into consideration the wants and infirmities of our nature, and shuts out from his view the suggestions of prejudice, must admit that a due attention to outward ceremonial is a wonderful help to fix the wandering thoughts, and confine the attention of the worshippers to the main object before them.

In estimating the matter, we must take it in its extreme forms, and judge between the most rigid simplicity, and the most elaborate ceremonial. Suppose we contrast a man, wearing the ordinary dress of the world, reading, from a platform or stool, a chapter of the Sacred Scriptures, without any effort at elocution, beyond bringing out distinctly the words of the sacred text; and this in a plain building, void of anything like religious ornamentation, merely contrived in its architectural proportions to assist the reader's voice, and that when he does read, he discourses plainly on some text, and that when he has finished his homily, the congregation, without help of organ or any instrument, join in an ordinary hymn; suppose, I say, we contrast this simplest form of Christian worship with the Ceremonial of High Mass in a grand Cathedral, there can scarcely be a doubt which will be more likely to impress the ordinary public.

Take a congregation consisting in the main of the poor and the uneducated, those in a word to whom it was our Divine Lord's greatest consolation that they had the gospel preached to them, and can it be maintained, that they will be equally impressed in both cases? Of course I am supposing that the natural emotions have not been schooled by puritanical training, and that those who are present are left entirely to their own unbiased feelings. I believe that no intelligent and honest man will have a doubt on the point. "It is only quite natural," he will say, "that the grand music and the pealing of the organ, and the rich vestments of the officiating priests, and the clouds of incense, and the clash of arms of the military present, and the bowing down of the whole assemblage at the more solemn parts of the ceremony, will produce a soul-subduing effect; and that this effect will be considerably heightened by the lofty nave and aisles, and the lights, and flowers, and decorations of the majestic building." " The meeting-house" or the " Tabernacle" may be as large as the temple in Salt Lake City, and its fittings all that is considered perfect in the way of utility and comfort, the acoustic principles duly attended to, and the ventilation carried out on the highest scientific principles, and the pews padded like first-class railway carriages, but the walls bare and bald of any decoration, no pictures on their broad expansive waste—no stained-glass windows, nothing, in a word, to appeal through sense to soul, what will be the natural effect of this simplicity? Alas! for the religious feeling or devout attention of those who are not over interested in the commentaries, and disquisitions, and numerous points of the learned preacher. It is not in human nature, that the many, unable to follow the discourse through its many mazes and subtle windings, should not yield to a thousand distracting thoughts. They will certainly grow weary of the solemn tones, and mope; and if they dare not look about, and converse with their neighbors, will in all probability slumber peacefully in the well-stuffed pews.

I know very well that, at one period, when prejudice and bigotry, the offspring of gross misrepresentation, had excited in the ignorant masses, a hatred of Popery, and it was considered a godly work to mutilate and destroy the costly treasures of art, with which ages of Faith had enriched the splendid Cathedrals of England and Scotland, that the barns and " pantile" structures were the cherished conventicles of the men who preached and sang and prayed aloud in the extempore style and with the nasal twang immortalized by Scott. But these days have happily passed away.

When I visited, a few years ago, St. Mungo's Cathedral in Glasgow, recently enriched, even in its crypts, with stained windows that are marvels of art, and saw just opposite the frowning figure of John Knox, who seems, in his bronze lineaments, to denounce this hateful restoration, I felt that a change had come over the spirit of this dream of Puritanism; and that sensible men were forced nowadays, in spite of long-cherished traditions, to pay public homage to the genius of Catholic Christianity.

It is only in congregations of ultra-puritans, on the borders of civilization, such as the " Doppers" of the Dutch Church on our remote frontiers, where men and women drawl out the psalms, as they did one hundred years ago, and are sustained in their noisy fervor by the energy of fiery Predikants, that people object to organs and the other adjuncts of solemn worship. Any one may see, from the style of ecclesiastical architecture adopted within the last generation in the colony, and the tendency of Christians of all denominations to decorate their churches and chapels, that there is really something after all in the good old Catholic notion, that the soul, in all that concerns the fitting worship of the Almighty, must be reached through sense.

Ritualism has not yet fully developed itself amongst us, in orderly ceremonial and elaborate choral services, with vestments and lights and incense; but an ordinary observer may perceive on all sides enough to satisfy him, that I am not arguing on any but sound principles, and the promptings of our best instincts, when I say that, apart altogether from the will and good pleasure of God, made known to us in Revelation, and viewing the matter only in its human aspects, the simplicity, as it is called, of un-Catholic worship is a mere pretence, invented in past days to excite and sustain odium against the practices of the Catholic Church.

But if we rise above the question of mere taste and right feeling, and ask ourselves what is the will of God as to our mode of worship, it will appear certain beyond doubt, that the same God, who instructed His chosen people under the old covenant in all the details of solemn worship, did also, in the person of Christ, instruct the Apostles, that these outward forms should be preserved by believers in their teaching. External ceremonies and outward forms of Religious service, suited to our wants and capacities, arise naturally from the Incarnation, and the whole sacramental system.

If we ask ourselves what was actually the mode of worship in the earliest Christian times, we find, in the old Liturgies, a direct and clear answer to the question. We do not know from the Sacred Scriptures, what were the special instructions of our Divine Lord on this point, but He who was so careful that every tittle and iota of the Mosaical dispensation should, as long as that dispensation was in force, be strictly complied with, must, while "giving commandments by the Holy Ghost to the Apostles whom He had chosen" (Acts i. 2), have fully explained to them His wishes on this important matter. "There are many other things," St. John tells us, which Our Saviour said and did "which are not written" (John xx. 31).

The practice of the Church, when she was free to act in the matter of building churches, and arranging her ceremonial, brings out what these instructions were.

From the time when Persecution ceased, and the Basilicas and other public buildings were handed over by the Imperial Government for Christian Worship, we know, from the records carefully preserved in all the churches, what this worship was. In the cities and towns remote from the great centres of persecution, there were, we may confidently believe, even in Apostolic times, solemn forms of external worship. Most commentators on the Apocalypse hold, that the vision of the golden candlesticks, and the altar with "the Lamb as it were slain" resting upon it, and the golden censer with its fire and smoking incense, and the assembled priests with the Venerable Pontiff presiding, seated on his throne, and the hymns and canticles, and the harps and musical instruments, was clothed in imagery borrowed from the ceremonial of the Church as it existed in his time, and that St. John made use of this imagery, so familiar to the Faithful, in order to help them to form an idea of the honor and adoration paid to our Divine Lord, by the Saints and Angels, in the sanctuary of Heaven.

A Protestant writer, Bingham says, in reference to these passages from the Apocalypse, "We have here seen the model of the worship of Christ as begun and settled in the practice of the Church in the first ages, and we shall find it continued in the same manner in those that followed immediately after" (Bingham, *Origines Ecclesiasticæ*, book xiii. ch. ii.). The learned Dr. Rock says on this point, "Such a remarkable resemblance exists between the more conspicuous outlines of this mysterious representation, drawn in so graphic a manner by the luminous pencil of the Evangelist, and those sketches of the celebration of the Eucharistic mysteries, incidentally pictured by the earlier Fathers in their letters and other writings, and even by Pagans in their remarks upon the ways and habits and practices of the Christians around them, or traced, with studious and minute accuracy, in the Liturgies of each particular church, that we are compelled to refer them to one original, from which they have all been copied with but very little and unimportant variation" (*Hierurgia*, p. 91).

It may have been that the Liturgy of the Holy Sacrifice, or the Mass, was modelled according to the Vision of St. John, the favorite disciple of our Divine Lord. In either case, as Dr. Rock remarks, the Liturgy or Mass bears deeply impressed upon it the type of Apostolical institution.

But it is in the cradle of our Christian Faith, in the Catacombs, that we find the most striking proofs that the Catholic mode of worship of the present day is most intimately connected with the worship of the early Christians. It is proved beyond all doubt by the eminent archæologists, who have made the careful examination, and minute description of these subterranean retreats, the study and work of their lives, that the Catacombs, early in the second century, were used by the persecuted Christians, not only as hiding-places and for the purpose of burial; but also for their assemblies, and for their united devotions and sacred rites. Guided by such lights as Boldetti, Bottari, Bosio, Aringhi, and D'Agincourt, and prepared by a careful study of the annals of early Ecclesiastical History, the visitor, who in these days descends, torch in hand, into this city of the dead, will at once discover unmistakable traces of the Altar at which the Holy Mass was celebrated eighteen hundred years ago. Aided by the emblems, and decorations, and frescos, on the walls of the little chambers, he can easily picture to himself, where stood the sacrificing priest, where knelt the pious crowd, and fancy he hears again the hymns, and alleluias, and strains of holy gladness, pealing through the vaults and passages.

How silly it is for men, in the face of evidence like this, to declare that the earliest worship was like that of the Puritans of the days of Cromwell! We see in the frescos of the Catacombs, pictures as old as those found in the ruins of Pompeii, overwhelmed A.D. 79 (our own Flaxman corroborates on this point the judgment of D'Agincourt), the very vestments of the priests, and enough to trace out distinctly the whole ceremonial of public worship.

With what different eyes would not those who scoff at the Mass, and the dress of the priests, and the lighted candles, and the bowings and bendings of the knee, regard these things, if they were convinced, that the sacred rite is the very same, in all its prominent features and essential parts, as that celebrated in the Catacombs according to the form prescribed in the ancient Liturgies!

But, as I have said already, this is a flippant and irreverent age. Faith in the august mysteries of Revelation is almost gone from those who will not hear the Church. There is no time to study the large tomes of learned archæologists, or the early annals of Christianity, or to inquire into the meaning of the rites and ceremonies, carefully transmitted through so many centuries; and therefore they are regarded by the many as trifling and contemptible.

"Why," says the sharp colonial youth, " should candles be lighted in the daytime? they are of no use when the sun is shining. Why should the priest stand with his back to the people, reading Latin which no one understands? What a singular way of preaching! Why not dress like other men? Why hold his hands extended? Was ever anything more absurd!"

But the priest is not preaching, he is performing a most solemn act of worship peculiar to the priestly office: and his people know well how to follow him, by their prayer-books through every part of the sacred rite. See how even those who cannot read are perfectly united with the rest of the congregation in every movement. They all, as one man, rise or bend the knee, or bow down in deep reverence; and these lighted candles, and all the ornaments of the altar, and vestments, have a symbolical meaning which speaks to the mind and heart of the initiated, who have been trained from infancy to understand every portion of the service. These are sacred things in their eyes who are properly instructed, honored in the glowing Faith of millions of saints, and venerated for ages by united Christendom.

There is something so preposterous and revolting to a Catholic in this ignorant association of utilitarian and business-like notions with the things of Faith, that he can with difficulty restrain his feelings of indignation, when they are rudely thrust on his attention by those who have never taken the pains to understand what they are so glibly talking about. It is not surprising that the well-instructed Catholic under these circumstances is tempted to believe, that these expressions of contempt and ridicule can have their origin only in horrible blasphemy, and supercilious scorn for the ordinances of God.

But in truth there is no thought of anything of the kind. They who speak so lightly or contemptuously of what we regard as most holy, are only expressing their matter-of-fact opinions about things which are meaningless to them. When they talk freely about the rites and ceremonies of Catholic worship, they are only expressing honest convictions, which have never been disturbed by even the ghosts and shadows of ecclesiastical learning, or the teaching of the Church. They know nothing about "the ages of Faith," and the grand thoughts that once formed the spiritual life of united Christendom.

I have often met with young people of this sort—who, I am sure had not the least idea of giving offence, by expressing freely to those about them their views on the silly and puerile and senseless things which they firmly believed they had noticed in Catholic worship. Poor deluded Papists! they must have sincerely thought, "what has bewitched you," that you cannot look at these things with the light of common-sense, and see through the foolery of all this playing at Religion!

How painful it must be to the really thoughtful and learned, who have travelled in many lands, and have, though not Catholics, picked up some information about the old religion, as they hear the dogmatic opinions about this religion freely ventilated, in train and cart, by young people, the amount of whose theology about the Roman Catholic belief might be summed up in the phrase—"the Pope is the man of sin and the Church he governs the beast of the Apocalypse." I am never disposed to be angry under these circumstances, and I know it would be rude to laugh, but one cannot help thinking that if there is one position, that makes an intelligent-looking individual more ridiculous than another, it is talking confidently, before those who are fairly educated, about things of which they know absolutely nothing. The notions of a raw Kaffir about the locomotive and the telegraph would be positively refreshing, compared with this barbaric "rushing in where Angels fear to tread."

If one could only reason with them, and explain what Catholicity really is—there would be some gratification; but alas! these minds are so full of the one idea on the matter, that they have no place for any other. Tell them, that the most gifted children of art devoted the best efforts of their almost inspired genius to adorn this worship so much despised by those who do not understand it; that painters, and sculptors, and musicians, devoted their whole lives to add one gem to the many that adorn the brow of the spouse of Christ, and they will look blank with amazement, and laugh outright at the folly, which could have suggested so stupid a waste of valuable time, and so profitless an expenditure of talents, that might have secured wealth and honor for their possessors. Describe to them a grand old Cathedral—or try to give them a notion of St. Peter's with its priceless treasures of art, and tell them that all this grandeur and prodigality of rich ornament in its glowing groups of statuary, and unfading mosaics, was simply to construct a temple worthy, as men could make it, of "the dwelling-place" of God Incarnate, and they will regard you as one who is an idle dreamer, and destitute of an atom of business capacity.

But who can blame them? they have heard over and over again that Popery is "a vain delusion," at its best—until this notion has become a settled conviction in their minds. It is no wonder therefore that they pity or despise the victims of this strange delusion; and judge of the extravagant folly to which it leads, as they would the vagaries of an idle and thriftless prodigal. They are not guilty of the sin of the unfortunate Apostle, who complained of the waste of the precious unguent, which Magdalene poured out on the sacred feet of our Lord; for he was covetous, and tried to veil his avarice under the hypocrisy of caring for the poor. No—these young people, who are ever asking,—what is the good of this or that in some beautiful Catholic Church, and pointing out how money might have been saved here and there, and are thoroughly utilitarian in their views, they are not hypocrites, nor are they misers. They are honest and outspoken, kind-hearted it may be, generous and amiable, and they make themselves ridiculous to Catholics, or scandalize them by their remarks on ceremonial religion, and works of art connected with the Divine service, only because they know absolutely nothing of a religion that is supernatural in its teaching, and in everything that pertains to the worship and honor of the great God.

We Catholics should be patient when our religious rites and ceremonies are as we think, rudely and irreverently criticised. Those who speak in this manner know not what they say. No harm probably is meant by them, even when they smile broadly and stare about them in our churches, and disturb those kneeling near, by their unseemly remarks. There is of course manifest in this conduct a want of good-breeding and ordinary politeness. But the whole ceremony and all its accessories is utter foolishness to them, they do not understand anything about it, and they do not even allow themselves to think that there may or can be anything worth knowing, underneath all that seems to them so childish and unmeaning.

If Catholics were always as devout as they should be in "the House of God," there would be much less of this seeming irreverence on the part of strangers. If, at the Holy Sacrifice, or Benediction, they tried to rise to the perceptions of Faith, when the Immaculate Victim is lifted up for their adoration, and to bow down with grateful homage to receive the blessing of the Emmanuel, non-Catholics, who visit our churches, would soon learn respect and reverence for our worship, and be led to inquire into the meaning of those rites which seem to them at first sight so strange and incomprehensible.

Let me suppose for a moment that, struck by the serious and rapt attention of the worshippers, and the sort of instinct which seems to guide even children through the solemn services, they were led to ask what does it all mean? and some friend were to offer them a prayer-book, and point out to them the different parts of the sacred ceremony, it would not be long until the thought would flash across their minds, that something, which they had never comprehended before, was taking place under their eyes. "What," they might be led to say to themselves, "if it be true that, under these outward rites, which we have been always taught to regard as senseless mummeries, there is enacted an awful mystery, and that God the Saviour is really present, veiled under the whiteness of the Host?" I can easily imagine the shame and regret which would overwhelm them for their irreverence.

Thousands are every day wakening up to this correct view of Catholic worship. They enter a Catholic church with much the same feeling of idle curiosity as would lead them to a theatre. They thank God perhaps that they are not like the superstitious crowd, who, at the signal of the bell, bow down and strike their breasts; and they smile at the spectacle of apparent fervor, and freely exchange with their companions their jests and mockery at every movement of the priest and congregation. But gradually as they note the unmistakable earnestness, and the ease with which all join in the forms of worship, and see that the indications of their superior wisdom are unheeded, and that sometimes their rude stare is met with a glance of pity, they begin to wonder what it is that can produce this reverent attention; and an impression is often made that is never forgotten, and which, if not chased away by frivolity and silly talk, is sure to lead to sincere and earnest inquiry. When the congregation manifests an edifying attention, and seems to realize the grand and awful nature of the Holy Sacrifice, it will be the means of effecting many a real conversion.

Worldly-minded people will of course account for all this in their own way. They will say, " Yes, no doubt the Romish rite is attractive, because it is purposely contrived to work on the senses." And they are right so far: it *is* attractive, and it *does* reach the soul through sense, and it has been so arranged from the very beginning, but only that it may raise the soul above the things of earth, and bring it into pure and sweet communion with the Spirit of God. It is meant precisely to do all this, and when not resisted by unreasoning pride and the force of prejudice, will always be a wonderful help to bring the well-disposed to a knowledge of the truth.

Men who have a contempt for Faith, as it is understood in Catholic Christianity, are always sneering at the credulity and superstition of Catholics. " Papists," they say, " will believe anything no matter how absurd."

I reply, Catholics will believe everything that is revealed by God, and taught by His Infallible Church, no matter how incomprehensible it may seem; and it is chiefly to awaken Faith, and to strengthen and develop it, by the aid of the senses, that there is all this pomp and ceremony in Catholic worship. Once this is clearly understood by strangers, and the frozen barrier of prejudice which chills anything like the ardor of true devotion, is broken through, a glimpse is then caught of the bright and Heavenly beauty beyond. Clouds and mists depart, and the thirsting soul is borne onward on the wings of desire to the fountain of living water, springing up, in the bosom of the Church, to life eternal.

There will of course be many difficulties, and trials, and obstacles, in the way, but they will melt into nothing before the ever-kindling light of eternal truth. Old thoughts will attempt to resume their influence, and turn from his course the honest inquirer. "This is the Church," he will say to himself, "that I was so long taught to hate as the mystery of abomination; this is the idolatrous, soul-enslaving enemy of Christ; this is the superstitious creed which debased and degraded the intellect for so many ages." These were once formidable objections, preventing him from looking in the direction of the Catholic Church; but now, that the possibility of the truth of Catholic doctrine, and the real nature of Catholic worship has flashed upon his mind, there arises simultaneously a suspicion that what he had so often heard, without question, may be altogether false. These ugly names and these solemn denunciations of Popery in every shape and form may after all, he begins to think, have been the offspring of interested zeal, and misrepresentation, and calumny. Better thoughts will follow in this struggle after truth. "If God has spoken to the Church, and revealed certain truths about His own nature, and the economy of salvation, these truths being beyond the reach of human perception, must be mysteries. Although I cannot comprehend them, I am bound, out of respect to God and to the infallible teacher appointed by Him to instruct me, to accept them reverently. There can be no degradation of the intellect in believing what we know with certainty to have been taught by Divine Truth itself.

"If Christians for so many ages agreed in adoring Christ really present in the Sacrifice of the Mass and in the Eucharist, and if the same belief was cherished by the Faithful in the very infancy of the Church, there can be no idolatry in adoring the Lord and Saviour present in this manner. The early Christians were taught by the Apostles themselves and by their immediate successors, and must have worshipped in a way that they knew was pleasing to their Divine Master. Surely they loved Him with all their hearts, who responded to the appeal of an Apostle with tears and lamentations, vehemently declaring that the Pagans might wring out their life-blood rather than force them to deny Christ. He must have loved them in return. He could not have been displeased with them, because they clung to the belief in His promise of being always with them, and testifying the reality and earnestness of their confidence in His Word, by their expressive worship. Nay He must have blessed them, as they clustered round the altars in the Catacombs, esteeming it their greatest happiness in the midst of cruel persecution for His name's sake, that they could partake of His Body and Blood and be made one with Him in the great sacrament. And if so, He must be blessing, with His choicest benedictions, those Catholics, who, in the face of the ridicule and scorn of an unbelieving world, cling to this old Faith, and honor His presence in their midst by an outward worship as old, in its peculiar form and ceremonial, as that clearly indicated in the earliest Christian monuments and the venerable Liturgies. If Catholics are wrong, it can only be, because they cherish notions too exalted of the Infinite power, and the Infinite mercy, and the Infinite loving condescension of God our Saviour. And, awful thought! if I am wrong in preferring the views and opinions of those who rebelled against the Old Church, and taught me to deride and blaspheme this mystery of Divine love, whither shall I fly from His wrath and where shall I hide my shame?"

This is the natural flow of thought that brings many into the bosom of the Church, who have been interested in inquiring into the meaning of her ceremonial, and in watching its effects on the souls of earnest believers. Thus it is that one ray of light, emanating from the sanctuary—is sufficient to indicate to a man who honestly desires to find out the truth, the hideous deformity of those spectres of the imagination, that rise up before him from the rank soil of long-accumulated prejudices.

It does not require much study or instruction to complete the conversion of any one, whom God in mercy has allowed to be seriously struck with the profound meaning of the ceremonies of the Catholic Church. He has got the key which unlocks the treasure committed to her keeping. He sees, by a sort of intuition, that the bowing and repeated genuflections, and the incense, and lights, and the rich ornaments, are all directed to one object, to show respect to the Saviour really present. The very peculiarity of the rite, so unlike anything invented and authorized by worldly fashions, and the changing caprice of men, commends it to his admiration.

It is, he sees, the time-honored ceremonial to be observed by His ministers and attendants in the presence of the Great King. As the Master of Ceremonies, and the Lord Chamberlain, in attendance on an earthly sovereign, direct all the minutiæ of the dress and movements of the privileged few, who pass in procession before the throne, or wait on Majesty; so, at the High Mass, there is the proper officer, to see that the Sacred Ritual, handed down from primitive times, is carefully observed. "And this then," he says, "is the clean oblation foretold by the last of the prophets; Christ, the priest forever according to the order of Melchisedech, is here at once priest and victim, and by the hands of the visible priest officiating at the Altar, is offering Himself to His Heavenly Father, to apply to the souls of the worshippers, the fruits of His Redemption." What a vision of marvellous beauty rises up before the mind of one thus initiated into the mystery of Catholic worship! This is the eternal, never-ceasing sacrifice, "offered up from the rising to the setting of the sun," not confined to one place, but celebrated over the whole world, not alone in stately Cathedrals, but in the little way-side chapel, or the Cave like that of Bethlehem, wherever there are assembled "the true adorers in spirit and in truth" (John iv. 23). And thus Catholics in every land, wherever there is a priest and an altar, can worship in a manner pleasing to God; for they can, while the priest performs the sacred action, each following his own devotion, say in the secret of their hearts —"Behold, O God our Protector, and look on the face of Thy Christ" (Ps. lxxxiii. 10); for His sake, here present in our midst, have mercy on us, and forgive us our manifold offences! And, as if this were not enough, each of the worshippers may take into his heart the spotless Lamb, and be made one with Jesus, a child of God and an heir to Heaven. How the vision grows in beauty and majesty, as, by a sort of instinct, he traces the connection between the Blessed Eucharist and the Incarnation, between the Sacred Heart and the Holy Communion, and begins to see one great Mystery unfolding itself from another; and perceives for the first time the wonderful invention of Almighty Love, whereby the blessed fruits of Calvary are brought home to every true believer, individually and personally.

How soon in his mind every dogma of Catholic Christianity takes its proper place! The whole sacramental system is, he sees, nothing more nor less than Christ really present in the midst of His people for evermore —passing along, blessing and touching with His hand those who stand in need of His help. Here bestowing the new life in Baptism; there strengthening by the gift of the Paraclete, the children of the Faith; now breaking the fetters of the sinner, and whispering sweet words of comfort—" Thy sins are forgiven, go in peace." Again he sees Him soothing the affrighted soul at the approach of the dread agony, " Fear not, it is I," who conquered death, and who will raise you up again when you have passed from this weary world; then communicating to His priests the same commission once given to the Apostles—" Whose sins you shall forgive, they shall be forgiven." " Do this in commemoration of me." " As the Father hath sent me, I send you;" and again in the Holy Sacrament of Matrimony blessing that happy union, which before God and His angels symbolizes the Union of Christ with His mystic spouse the Church. Mary the Mother of God at once rises to her honored position, Queen of Heaven, Faithful Guardian of the Incarnation, and because of her free-will she became " the hand-maid of the Lord," and enabled Him to show visibly His great love for man, made the dispensatrix of His special grace and favors. And scarcely has he beheld this bright vision dawning upon him than, like the Shepherds on Christmas night, he beholds the blessed angels and saints of God, fulfilling their happy functions of messengers of peace, rejoicing at the conversion of one sinner, smiling upon him and inviting him, at all sacrifices to enter into the one fold.

And then there is another vision, full of comfort to such a one as this. The ties that bind him to father and mother, brothers, and sisters, and dear friends who may have passed away, are not severed. They, he believes, loved God in their own way, and though they were not externally united to the fold, they really desired to do in all things the blessed will of God, and so, before they were called to judgment, they may have received the great grace of true Faith and thus are saved "yet so as by fire;" and he learns that he may pray for them, that the time of their suffering may be shortened, and may hope that everything he does to please God, and offers for them, may soothe their sorrows, and hasten the moment of their deliverance. In a word, the simple understanding of the nature of Catholic worship, is in itself sufficient to give the sincere and humble inquirer after truth, a glimpse of the supernatural life, which every Catholic may enjoy in this world.

True, there are many Catholics who do not realize these privileges, and there are, unfortunately for themselves, some, who having been brought from darkness into light, have sinned against the light, and fallen back into darkness again. It is scarcely possible that they, who trifle thus with Faith, the most precious of God's gifts, will escape the everlasting wrath, should the dread summons to judgment find them "sitting in darkness and in the shadow of death."

I hope, in the next chapter, to give a brief sketch of that misrepresentation and caricature of Catholic Christianity, which is assailed by those, who, while they imagine they are attacking the Catholic Church, show, by their objections, that they never had any perception of its real character. There are some also who having once enjoyed the happy vision, allowed it to fade away from their view, and perish by the wilful neglect of their spiritual duties. These are most to be pitied, for they sin against the light, and allow themselves voluntarily to be blindfolded by the spirit of the world. They abuse the Church with a fierceness that extinguishes remorse, and suffer their desolate and despairing souls to be trampled upon by the legion of low and earthly desires, and the hordes of wild speculations, that invariably overwhelm and hopelessly extinguish the expiring embers of a lost Faith.

CHAPTER VIII.

Catholic Christianity Misunderstood by Freethinkers.

IN the preceding chapter, I have endeavored to fix the attention of my readers on the supernatural character of Catholic Christianity; because it is this which eminently distinguishes it from all other forms of Christianity; and because it is the very quality which most exposes it to the assaults of Rationalism. Amongst the Christian sects outside the Catholic Church, there is practically nothing of the supernatural.

In some sects there is indeed a claim to supernatural guidance of a sensible kind. The Divine Spirit, they say, bears testimony to Himself in the work of conversion, and manifests to the converted soul the sweetness of interior peace. This is however merely subjective, confined to individual experience; and from the very nature of the case, open to delusion.

Worldly men regard this religious excitement as a sort of madness, that may produce the most deplorable effects on the unfortunate being who is possessed by this spirit of delusion, and highly dangerous to the nervous susceptibilities of others who witness the effects of this passing frenzy.

It is not of the supernatural in this sense, I speak, but of that which is objective, or resulting from positive dogma. The whole of the doctrines of the Catholic Church are most intimately connected with the unseen world. An earnest Catholic lives in a very atmosphere of Faith. God and His providence is ever near him. He feels that "in God, he moves, and has his being." He almost hears the rustle of Angelic wings. He knows that at solemn times his Divine Saviour stoops to him. He communes with the sainted dead, and the suffering Church of the faithful departed. This is what the Rationalist cannot in the least understand, and most non-Catholics are in the same position. It is foolishness to them, and downright superstition. There was a time however when the entire Christian world felt the Spirit of God pervading not only the whole mystic body of Christ, but diffusing itself through every member of the vast fold; not alone in their midst when gathered together for prayer, but ever, at all times, and in all places. Then men walked in God's presence, feared to offend Him, and aspired to commune with Him lovingly. We are, however, gravely warned that these were "the dark ages," and reminded constantly, by the leaders of Free-thought, that we now live in the light of the nineteenth century, when all these old-fashioned notions have passed away forever. These convictions live with undying life, however, in God's Church still, and they are the natural outcome of her Faith.

This is the chief reason why Rationalists assail the Church. As a rule, educated men of this class have nothing to say about "Antichrist," and "the scarlet woman," and "Idolatry," and "Blasphemy," and "the abominations"—subjects still most dear to ignorant Christian fanaticism. They are kind and respectful to the old Church: they pity her because she will, they say, keep to her old-fashioned ways; and they would be delighted beyond measure if she would only take up some at least of their notions of progress. " Poor old thing !" they seem to say, " she is so good, and so respectable, so hallowed by the traditions of nineteen hundred years, so free from the silly airs and pretensions of these vulgar Christian upstarts of yesterday, so sound in her moral principles of right and wrong, so conservative, so unchangeable! What a pity 'tis she is so obstinate in her views. She will cling to these antiquated notions of the Mosaic narrative, and pay no heed to the demonstrations of our scientific men, and close her eyes and ears to the marvels of discovery. And then, worse than all, she is so intolerant. She would, if she dared, persecute to the death all who presume to differ from her, and when she cannot crush her opponents in this way, she will try to satisfy her impotent rage by consigning them without exception to eternal flames. She does not seem to perceive the folly of imagining that men of learning are to be frightened, like children, with these insane threats of a future, of which we can absolutely know nothing. It makes one miserable to hear her talk so confidently of a Personal God, and Saints and Angels, and miracles and mysteries, as if we had not 'changed all that,' and demonstrated that whatever is beyond the reach of our telescopes, and microscopes, and spectroscopes, and the power of our combined scientific apparatus, cannot, by any stretch of the mind, have a real existence. No doubt she is very angry because our Railways and Telegraphs are disturbing her repose, and our grand discoveries in Electricity are putting to flight the hobgoblins, on which she feeds her crazy imagination. If she would only confine her attention to these trifles, about which this generation of progress is only amused, and gratify the morbid taste of her infatuated votaries with tales of Hell-fire and such like nonsense, one could bear with her insane fancies, and set them down to the natural dotage of an existence prolonged beyond all natural limits. But then she is mischievous, and uses all her influence, which is no doubt something superior to any power on earth [the immortality of the Church and her widespread influence are hard facts for the infidel], to check the onward march of mind, and the advance of true civilization. She will oppose our wise laws about education, and marriage, and those other national institutions, with which she has nothing to do, and meddle with our arrangements about liberty, and equality, and the rights of men, and the rights of women, and what not, that one loses all patience, and would wish her sunk forever in the depths of the sea."

This is I think a fair statement of the views of Free-thought about " the everlasting Church ;" and I mean to point out how utterly mistaken they are, and how unreasonable is the hatred to which they almost insensibly give rise, in the minds of the impatient and noisy unbelieving crowd that worship the idol of the hour, and would, if they had their way, plant again the goddess of reason on the Altar of the one true God.

What I meant to show in the last few pages, is that the dislike, and hatred, and contempt for the Church, that sooner or later develops itself in the minds of Free-thinkers, is altogether different from the no-popery fury, which has assailed the Church for the last three-hundred years. The Church is an object of dislike to the leaders of Free-thought, not because of the calumnies of times past, now constantly refuted by the laborious research of able and unprejudiced scholars; not because there were said to have been bad popes; nor because the theology of the Church, misrepresented by her enemies, was offensive on grace, and free-will, and justification; not even on account of the grosser charges of idolatry and trafficking in holy things, which were so freely urged against her by the early reformers; but simply and solely because she at the present day is believed, by her stanch and rigid conservatism, to stand in the way of the realization of those Utopian schemes of communism and socialism, which are the unhallowed fascination of this unbelieving and frivolous age.

It will be interesting then to consider the grounds of this fierce hatred. This narrows the question considerably. We have not to enter upon the ocean of ecclesiastical history, and overhaul every cargo of offensive rubbish fished from the surface of political events, and floated by the perverse ingenuity of party zeal. We may leave the past to take care of itself, and devote all our attention to the facts and principles of the present hour.

Is it a fact then, in the first place, that the Catholic Church stands in the way of scientific research? I say decidedly—no. From my own limited reading, and from my own experience of the development of scientific education in our colleges and schools, I can bear unfaltering testimony to the very contrary. It has been my good fortune to have met, amongst the Catholic clergy in England, Ireland, and on the continent of Europe, some of these giants in the vanguard of scientific progress, men whose brilliant discoveries are known to every learned institute in the whole world.

There are few students who have not heard of the renowned astronomer Father Secchi, or the distinguished microscopist, the Abbé Count Castracani. I have conversed with them both, and learned from them something of the profound interest with which their discoveries were received by their scientific brethren in the priesthood. I often look back with unfading pleasure to the scene of Doctor Callan's scientific triumphs, in the college of Maynooth, when eminent men in physical science gathered eagerly to witness the progress of his discoveries and inventions in Galvanism, and Magnetism. It was a delight ever to be treasured in memory, a visit to the magnetic observatory of the Jesuit college of Stoneyhurst. The Astronomer Royal in England holds Father Perry, and Father Sidgreaves, amongst the most eminent of his observers. So great was the success of the Jesuit college in the Rue des Postes in Paris in competing with the Polytechnique, for the best prizes in science and the higher mathematics, that a commission of learned scholars was appointed by the late Emperor, to examine into the course of the studies in this college, and to import the fruit of their investigation into the favorite scientific college of France. When I was in Paris in 1875, I met a young French priest of the order of Oblates, who was editing a polyglot dictionary of the different dialects of the Esquimaux, and who, though not over thirty years of age, was appointed to lecture at the different scientific assemblies gathered from all parts in that year, in the capital of France.

Whoever has visited any of the great Catholic Colleges in Great Britain, or on the Continent, will be amazed at the splendid museums, and costly scientific apparatus to be found in every one of them. If I had a list by me of eminent mathematicians, and workers in Natural Philosophy, I could give an array of names with the prefix of Abbé, or some such word indicative of the priesthood, that would prove beyond doubt that the Catholic

Church has now, as ever, her representatives in fair proportion to other creeds, and in high position also.

Why should she not? seeing that her clergy, Regular and Secular, are eminently qualified by their ordinary studies to enter on this particular course if they are so inclined; and that those who are not actively engaged in mission work, have more time and better opportunities, in the libraries and laboratories of the numerous colleges, than the generality of other students; seeing also that the shortest way to distinction, and to the esteem and approval of the great dignitaries of the Catholic Church, is success in those branches that are now so popular.

Then it must be remembered that "the science of sciences"—Theology, necessarily includes all the facts, and theories, and objections, gleaned in the fields of scientific research. He can scarcely be considered a profound theologian who is not *au courant* with the latest discoveries in Geology, Chemistry, Medicine, Archæology, and the laws that govern the physical world.

People are sometimes amazed by the accurate knowledge displayed by barristers, when the case in which they are engaged is connected with some other learned profession. But students know well, that it does not require much time or labor, for a clever man to read up all that is necessary for the thorough understanding of any particular branch of science. The real wonder is to find so many theologians, who seem to have accumulated, in the course of forty or fifty years' study, everything that is essential to the full understanding of all the sciences; and who are able to lecture, at an hour's notice, *de omni re scibili;* and run the gauntlet of a public thesis which will include the objections that can be raised from the discoveries of every branch of science against revealed religion.

There is not one of the great Catholic colleges in Europe, and America, which will not furnish its quota of these learned men. Why—I say again, should it not be so? Will it be said that the Church is afraid of the light? she, the city on the mountain, that for nearly nineteen hundred years has been the object of assault of all the ungodly powers of earth and Hell! Ah!—no, she is too experienced in conflicts of every kind, to hide her head at the approach of any enemy, however inflated he may be with that knowledge "that puffeth up," she heeds not the angry frown, and the scorn, and contempt of the unbelieving Philosophers of this proud age. Greater men than any this nineteenth century can boast of,—men who, in the schools of Athens, and Rome, and Alexandria, had been trained to think and reason profoundly, bowed down before her learned priests, and acknowledged themselves overcome.

Our scientists are so full of theorizing, and making much of every chance discovery that falls in their way, that they have not time for the tedious process of thinking out a subject. They are so captivated with every fresh invention, that they forget the theories and conclusions announced so dogmatically a month or two before. If in their hurried course, they should chance to stumble on a fact not hitherto known, they are so jubilant and triumphant, that they do not perceive that, while they are making merry at the expense of Religion, the scientific sons of the Church have already seized upon the fact, and turned it to the advantage of Catholic Christianity. They do not know when they are beaten; and it is only when their over-excited fancies have plunged them into some absurd conclusion, that they become aware, by the laughter and derision caused by their ridiculous position, that they have run counter to common-sense, and perpetrated the stupid blunder of arguing against what every one but themselves knows to be quite certain.

There is such a thing as too much light. The mind under such circumstances becomes dazed. Just as the physical organ suffers, and temporary blindness ensues, when the chamber of the eye is over-filled with the luminous medium, so the mind itself seems to break down, when no restraint is offered to the flood of fancies let in upon it by a disordered imagination.

There is no place for wild theories in the mind of a sound Catholic philosopher. If there seems to be a jarring or conflict between some unexpected discovery in nature and Divine Revelation, he feels at once the conviction that the contradiction is not real. He knows beyond doubt that what Divine truth declares, either by direct Revelation, or in the book of Nature, cannot be in conflict. And therefore he calmly considers how the seeming discrepancy can be reconciled.

It most frequently happens, as I have already said, that while the unbeliever is rashly exulting in a supposed victory over revealed truth, the Catholic finds in this object of misplaced joy, a confirmation of his faith. Whoever will read attentively " The Lectures on Science and Revealed Religion" by Cardinal Wiseman, will discover many remarkable instances of this fact.

There is one that just now strikes me, and as it seems to put the point very clearly, I mention it. I have, in the early chapters of this book, quoted Mallock. In Chapter XII. of his work—" Is life worth living ?"—he puts the objection from historical science against the Bible very strongly—that the histories of other religions are strangely analogous to the history of Christianity. It is an old objection, as indeed are all the objections now so confidently urged by Free-thinkers, all, every one without exception, "as old as the hills." The force of the objection is to show that all religions had a common origin; and that Christianity, with all its mysteries and supernatural dogmas, can be clearly traced in the sacred books of Religions, that existed in the world long before the time of Christ. It is a favorite objection with the "poor imitations of polished ungodliness." It was put to me once, in a railway carriage in the colony, not indeed so strongly as Mallock puts it; for my young antagonist had not seen the book. I first showed him the objection in all its force. "Two centuries before Christ, Buddha is said to have been born without a human father. Angels sang in heaven to announce his advent; an aged hermit blessed him in his mother's arms; a monarch was advised, though he refused, to destroy the child, who, it was predicted, should be a universal ruler. It is told how he was once lost, and was found again in a temple; and how his young wisdom astonished all the doctors," and so on through the remarkable events in the early life of our Divine Lord. "You see," it is argued, "the Buddhist religion and the Christian had a common origin, neither can be from heaven." How all this apparently powerful and overwhelming argument melts into thin air, as we read, in the Lectures of the Cardinal (vol. ii. 26), the clear proofs established by Bentley, that this legend in the life of Buddha was artfully framed by the Brahmins in the seventh century, and inserted fraudulently in their sacred books. What seemed to be a serious difficulty only shows, that even the Brahmins regarded the Christian religion as something far superior to their own, when they stooped to this low trick to give their own legends greater plausibility.

So far then is the Catholic Church from regarding true science as an enemy, that, on the contrary, she cultivates science, and fosters, and cherishes it, as a splendid auxiliary.

Next it is urged that she is obstinate and intolerant. Well, a very short answer meets this difficulty. Truth is necessarily intolerant of error. It could not be Truth at all if it did not maintain itself against every approach of error. They are as different from each other as light is from darkness. If it be true that God the Son, the second Person of the Blessed Trinity, became man, and that our Divine Saviour is God, it is necessarily false, abominably and blasphemously false, that He was only a man. If He saved us from hell, and the power of the devil by His Atonement, then this Atonement cannot be the dreadful thing it is said to be by the advanced Rationalist. If it be an invention of Almighty Love to unite us to our Divine Saviour in the Blessed Eucharist and the Holy Communion, it must be a hideous and revolting insult to this Divine Saviour, to treat this most Holy Sacrament with irreverence. If it be true that the sacraments have been instituted by Christ, to apply to our souls the fruits of His abundant redemption, they who scoff at these sacraments, are evidently exposing themselves to the wrath of God; for " God is not mocked " with impunity. If there is a personal God, then Atheism is inconceivable madness. If man has an immortal soul, it is worse than absurd to say that he is only organized matter. If there be another life, " the bag of bones" theory, and the life of a brute and the death of a brute is the extreme of folly. If there be a Hell, how awful is the daring of those who, on its very brink, defy their Maker to punish them eternally! Such extremes can never meet; therefore truth must reprobate, and hate and abominate error as the greatest of evils.

But the Free-thinkers go on to say—yes, but the old Catholic Church hates not only error, but those who profess error, and would persecute those who differ from her, if she dared, and actually consigns them all to eternal flames. I say distinctly—no. The Church is as faithful to her principles of loving mercy and pity for the unfortunate, who are in danger of being lost, as she is faithful to her trust in preserving the dogmas once committed to her keeping by her Divine Founder. It is not the Catholic Church, as a society of men framing laws according to the best of their judgment, it is the Catholic Church inspired and directed by the Spirit of God, that declares it to be a solemn and eternal truth, that "without Faith it is impossible to please God," and that "he who believeth not, shall be condemned." So God Himself has willed it. This is His law, and not the law of men. It is her Divine Founder who has said, "The wicked shall go into everlasting fire."

The Catholic Church firmly believing that this is the terrible sanction of the Divine law, constantly proclaims it. If she did not proclaim it, she would be infinitely more guilty than the wretch, who, seeing a fellow-creature blindly advancing with unguarded steps to the edge of a precipice, and having it in his power to warn and save him, let him go on to destruction. Surely such a man would be a murderer, as certainly as if he deprived his victim of life by an act of positive violence. I say that the Catholic Church would be infinitely more guilty than this murderer, if she did not, "in season and out of season," repeat her warnings, because the fate of those who die impenitent is fixed for all eternity. The unfortunate being who falls over a precipice may have a momentary consciousness of his fate, and so yield to the instinctive cry of suffering humanity, and say, if not with the lips, in his heart at least, " God have mercy on me, and forgive me!" Who will judge and determine, that God, Who has implanted that instinct in every human being civilized or savage, will not hearken to it? Certainly it is not the teaching of Catholic Christianity that one who has cried aloud for mercy, though it be only in his utmost need, shall not receive mercy. She does not judge at all of individuals; but she declares, with all the force of her authority, that the unbeliever who defies God to the last, and perishes with the proud cry of the demon on his lips—" I will not serve"—shall share the fate of demons for ever and ever.

If the Free-thinker will press his objection, and take up the old gossip about the Inquisition, and " the fires of Smithfield" and all that, I could only smile at this evidence of ill-humor, and when he had time to recover his temper, would remind him, that in the ages of Faith, when men valued their eternal salvation above all earthly blessings, they were wont to be indignant and unsparing against those who endeavored to stir up religious quarrels, and dissensions, and to form sects; because they believed with the Apostle, that they who do such things would neither themselves "obtain the kingdom of God" (Gal. v. 21), nor suffer those who listened to their corrupt teaching, to secure this blessing.

I would tell him that times change, and the fashions and ways of people with them; that laws are not now so Draconian in their spirit as even half a century ago, when the theft of sixpence worth was punished with death; that we cannot judge of the spirit of the present times by what we read of the past, nor the fierce intolerance of other times by the more gentle and large-hearted feelings of to-day. I would try to make him understand that there was a great deal to be said about the cruel persecutions of those very people who charge the Catholic Church with intolerance; that worldly policy, and the plans of Governments had much to do with the Inquisition; and that, as to the massacre of St. Bartholomew and the other terrible things, which have been so often cooked and rehashed that they remind one of the twice-boiled cabbage or "*thanatos*" of the Greek writer—they are things of the past, about which men might dispute their whole life long, without coming to a satisfactory conclusion. They are enough to sicken to death any one with the least pretensions to scholarship, who has attempted to wade through the broad shallow waters of conflicting testimony, and bitter argument, that surrounds questions of this sort. Let us keep to the present. Free-thinkers may feel quite assured that the spirit of the Catholic Church towards those who blaspheme the Saviour, and make a mockery of His sufferings, is all expressed in that Divine prayer— "Father forgive them, for they know not what they do!"

"But why will the Catholic clergy talk so constantly about the supernatural and mysteries? What can they know about such things? And why make so much of miracles and apparitions, in which no sensible man can believe? and why encourage pilgrimages, that foster these delusions? Why will they not confine themselves to that sum and substance of all practical religion—contained in the words of the Apostle—'Honor all men; love the brotherhood; fear God: honor the king'? (1

Pet. II. 17.) Why endeavor to bring forward, into the light of this nineteenth century, such old wives' stories of the dark ages about the Devil and Spiritism. All this is enough," they excitedly remark, "to bring her teaching into contempt, and to make her hateful to men of intelligence and education."

I have already explained the nature of mysteries; they are the natural outcome of a Religion which professes to give us the message of the Infinite about His own nature, and His relations to His creatures. If there were not mysteries in such a Religion, it would be on the face of it a clear proof that this Religion was earth-born, and the invention of men. I have also explained that miracles, or extraordinary interventions of Almighty power, preventing in certain cases the ordinary effects of natural laws, is the obvious and necessary consequence of a firm belief in the Providence of a supreme being, who by His goodness is bound to care for the creatures He has called into existence.

The Catholic Church believes in a good God, who has taught us to call Him "Father;" and in whose immensity "we live, move, and have our being." Catholics believe in a God who has made us free, and who would not, much as He desires the salvation of all, interfere in any way with the exercise of their liberty. Therefore it is that the Church is never weary in impressing on the minds of her children that this God, as His Son our Saviour taught us in express words, knows us by name, has counted the very hairs of our head, and loves each of us infinitely more than the wild flowers of the field, which He has clothed with so much beauty. We Catholics are taught to believe that whatsoever we ask in the name of Jesus Christ, it will be given us; and that if we have Faith and unbounded confidence in Him, the powers of nature shall not stand in the way of the accomplishment of our wishes. Will not a God, who has made us these gracious promises, fulfil them? It is no trouble to Him. He knows all things without an effort. He is present everywhere, all created things, save man, obey His will. We could not believe in God, if we did not also believe in His Providence, and in the working of that Providence in the supernatural way of miracles; and there can be no truth of this belief that can more practically concern us, or which we should keep more constantly before our eyes.

Pilgrimages, and processions to Holy shrines, are only the outward expression of our Faith, a most admirable means of keeping it alive within us by mutual edification, and of proclaiming this Faith to others, who do not believe this consoling doctrine of an ever watchful and loving Providence, that they, seeing these things and the wonders that are wrought, may glorify God who is so amiable and condescending to those who trust in His loving care, and in the day of trouble, call upon Him. I have spoken with those who have been present at wonderful cures, instantaneously wrought in favor of the sick and infirm. They assured me that, never before did they so realize to themselves what this Faith in the unseen Guardian and Sustainer of their lives actually meant, as when the touch of His healing power was in a moment manifested to a great multitude, and they heard them, as in the days when our Saviour wrought His miracles, cry out, as if with one voice, "Lo! God again hath visited His people."

Farther on in this book, when I treat of the phases of modern unbelief, I shall have something to say of this accursed Spiritism, which is following the track of avowed and open infidelity, and feeding the delusions of those who, rejecting Revelation, are endeavoring, by unholy rites, to peep into the secrets of the future life.

There is another objection to the action of the Church on society, which more fittingly comes in here: "Why," say her enemies, " does the Church interfere in the affairs of this world? Can she not confine herself to her spiritual functions? And, since, she will obstinately believe in the supernatural, why not satisfy her longing for preaching and teaching, by subjects connected with this higher sphere? What has she to do with our civil laws, and social relations, and material progress, and above all why will she attempt to circumscribe our national liberties?"

Let me first of all say that the Catholic Church has ever been the enthusiastic defender of the true liberties of oppressed nationalities: in the next chapter, I mean to show why the Catholic Church, in the discharge of her important mission, " to preach the gospel to every creature," is bound to watch and guard, as the apple of her eye, the educational interests, and the domestic and family relations of all classes of her children. It is only misconceptions of the great principle of " Divine right," that lie at the bottom of the strong prejudices which prevail amongst Free-thinkers against what they love to call " the despotism" of the Church. Because the Pope is a sovereign ruler, it is inferred, that all the sympathies of Catholics must be in favor of Monarchy. The Sovereign rules, according to Catholic theology, by right Divine, therefore, it is argued, any departure from this form of Government must be regarded as direct opposition to the Divine will.

Never was there a greater mistake. The governing power, let it be monarchical or republican, let the ruler be Emperor, Empress, King, Queen or President, is, on Catholic principles, the visible representative of God, for the maintenance of that order which is essential to the existence of Society. God has made man to live in community: language alone, which distinguishes man from all other creatures in this world, proves this. But men cannot live together in any form of community without a head or ruler. In its most elementary state, or the family, human beings, to live together in peace and unity, must have a head, the father of the family. The tribe must have its chief; the nation must have its ruler. These are absolute truisms. No one with a grain of common-sense will argue, that every member of a community can do as he or she pleases: there must be mutual concessions of individual right, else the family even will be like a bear-garden. In the maintenance of order in the family, the father rules without question or doubt. But when the family swells into a tribe, and the tribe into a people or a nation, the appointment of a ruler, and the form of Government, are left to the choice of those who require to be governed. The Catholic Church has never interfered with this choice, unless when invited to do so by the people themselves, and in the interests of order. When all Christendom looked up to the successor of St. Peter, as the vicar of Christ, the real master and ruler of the Christian Commonwealth, the Holy Father was by the free consent of nations, the supreme arbiter of disputes, and his decision was received as the law of God. But in whatever way the ruler was elected, whether he was an hereditary Sovereign, or one chosen by the votes of the majority, once in the position of authority, he ruled as the representative of God ; and his authority was binding on the consciences of his Christian subjects. They obeyed him, not because he was popular, not because of his good and amiable qualities, not through fear, not for wrath, "but for conscience' sake."

This is what is meant by "Divine right" in the teaching of the Catholic Church. The ruler, call him by whatever name you will, should " carry the sword," and indicate order, according to the laws of his people; not by virtue of any contract, not because the subjects gave up the right over their own lives, for their lives do not belong to them, they belong to their Creator ; but because the ruler held authority and right from God.

An effort is sometimes made to prove, that the present persecution of the Church in France, is owing to the fact that the pastors of the Church in that country are opposed to the Republican form of Government. There may be strong feeling on this point; but the principle I have stated is as firm as the rock on which Christ founded His Church. The government *de facto*, the choice of the nation rules by Divine right; and he who rebelliously resists this authority, "purchases to himself damnation." If there has been no free choice, if a nation is robbed of its inherent rights, and compelled by brute force to submit to a ruler, there is question then only of patient submission, until there is a reasonable prospect of rectifying the cruel wrong. Catholic theologians have laid down principles on this point, which should find favor with every one who values true liberty.

There is nothing, in the history of the times in which we live, to show, that the Catholic Church favors one particular form of government more than another. One thing is quite certain that Catholics who enjoy the freedom of the children of God, who are not harassed and disturbed on account of their religious principles, feel nowhere more at home than under a republican form of government. Never in the history of the Church, have her institutions expanded so amazingly, and so rapidly, as in the United States of America. "If," as Father Müller puts it, "a great pope could say in truth that he was nowhere more pope than in America," every Catholic can and does also say with certainty " Nowhere can I be a better Catholic than in the United States."

The questions of Education and Marriage require a chapter to themselves. I think it will not be difficult to show, that Catholic Christianity, in contending for the rights of a Christian education, and the indissolubility of the marriage-tie, is only fulfilling a most important duty, and in no way hindering the real progress and happiness of the human race.

CHAPTER IX.

Catholic Christianity in Relation to Education and Marriage.

THE Catholic Church has always maintained, that it is an essential part of her mission from above, to watch over the education of her children. This duty is necessarily implied in the words—"Teach all nations." Teaching does not mean simply to instruct in science, and literature, and languages, and all that knowledge which is useful in the affairs of this world; its most important aim should be to fit man for the great end of his being, that life which is eternal. Education properly understood should direct itself mainly to the formation of character on sound moral principles; so that children may, from the first use of reason, be trained to fear God, and love Him, to honor and obey their parents, to curb their young passions, and hate sin, and thus grow up to be good and useful members of the community, and to be made fit for the kingdom of Heaven.

There can be no reasonable prospect of educating in this sense, unless Religion is cultivated in the young mind, as well as other plants of knowledge; and therefore the Church has always insisted, that in her schools, as well as in the family, the young shall be taught to know God, and be faithful to His law.

This principle finds no favor with those who regard material progress as the chief end of human life. The future is, according to the views of Free-thought, quite uncertain. It is one of those things about which, Rationalists and Agnostics say, we can know nothing positive, and therefore, they argue, man's whole attention should be devoted to what is real and tangible. As the Church declares, in the very words of our Divine Lord, that salvation is "the one thing necessary," and makes this grand principle the basis of all her teaching as regards the welfare of her children, the unbelieving world fiercely maintains that the main point of human life should be to make the best of our short time on earth, in securing for ourselves whatever we can of the good things of this world. "The present only is ours, let us enjoy it wisely while we may; the future must take care of itself."

Of course, where there is so direct a conflict about the main object of life, the deductions from these opposing principles must manifest themselves clearly and distinctly; and so the Church and the world are at open war on this question of Education. Hence the two systems, Education grounded on religion, or denominational, and education, or rather Instruction, from which all religious teaching is excluded, commonly called secular and undenominational.

I would briefly consider the matter as regards social progress. Has Free-thought good and sound reasons for denouncing the Catholic Church as the foe of material progress, and the happiness of peoples, because she requires that Religion shall necessarily be associated with other instruction in the elementary schools? I take it for granted, that the most advanced leaders of unbelief will not think of carrying the question into the bosom of the family. They will most assuredly not dream of interfering with good fathers and mothers, who do their best to infuse into the minds of their little ones that holy fear of God, "which is the beginning of wisdom," and who endeavor to train them "to avoid evil and do good."

Indeed the advocates of secular education, as a rule, rather insist on the necessity of this domestic religious teaching, when they would show that their system does not necessarily exclude religion altogether from the minds of youth. The care of parents, supplemented by Sunday-schools, will, they would have us believe, supply the want of religious training in the school-room. I may note here that this is in reality a complete fallacy, and well known as such by all who have practical experience in the bringing up of children. Parents are bound by the Catholic Church to teach their children the catechism, and their prayers, and religious duties, even when these children receive daily instruction in good Catholic schools; for if the impressions produced in school are not fixed in the mind, and confirmed by home-training, they will scarcely take firm hold of the youthful conscience. But there will be little or nothing to establish there, if a considerable time is not allotted in the school to daily religious instruction. Amongst the poor, who have to work hard from morning till night, even the best disposed parents can do little more than hear their children say their morning and evening prayers, and repeat the commandments, and some of the fundamental truths of religion. Many are not competent to explain the catechism. When we see how this duty is neglected by the rich who have education and plenty of time to inculcate religion, it will be understood at once that religious instruction confined to the family, or to the hour or half-hour in the Sunday-school, means, no religious instruction at all. At best, the few moments devoted to this work at home and the hour or half-hour once a week in the Sunday-school, serve only to keep alive the tender flower, planted and watered with assiduous care by pious hands in the hearts of the young.

But to return to the argument which would exclude Religion from the schools, I will first of all, as I have done all through in treating the objections of unbelief, put the points opposed to us as plainly and as forcibly as I can.

I think the opponents of religious education must reason somewhat after this fashion. "Ignorance, in any large section of the population of a state, is a positive evil of the most formidable character. If men cannot read and write and know how to use their brains, they are mere drones in the busy hive, they can feel no interest in the common weal. They must, from the very nature of the case, be intensely selfish; they must be forever wrapped up in their own unprofitable thoughts. They can do very little to benefit themselves, and they cannot help others. They are constantly exposed to the danger of being made instruments of social mischief, and the dupes and tools of designing persons, and consequently they become a source of trouble and expense to the society that harbors them. They can know nothing of sound sanitary laws and wise regulations, to promote the health and comfort of the community; and so they may, at any moment, become plague-spots, and centres of disease, and rot in filth and squalid poverty, a misery to themselves, and a fruitful source of danger to their fellows. There must therefore be no class in the State that shall not be educated. If any, through laziness or indifference, or blindness to the advantages of knowing how to read and write and cipher, will hang back, and keep their children from the public schools, they must be compelled to send them. Now, Religion stands in the way of this public benefit. If a school is denominational, or endeavors to propagate the religious views of any sect, forthwith there is an outcry against State education. Parents will justly complain that they are compelled, by fine and imprisonment, to send their children to schools, where there is interference with the rights of conscience. Hence we are bound in the interests of the common good, to keep clear of Religion altogether. If children are taught in our public schools only to read and write and some of the branches of ordinary knowledge, there can be no well-grounded complaints, if the Government insists that all must be compelled to partake of this perfectly harmless benefit. This is the only way in which the difficulty of diffusing elementary education through the masses, can be overcome. Parents if they set such value on Religion, must teach it at home. Children can learn quite enough of it in the Sunday classes of the particular denomination to which they belong. But we cannot, and we will not be thwarted in our plans for the general benefit, by these religious differences and unseemly squabbles."

This is about what it comes to in the views of those who contend for purely secular and compulsory education. And, because the Catholic Church denounces this system as unchristian and "Godless," it is considered as proved beyond the possibility of contradiction, that she stands in the way of real progress.

I suppose that those who reason in this way would go farther, and urge that some education is better than none at all, and since the State has a right, in self-defence, to protect itself against the evils of ignorance, it is the duty of "the powers that be" to sweep away all the barriers that stupidity, or fanaticism, or superstition, can raise in the way of wholesome legislation.

To all this reasoning, which seems very specious and satisfactory, I would reply, Let us examine what are the actual effects of this "godless" system. This is the most satisfactory of all tests. Compulsory education, in which religious instruction has no part, has been tried for a considerable time in many countries; has it been productive of the good expected from it? Suppose we examine the working of the system, and its results, on the Continent of Europe, and in the "common-schools" of America, where it has been in operation for about half a century, we will be enabled, in the simplest and easiest and most sure way, to form a judgment on the question.

I contend that these results present abundant reasons for admiring the wisdom of the Church, and condemning the short-sighted policy which would have us regard secular compulsory education as a panacea for all the evils of society. This system, judged in its effects for the last forty or fifty years, has proved worse than a failure—an aggravation, rather than a remedy, for the evils complained of.

In Prussia, where the system was first enforced, and rigidly carried out, in accordance with the military spirit that directs all the institutions of that country, the secular plan has been long ago abandoned. At first, the statesmen, who directed this important work, believed that secular education was the only plan by which they could overcome the difficulties caused by religious differences, and the public schools were in the beginning, purely undenominational. But it was soon found, although the Religious differences are less in Prussia than in most other countries, from the fact that only the two great principles of authority and free inquiry are recognized, no regard being paid to the subdivisions of peculiar sects— it would not work. There for a time, the teachers were chosen in equal proportions from the two Religions, Catholic and Protestant—and the schools were called " simultaneous." This it was hoped would quiet jealousies. It did so in fact, but it was found, when the teachers were prevented from giving any religious instruction, that a fatal indifference to all religion was the consequence. Freethinkers would no doubt hail this result as a sign of hopeful progress, indicating the advent of a sort of religious unity. But the Prussian Government did not think so. The men at the head of the educational department clearly saw the deplorable effects of forgetfulness of God, and the claims of conscience. This state of mind soon manifested itself, by the absence of all respect for authority, and the wide spread of revolutionary theories, and secret societies, and ever-growing scandalous immorality.

As early as 1822, the minister, Von Allenstein, in the Cabinet rescript for that year, April 27th, calling attention to this state of things, gave expression to his views in favor of a return to denominational education. " Experience has shown," he says, " that in these secular schools, the chief matter of education is not sufficiently cared for; and it lies in the nature of the case that it cannot be. The intention of these schools, to wit, the promotion of tolerant feelings between the members of the two communions, is seldom or never attained." Speaking at a later period, he says—" The time which has elapsed since 1848, appears to have wrought a general conviction among all practical men, that the denominational school is the only school that is at present possible in Germany." The Government in consequence changed its system, and established schools where Catholics and Protestants might be taught under the direction of their own pastors. The elementary schools in Prussia have been, for nearly thirty years, purely denominational. If the school is for Catholics, the teachers are Catholic, and the books Catholic: if the school is Protestant, the books and teachers are Protestant.

I believe that the harmony, and good feeling shown by Catholics and Protestants, during the late war with France, the healthy spirit of patriotism, and the earnestness of purpose that animated all ranks of the Prussian army, can be easily traced to the admirable system of education adopted by the government, and the principles of social order, respect for authority, and trust in God's providence and blessing, produced by sound religious training.

Any one can mark the fatal consequences of banishing Religion from the schools in France, in the misfortunes that have beset this misguided country. When "the citizen king" drove out the pastors and Religious from the schools, it was not long before he reaped the fruits of this destructive policy. "In the broad glare of the Revolutionary history of 1848," says J. C. Colquhoun, "in that chaos of confusion, delirium, and dreams, when socialists raved, and the infidel mob plundered, the leaders were the schoolmasters, and their scholars were the masses." To what other cause can be attributed the miseries of the days of the Commune?

When I read the admirable work of Maxime du Camp—"*Les Convulsions de Paris,*" I could easily see, that it was in the neutral schools that were trained those demons in human flesh, who excited the horror and detestation of the entire civilized world. The wretches, from whose minds the State had trampled out the notion of God, and right and wrong, and anything like morality, became, in the brief period of their sovereign power, more thoroughly brutish, than the most ferocious savages, that have ever contended with civilized nations.

In reading the account of the reign of the Commune, one cannot help thinking of "the dangerous times" predicted by the Apostle, as signs of the "last days" of the world,—"men shall be lovers of themselves, covetous, haughty, proud, blasphemous, disobedient to parents, ungrateful, wicked, without affection, without peace, slanderers, incontinent, unmerciful, without kindness, traitors, stubborn, puffed up, and lovers of pleasures more than of God" (2 Tim. iii. 2, 3). Every downward step, in the ladder of impiety and unmanly wickedness traced by the Apostle, has been formed in these neutral schools, where a government, that once was Christian, proclaims —"There is neutrality as to the existence of God," and where the State forbids "even the mention of His Holy Name."

The "common schools" were to have done wonders for America. Ignorance, it was said, is the Mother of Vice, and when every citizen of the United States knew how to read and write and cipher, then there would commence a sort of Millennium of prosperity. They banished God and religion from the schools, that they might make education compulsory; and now, after about fifty years' experience of the working of these schools, what is the moral state of American society? I will give a few statements of what American writers say on the subject.

I may not mention in this book the thousandth part of what I have read on this painful matter; nor do more than hint at the fruits of Godless education, which are poisoning the noble energies of a people, who, half a century ago, promised to be the leaders in the march of real freedom, and the true progress of humanity. One is saddened and humiliated, as he turns over the pages that record a material prosperity such as the world has never seen, side by side with a decadence in morality that might rival the worst days of expiring paganism. It is estimated that about half the population of the United States, or thirty millions, have set up the idolatry of wealth—and the pleasures and comforts that wait on this god of the earth, in the place of our Divine Redeemer. Probably more than this number profess no distinct Christian belief, and have broken altogether with the venerable traditions of Christianity. How far this affects sound morality is apparent to any student of history, who pictures to himself the sad days before our Divine Lord appeared on earth, when, "men professing themselves to be wise, they became fools" (Rom. i. 22), "and God gave them up to the desires of their heart."

Abundant evidence is furnished by the organs of public opinion, that such are the sad consequences of endeavoring to push the Almighty out of His own world, and to keep away from Him the little ones, with whom He loves to dwell. "Society in New England," says the *Cincinnati Enquirer*, "if we are to credit the data of physicians, is but a mass of sores, the poison of which is so virulent that—[here some grievous crimes are detailed] —are scarcely considered crimes, so common, so everyday an occurrence have they become."

The *New York Express* makes the following notable statement—" From the absence of all religion in education what follows ? Another consequence not less fatal.

It has banished religion from the entire life of the great majority of the American people—there are about three fourths of the whole population who belong to no church, profess no religion, are in no way occupied with the destination of the soul, living as if it were certain that man had nothing to expect beyond time, more than the brute." "This absence of moral restraint," says the *New York Express* of the 6th February, 1869, "has produced the same effect on morality, as the same cause produced, one thousand eight hundred years ago, in the decrepit Rome of the Cæsars. In the older States of Maine, and Massachusetts, the number of children is incomparably less than it was; the proportion is so enormous, that we dare not publish it."

In the *New York Times* of the same date, we read— "We Americans by birth are decreasing rapidly. For the last ten years, the number of marriages has decreased in an appalling manner." "Statistics," says Father Michael Müller, a Redemptorist, "have been frequently published to show, that, in certain States of the Union, and in certain districts of those States, the births did not, and do not, equal the deaths; and were it not for the foreign population among us, many of those districts, and not a few of those States would be depopulated in a few years. Massachusetts and New York lead the van in this criminal record." The same author quotes the statements of several Doctors, eminent in their profession, giving their names and addresses in full, and the statements are most alarming to all who feel an interest in the growth and prosperity of the great Republic. An idea of the nature of what these men say may be formed from one passage—" In some of our large cities, a lady who is the mother of more than two children is looked upon as unfashionable;" or from the following extract of a letter addressed by Dr. M. B. Wright in 1860, to the Medical Society of Ohio, "The time is not far distant when children will be sacrificed among us with as little hesitation as among the Hindoos, unless we stop it here and now." That the horrible immorality, to which these statements point, is intimately connected with the absence of moral and religious training in the "common schools" is abundantly proved, by the revelations made from time to time in the public newspapers of the conduct of the pupils.

Some years ago, the *Boston Times* published full details of the development of shocking depravity in one of the public schools of that city. It is not so long ago, that the leading papers in New York were obliged to denounce revolting scandals connected with these establishments. I forbear to transcribe statements that lie before me, from the chief newspapers in Chicago, and which were corroborated by the *Daily Sentinel* of Indianapolis, the editor declaring that what was said of the "common schools" in the Chicago newspapers, was true of the schools in this city also. When I read in this book of Father Müller, that the moral character of the Public schools in many of the cities of America had sunk so low, that even the public courtesans disguised themselves in the uniform of these establishments, in order the more surely to ply their foul avocation, I felt that this was saying all that could be said with prudence, to show the fatal tendency of education, when completely severed from Religion and God, to ruin the morality of the rising generation.

Any one of common intelligence can see at once that, when it requires constant care and watchfulness to maintain purity and innocence amongst children who are carefully taught to fear God, and say their prayers, and go regularly to the Sacraments, it must be next to an impossibility to preserve morality, where every salutary restraint on the conscience is ignored or ridiculed. Happily there are natures that spurn the filth of gross criminality—the children of good mothers who shrink instinctively from anything that offends moral purity; but let even these be exposed, for hours every day to the heavy atmosphere of feverish sin, and sooner or later they will be affected by the contagion. I think I have said enough to show that schools without Religion, and where the name of God is never mentioned, or as they are very properly called " Godless schools," are not hot-beds of morality.

I have not entered into the theory of the question ; it is too large to be touched upon in a book like this, meant only for the passing reader. The proof of my position, that I have briefly set forward, is the plainest and most convincing—" By their fruits you shall know them."

The Church is not opposed to the spread of education, but this means sound education, in which the moral character is developed by Religious teaching. Any other education tends only "to bring out" the evil propensities of youth, and is, as regards the progress and well-being of society, worse than useless. Mere instruction in the rudiments of education will not check the growth and spread of the vices, which are the desolation of healthy society.

Mr. Clifford, several years Governor of Massachusetts, where the "common schools" have been more pushed forward than in any other State of the Union, very wisely remarks, " Without the sanctifying element of Religion, I am by no means certain that the mere cultivation of the intellect does not increase the exposure to crime, by enlarging the sphere of man's capacity to minister through its agency, to his sensual and corrupt desires. I can safely say, as a general inference drawn from my somewhat extensive observation of crime and criminals, that as flagrant cases, and as depraved characters have been exhibited among a class of persons who have enjoyed the ordinary elementary instruction, in our New England schools, and in some instances in the higher institutions of learning, as could be found by the most diligent investigation among the convicts of Norfolk Island, or at Botany Bay." "You may alter the nature of crime," says the Marquis of Salisbury, in the debate in the House of Lords, March, 1869, "you may change the paths by which the criminal will proceed, but crime is a consequence of moral depravity, and the mode in which it will be committed will be a matter of calculation with the criminal, no matter what amount of education may be given him in our national schools."

The fact is, as all thoughtful men will admit, to educate without attempting to form the moral character by the aid of Religion, is only to put polished weapons into the hands of those who, from evil inclination, or wicked associations, are the worst enemies of social order.

Some people run away with the idea that free schools for the poor are one of the fruits of modern civilization. But the Catholic Church, long ago, was the first to establish schools for the free education of the people. "As early as A.D. 529," says Father Müller, "we find the Council of Vaison recommending the establishment of public schools. A Council at Rome in 836, ordained, that there should be three kinds of schools throughout

Christendom: episcopal, parochial in towns and villages, and others, wherever there could be found place and opportunity. The Council of Lateran, in 1179, ordained the establishment of a grammar school in every Cathedral, for the gratuitous instruction of the poor. In the present day, in every street in Rome, there are, at short distances, public primary schools for the education of the children of the middle and lower classes. Rome, with a population of about 158,000 souls, has 372 public primary schools, with 482 teachers, and over 14,000 children attending them; whilst Berlin, generally believed to be far in advance of all other cities in the work of primary education, and with a population double that of Rome, has only 264 such schools."

I argue then, from the fruits of "Godless education," that the system is opposed to real progress. Let every member of the community be taught to read, and write, and cipher, by all means I say; but at the same time, let the chief element of sound education be carefully attended to. If the governments of civilized nations will only help the Catholic Church in a liberal spirit, there will be no need of compulsory laws to push forward general education. As a rule, Parents will discharge their obligations, and the Church is never weary in teaching the importance of this primary obligation. But if the Church is fettered, in her efforts to provide a sound religious education for her children; if Catholics are unjustly compelled to support schools where no religion is taught, and deprived of state aid towards the support of their own schools; if this burden is flung upon the poor, and consequently there are not schools enough for their accommodation, it is a cruel wrong to attribute this want to a spirit of opposition to real progress, and to charge the Catholic Church with an obstinate and unreasonable determination of raising obstacles to the action of enlightened legislation.

The Church seeing clearly the evil of " Godless education," is bound to use all her influence to oppose this evil. No one will contend that, if the State chose to force one Religion on its subjects, they would be bound to obey so tyrannical and despotic an order. But no Religion is worse by far than the religion of a particular sect of Christians; and therefore, in opposing secular and godless schools, the Catholic Church is only struggling for that religious freedom, which should be the glory and the pride of all good governments to maintain. Hence I conclude that the prejudice against the Church, arising from the fact of her opposition to undenominational education, is utterly groundless; and that, far from hating her for her sturdy determination to resist, in every shape and form, what she considers as one of the most blighting curses of modern civilization, honest men of every shade of belief should honor her, as the faithful guardian of the rights of civil liberty.

As regards the question of the indissolubility of the marriage tie, and the steady determined action of the Church against civil marriages, and divorce, I need not say much. Any one who observes the tendencies of the present age to facilitate in every way the separation of husband and wife, for the most frivolous causes, and the effect of these separations on the family, and the individuals who sue for divorce, and on the general tone of morality, where these things are fashionable, far from condemning, must admire the action of the Catholic Church. To oppose the violation of the bond of marriage is to struggle for real and enlightened progress, and to stand in the way of the rapid descent of Christian society towards the depths of Pagan degradation.

"It is," says Father Müller, "the holy sacrament of Marriage that gives sanctity to the family, and strength to civil society. It is the Catholic Church alone that has always regarded the Christian marriage as the cornerstone of society; and at that corner-stone, the Popes stood guard for eighteen centuries, by insisting that Christian marriage is one, holy, and indissoluble."

"If the Popes," says the Protestant Von Müller, "could hold up no other merit than that which they gained by protecting monogamy against the brutal lusts of those in power, notwithstanding bribes, threats, and persecutions, that alone would render them immortal for all future ages."

It would be going beyond the boundary I have marked out for myself, to discuss the question of the indissolubility of marriage; or to point out the noble action of the Church in past ages, in defence of the sanctity of this "great sacrament." I will merely say, Watch the effects of a wider departure from the principle of the Catholic Church, in these days of the latter part of the nineteenth century, and judge if they are reassuring. Is it not a fact that, since the newspapers began to teem with public scandals connected with the new Divorce Courts, thoughtful men shudder at the signs of the times, and earnestly pray that the ever-swelling tide of evil, which threatens the purity of the family, and the stability of the state, may in some way or other be checked or averted? At any rate, it seems to me, that it is only when men look in the direction of communism and socialism and free-love, as the goal of progress, that they can derive satisfaction from the heavings, and throbbings, and feverish restlessness, which, at the present time, characterize the movements of the masses of humanity. I have said enough to show that the Old Church is true to her principles of social order; and that Catholic Christianity in opposing " Godless Education," and Divorce, is in no way the enemy of real progress.

CHAPTER X.

Catholic Christianity as Opposed to Emotional Christianity.

ALTHOUGH I have given all the attention possible to express my convictions on the present state of the controversy between Catholic Christianity and the fashionable infidel theories of the day, I feel, on looking back on what I have written, certain misgivings, which affect not only the hurried style of the composition, but even the matter itself, as it may be judged by others. I have tried to set the objections of unbelief not only fairly, but even strongly before the public; and sensible men who may look over what I have written may say—" Is it prudent to enlighten the public generally on such points; may it not disturb simple Faith ?"

Well, I can only say, as the result of my experience in this colony, and I suppose the views of colonists on such subjects are the same over the world, that there is not the least danger in thoroughly ventilating thoughts and notions that have found their way early into the minds of precocious youth, and that have been seething and festering there throughout their lifetime. It is an undeniable fact that want of reverence for the traditions of the past is a marked feature in all new countries. A colonial child will laugh at stories of legendary lore that edify the developed minds of people who have lived in an atmosphere of the Faith. Colonists, as a rule, are sharp in picking up fragments of heterogeneous knowledge, and whether it concerns holy things or the opposite, morality or scandal, which minds regulated by the staid and sober habits of quiet home dare not mention, they are full of eagerness to know all about them.

I heard an old lady, the other day, tell the advice she received from her grandfather, when she was a child in England. " My Dear, whenever you chance to pick up a bit of scandal in the streets, drop it in the sewer, for it is a filthy thing, and not fit to enter into a decent house." Such morality would, I fear, be somewhat beyond the mark of a young colonist of either sex. They might marvel at such prim and high-stilted and old-fashioned conceits; but inwardly conclude that these old people knew very little of the ways of the present world. "To know something about everything, and to pick up every fragment of knowledge that comes in your way"—seems to be the maxim of those who from early life, have to think, and take care of themselves.

Young people here and in America, and the new continent in the far East, and wherever the old civilization of Catholic Europe is grafted on a new stem, speak with a confidence and an assurance about all the "ologies" that would fill their ancestors with amazement, not unmixed with grave anxieties. Though their intimate acquaintance with the secret things of nature would be startling to European civilization, their dogmatism on Religious subjects goes far beyond the widest experience of the "Household of the Faith" in older countries. The total disregard of traditional landmarks, and the almost complete ignorance of sound principles of Theology, launches them out fearlessly on the wide sea of religious speculation; and urges them to seize with avidity every morsel and scrap of floating opinion that may present itself to their notice, in the shape of paragraphs of every new publication, that comes within their reach. Novelty has a special charm for them; and the last outcome of Freethought, which would sink and perish unheeded under the surging ideas of new theories at home, is rare food for the bold explorers of Greater Britain beyond the ocean.

It seems to me that the only safe way to satisfy this passionate desire for daring discovery is to meet it bravely and openly; and this plan I have endeavored to pursue throughout my book. I have invariably put the objections of unbelief as strongly as I could, more forcibly perhaps than they would present themselves to persons almost totally ignorant of the important consequences involved.

It is a mistake to say to a precocious and inquisitive child,—"I cannot now explain to you fully what your question means; by and by, when you have studied and learned more, I will tell you all." Prudence of this kind is apt to be mistaken for ignorance, or stupid fear. Impetuous youth will not be checked in its investigations by answers of this kind; and the colonial youth, who is all on fire with the ardor of hungry and unsatisfied longings after the mysterious, will plunge recklessly into depths from which he may never afterwards arise.

I remember once hearing of a smart young fellow, in this part of the world, who having his curiosity excited by something he had heard of the Transit of Venus, pressed his father with question after question, till the old man was feign to escape the importunity of the eager inquirer, by telling him, that in the course of time, his difficulties would be satisfied. The youngster was equal to the occasion, and in true new-world bluntness, replied,

"If you know nothing about it, buy a fellow some books that will explain it."

If what I have said in justification of stating openly the objections of Infidel writers, and the peculiarities of the countries, where my experience has been gleaned, for more than a quarter of a century, be not fully understood in the land of my birth, I am convinced by the experience of old friends in that dear old land, remarkable for their prudence and foresight and the profitable use of this experience, that the time is fast drawing nigh, when the open attacks upon revealed religion must be met even there in the same spirit of open and unreserved satisfaction.

There is another objection which far more strongly suggests itself to me. Having put the arguments of unbelief plainly and forcibly, have I answered them with that fulness, and that amount of learning which the subject demands? I will at once confess that, though I prepared myself by careful study, and extensive reading, to meet these difficulties at every point, I have felt most keenly the want of that acuteness and dialectical skill which the mind acquires by constant practice and polish in the schools, and which is altogether beyond the reach of a missionary Bishop. The answers were clear enough to my mind, even from the recollection of the treatises which I studied in college, more than thirty years ago; but to put them with the precision and power of a master in theology was something I could not attempt.

It seemed to me therefore, that my best efforts should be directed to give the answers in a plain and popular form; and this I have tried to do to the extent of my ability. No doubt I have done it often clumsily, and repeated in one form or another the same answer. But I satisfied my misgivings on this point, by the consideration that my book was meant for readers, who, under the influence of the spirit of the age, would merely glance over its pages; and that if what I said in one chapter failed to arrest attention, the same explanation of the difficulty, in another form, might be successful.

Hence I eschewed anything like the assumption of profound theological learning; and put my trust in my own honesty of purpose, and the good-will of my readers, and most of all, in the blessing and grace of God, which can give a sort of sacramental efficacy to the simplest materials, which are devoted to promote His honor and glory. The most striking conversions that I have met with in the course of my experience, have been due, under God, not to what the world would call wisdom, but to the simplicity of an earnest desire " to hear the word of God and keep it." I have known cases in which, not a learned discourse and cogent argument, but some of the most ordinary devotions, and ceremonies of the Church, the incense offered at the Altar, the Rosary, and the invocation of the Holy name of Jesus, were the key that unlocked hearts long closed to the impulse of Divine grace. I must only hope and pray that a similar blessing will be conferred on many who read this book, with the intention of acquiring, by its means, some useful knowledge about Catholic Christianity.

It will be seen at once, by those who turn over its pages, that I have studiously avoided the old paths of polemical disputation, so long used in the contest with religious sects. All that can be said to guide readers through these devious and ever divergent ways, has been said over and over again; no doubt with a certain amount of satisfaction to the sapient writers, but only to weary and distract those who studied their writings, in the hope of meeting with explanations that would clear away their doubts. He who would imagine to find "the narrow way that leads to life," by comparing disputation with disputation, and attempting to reconcile facts of history with their distortions, and truth with its infinite misrepresentations, would end his weary life, as it was begun, in utter bewilderment; and be tempted, often in its course, to give up the task in despair, and fling himself hopelessly into the rapidly flowing current of total indifference.

There is another difficulty, and as it is of considerable importance, and naturally arises from what I have said in preceding chapters, I will dwell upon it more at length. It may be said, "You have labored hard to draw a charming picture of Catholic Christianity as a whole; you have shown how all the mysteries of this Religion, and its sacramental system, and its worship, emanate from, and circle round the Incarnation. There is no doubt that a Religion, so united in all its parts, bearing its supernatural fruits to every soul that desires them, making us one with our Divine Redeemer, and sharers individually in His plentiful Redemption, is in itself transcendentally beautiful; and, if it could be received with entire faith and confidently relied on, quite calculated to satisfy the longings of every heart that desires life everlasting. But, at the same time, you have warned us repeatedly against a religion of feeling, that gratifies our emotional and sentimental tendencies. If we accept your warning, everything you have urged, and it may be exaggerated in its favor, should naturally make us distrustful. May we not, if we yield to its attractions, be caught by some potent spell, that, by its fascinations, will effectually blind us to the simple and unaffected charms of pure unalloyed truth?

"In other forms of Christianity, we can discover beauties that fill the soul with satisfaction, and give us peace, and an assurance of salvation, and promise to make us feel even sensibly the abiding presence within us of the Holy Spirit of God. In these we find no elaborate ritual; we are taught indeed to unite in prayer, and to help each other by mutual fervor: but the prayers are in a language we understand, and there is no formality about them. The minister who conducts a form of worship of this kind yields to the impulsive gushings of his own heart, and we sweetly communing with him, are borne, by his glowing language, on the wings of Divine love, till, soaring far above the things of earth, we feel safe and secured from sin and temptation in the bosom of God. Here the end at which your religion aims in its material sacraments and outward ceremonies, is attained at once. Surely simplicity marks all the ways of God; and the Religion that attains its chief end, union of the soul with its Creator and Redeemer, is more likely to be acceptable to Him, than one that appeals to us through every organ of sense, and requires so much labor and instruction to understand it. And yet you will say that this emotional and delightful Religion of feeling is not real, that it mocks and deceives us. Is it not wiser then to cling to the simple Religion of nature—to bask in the sunshine, to gaze on the loveliness of the varied landscape, to inhale the sweet odors of the wild flowers, to drink in the harmony of the rippling stream, and the song ever fresh and ever new of the world of life around us, till we 'feel good all over?' Here at least we are safe, there is nothing to delude us, and the mind, as well as the body, is rendered healthy and vigorous."

On this point, as in the case of every objection, I have put the difficulty as forcibly as I could. And what is my answer? Just as this sensuous enjoyment of nature leads to nothing but the animal gratification of those who either have never learned, or having learned, disdain "to rise through nature up to nature's God;" so do these emotional forms of Christian worship, which I have just described, end in meaningless or fatal delusion. They deaden the higher faculties of beings created to know and serve their Creator, and leave them in a state of almost hopeless languor and profound indifference to duty. These gushing extempore prayers, and the emotions they excite, and this seeking after sensible indications of the presence of the Holy Spirit, while they satisfy the longings of pious natures, too often betray their most earnest and zealous votaries into the hands of their worst spiritual enemies.

The essential difference between these forms of Christianity and Catholicity consists in this, that, whereas, while Catholic worship leads us, through sense, to commune with God, presents to us something real, and carefully fixes our thoughts and feelings on this reality; this religion of emotion ends, as it begins, in mere sensibility, and vapid piety aimless and objectless. Feeling is the "be-all and the end-all" of this imaginary fervor, and with the subsidence of feeling, all the seeming ardor in the service of God fades away.

I firmly believe that there is no more dangerous illusion, and no greater enemy to the Religion established by Christ, than a creed that encourages spasmodic piety of this kind. The worst of it is, that it involves the souls who trust in it in the gravest dangers. If it be true, as the Wise Man tells us, that "no man knoweth whether he be worthy of love or hatred" (Ecclesiastes ix. 1), and if St. Paul warns his obedient children of Philippi, "to work out their salvation with fear and trembling" (Philipp. ii. 12), there must, on the very face of it, be danger to the soul in any form of religion that promises its adherents a positive and sensible assurance of the certainty of their salvation.

I do not doubt for a moment that souls glowing with apparent fervor, may, and do feel, something like a supernatural emotion that gives peace to the soul. But there is a peace that is not real peace according to God. "Satan himself transformeth himself into an angel of light" (2 Cor. ii. 14). The Catholic Church has ever set her face against delusions of this kind; and her most distinguished saints have laid down rules for the guidance of earnest Christians, in that most difficult sort of supernatural knowledge which, according to St. Paul, ranks next after the power of performing miracles and uttering prophecies,—"the discerning of spirits" (1 Cor. xii. 10). What can be a more dangerous delusion for a Christian, who believes that at the day of judgment he must render an account for every idle word (Matt. xii. 36), than to imagine that, in a moment of what may be, if not a diabolical illusion, at least a certain pitch of nervous excitement, all his sins are cancelled? What can be more opposed to this pleasing conviction than the words of our Divine Lord, constantly preached by the Catholic Church, alike to the just and sinners,—"unless you do penance, you shall all perish" (Luke xiii. 3).

But I am not arguing with Christians who are non-Catholics; I am defending Catholic Christianity against the unbeliever, who fancies he discovers in Catholic doctrine, an enchanting solace as false and delusive as that which he sees in other forms of Christianity.

"This is your grand comfort," he says, "that through union with Christ in the sacraments you find peace of soul. Other Christians not only promise, but give a positive assurance of this peace, without any sacraments at all: and if this peace be a delusion in one case, why is it not one in the Catholic Church also?" And he goes farther, and, here is the very point of his argument, "We know and are certain," he says, "that all this so-called peace in those who say they feel an assurance and sensible conviction of its attainment, is a mere exaggeration of feeling. We know that the greatest reprobates, whose hearts are wedded to iniquity of every kind, can lash themselves into this state of emotional fervor, and see visions, and hear the voice of what they call the Spirit of God assuring them of pardon. They are clearly mistaken; and so may the pious Catholic also be deceived; and therefore this Religion, which you have described as so beautiful and charming, may be found after all to be a mere idle dream, which, when thoroughly sifted by sound reason, contains within it not one grain of substance."

I have already said, in noticing this difficulty, that the object before the Catholic, when he feels himself carried away by feelings of fervor, is something real, fixed, and definite. He cannot be deceived, because "he is taught of God." The living and speaking voice of God reaches him through the infallible Church, assuring him that he may aspire to a perfect union with God in the Blessed Sacrament. He may indeed be deceived in all that regards his own dispositions; he may not have "proved himself" sufficiently. Notwithstanding the help and light afforded him in the holy tribunal of penance, his soul may still harbor secret attachments to sin. Though he knows perfectly well that the occasions of sin must be cut off, and the injury done to the neighbor in character or property rectified, before he dares to approach the holy table, still he may hope with confidence proportioned to the earnestness of his purpose of amendment, and to the judgment of his confessor in the reality of that earnestness, that he does not deceive himself.

The Catholic Church teaches, as the very A. B. C. of her doctrine of the possibility of being "made partakers of the Divine nature," what St. Peter so plainly sets before us, when he points out "the very great and precious promises of this supernatural union" (2 Pet. i. 4–10). That those who aspire to it, "must fly from the corruption of that concupiscence which is in the world." Not Faith alone will suffice, according to this Apostle, but the earnest Christian must labor diligently "to join with Faith, virtue, and with virtue knowledge,"—that is to say the real knowledge of self—"and the abstinence, and patience, and piety, and charity that spring, through God's grace, from this saving knowledge." Without this labor and diligence, though his heart might feel all aglow with the ecstasies of Divine love, he would be, as St. Peter says, "blind and groping, forgetting his old sins," and destitute of that deep sense of his own unworthiness, which leads those who truly love the Saviour, and desire to be made one with Him, "to labor the more, that by good works, they make their calling and election sure." When union with God in the Holy Communion is preceded by this proving of one's self, then indeed the Catholic "doing these things," may hope "not again to sin at any time" (2 Pet. i. 10).

There is a wide difference here between Catholic Christianity and that intimate persuasion, and sensible conviction of imputative justification, which was the bright discovery of the unfortunate Luther, when he had grown tired of good works, and weary of his solemn vows, and felt himself impelled by his strong passions to cast away the anchor of Christian hope, to turn his back on the light of true Faith, and steer forth on the wide waters of Free-thought.

God help those who set up his grand theory, so charming to perverse nature, before the hard teaching of Christ and His Apostles; and so refuse to bear the cross daily after their Divine Master, nor see to do themselves that salutary violence, which is necessary for the attainment of the kingdom of Heaven (Matt. xi. 12).

I have said that there is no more dangerous illusion, nor a greater enemy to Catholic Christianity than this sentimental religion of mere subjective feeling. No more dangerous illusion, because, founded on the fanciful and prejudiced interpretation of some texts of Scripture, it may be, and often is, a real temptation of the devil. Dangerous too, because it seems to satisfy the souls of earnest men and women, who mistake its unwholesome and frothy excitement, for the substantial " Bread of life." Still more dangerous, because it puffs up the soul with presumptuous pride, and, while whetting the appetite for sensual enjoyment, by developing a highly wrought sensibility, it impels its unfortunate votaries into the very whirlpools and rapids of sore temptation.

There are, I am convinced, thousands and tens of thousands of earnest and sincere Christians, outside the Catholic Church, who, fed on this garbage, have gradually lost all taste for the Heavenly food of the Blessed Eucharist, become utterly sensual, " perceive not the things that are of the Spirit of God" (1 Cor. ii. 14), and learn to deride the great gift as " a fond delusion," and a thing to be discarded as foolish and unreal. Most of these certainly would be saints, in the true acceptation of the term, and as it is known in the Church of God, if they had learned betimes to be guided in all humility and docility by the fond mother of all the living, whom our Divine Lord has left us to teach what we must do to please Him.

And what greater enemy to Catholic Christianity can there be than this flaunting, presumptuous, self-justifying and Pharisaical piety, which, without mission from above, rudely intrudes itself on public notice, and fancies that it is only doing the work of the meek and lowly Jesus, when it flings aside the control of ordinary prudence, and challenges vice and worldliness, in " the very torrent, tempest and whirlwind of its passion"?

Such "out of season" cant must often lead to profanity. I remember a fact bearing on this matter which may set my meaning in a better light. When the soldiers were blockaded by the Boers at Durban, and all Grahamstown was in a state of intense excitement as to whether the men of the Twenty-seventh Regiment, who had to a man volunteered, and gone to the relief of their comrades, would arrive in time to save them, a gentleman connected intimately with many military friends then in extreme peril, was met by a sanctimonious old character not favorably known in the city, who accosted him with the words—" Have you heard the joyful news?" —" No, what?" exclaimed the gentleman, from whom I heard the incident.—" The Lord came down on earth to save sinners, and you among the number." I leave my readers to imagine the disgust excited by this ill-timed announcement.

When men of the world, who have renounced Revealed religion, identify this bold and pretentious mode of piety with Christianity, it is no wonder they are led to hate and abominate Christianity itself. They forget or ignore all they may have heard of that higher form of belief, which is ever calm in Faith, strong in Hope, and Majestic in its noble and self-sacrificing charity, and which, endeavoring to screen its charms from public gaze, reserves all its beauty for the eyes of the great King. They feel stung to the height of indignation at this sanctimonious wordiness and hypocrisy, and deeming all Christian forms of religion the same, they prefer to commune with the poetry of nature, than to bow down and worship with men who can picture to themselves a God who could be imposed upon by this outward show of unreal and hollow professions of piety. It is not surprising, under these circumstances, that many highly-gifted men and women, deceived as to the true character of pure Christianity, and putting this empty sentimentalism in its place, have assailed it with the most bitter invective.

I may not quote Ingersoll's "vision of judgment;" it is too irreverent, as expressed in his own words. But from the idea which I will give, it will be seen at once, that the power of men of this stamp to upheave Christianity in the minds of some, by force of ridicule, arises from the complete misapprehension they have wilfully or foolishly formed of the reality.

"Smith," the hard-working laboring man, honest, sober, and industrious, and devotedly attached to his wife and family, is ignominiously cast into outer darkness because he has not been a reader and distributor of tracts, and is not familiar with sanctimonious and unctuous phrases. While the other "Smith," who has robbed his employers, coveted, and carried off his neighbor's wife, and softly yielded to temptation by "trying fire" and other nefarious practices, is raised to the clouds and gifted "with a harp," because he had cleverly succeeded during life in veiling his iniquity by assiduous attention to prayer-meetings, and other such practices, as have, in these days in which we live, marked the career of some of the most notorious swindlers and forgers, and robbers of the poor, that ever disgraced the fair name of a nation boasting of its righteousness.

If Charles Dickens exalts *bonhomie* and natural virtue above the supernatural, it is only because his strong prejudices prevented his acute perception from examining into the real nature of Catholic Christianity. Had he allowed his honest nature to yield to the sweet attractions of Divine grace, he would have developed in all likelihood into the *beau-ideal* of a Catholic gentleman. No doubt he had glimpses of the truth; the purity of his conceptions of female excellence, as shown in his heroines, like those of the poet Longfellow, could only spring from a sort of intuition of human nature, exalted above ordinary weaknesses by the supernatural gift of God. Dickens has severely lashed that form of Christianity which I have just noted, and though he made bitter enemies by the severity of his chastisement, he has done much to check the morbid admiration for "pious" criminals that was, in his time, fast becoming fashionable.

They who have read the account of the "two interesting penitents," given in the 33d chapter of "David Copperfield," cannot but loathe and detest the caricature of real piety exhibited in Uriah Heep and Mr. Littimer. How exquisite is the satire on wretched hypocrisy, conveyed in the parting words of the latter to the magistrates visiting the prison : " Gentlemen, I wish you a good day, and hoping you and your families will also see your wickedness, and amend"! Or in the words of Heep about his mother—" I am afraid she ain't safe, immortally safe, sir. I should wish mother to be got into my state, I wish mother had come here. It would be better for everybody, if they got took up, and was brought here"!

This is hard hitting; but, as the clever writer says,— "Perhaps it is a good thing to have an unsound hobby ridden hard; for it's the sooner ridden to death." Of course Dickens caricatures this mock Christianity, as he does the other nuisances of society: but ridicule is a powerful weapon, when wielded by a master-hand, and applied to real evils—the best remedy perhaps, and the most appreciated in this unthinking age.

They who know anything of Catholic Christianity, will never charge it with infusing into its penitents, self-justification, forgetfulness of one's own sins, and affected pity for the sins of others. The attacks of such as these, who have studied even hurriedly our books of instruction, and got to know the rudiments of Catholic morality as regards repentance, will be directed against another point altogether. Our system of repentance, this rigid adherence to the teaching of St. Peter, as quoted above, is according to their notions, much too strict. Confession is held to be " a cruel butchery of the soul," and penitential works and austerities, misplaced and profitless severity towards self. Even if they catch a glimpse of the beauty of that union with God, which is the object of our Faith, and Hope, and Charity, they exclaim against the great price which we require, in the securing of so splendid a privilege. Catholic doctrine is, in their view, unnaturally harsh and repulsive: it interferes with the comforts of life ; it disturbs the peace of families.

"Why should religion," as I once heard a good-natured and kind-hearted English lady say, " have anything to do with one's regular meals, upsetting and disturbing them ?" " Why," again, it is said, " should young persons leave the bright world, and shut themselves up in convents?" This hard Religion turns people against their own dearest friends, and extinguishes charity. And, after all, what is Religion without charity? Is it not, as St. Paul says —" as sounding brass or a tinkling cymbal"? (1 Cor. xiii. 1.)

I will answer these and cognate charges, in the words of Cardinal Manning, "The love of the neighbor springs from the love of God; the love of kindred, the love of friends, the love of all that are about us is a part of the love of God. As radiance is a part of light, so the love of mankind flows in a direct stream from the love of God. Therefore aversion from creatures" (the perfection of Christianity according to Catholic teaching) " means this, that there are no undue attachments, no dependencies, no bondage to creatures, even to the purest and the best. The soul is in perfect liberty, because it is united with God ; it loves every one, each in his measure, and fulfils every duty of charity with a delicate tenderness greater by far than the love of those who love God less. In the measure in which we love God, in that measure we shall have more heartfelt love to all that are about us. A father will be a better father, and a mother a better mother; son and daughter will be better children; they will love each other more, and friends will love one another more in the measure in which they love God more. Therefore aversion from creatures means a rational and measured love which sets us free from all undue attachments."

If this were more insisted on in practice outside the Catholic Church, Infidels would have far less to say against any form of Christianity, than unfortunately they can urge at present, when the doctrines of free-love, and other similar fashionable theories, are spreading so generally. An appeal to the instincts of fallen human nature is a sorry argument against the Divine religion, which our Lord has delivered to us. Though He has been pleased, through our senses, to draw us to Himself, and enable us to feel the regenerating influence of His presence amongst us, He has not shrunk, through delicacy for our natural feelings, from declaring that He has not come to send peace, according to our notions, upon the earth; but what is, on the contrary, directly opposed to these feelings, " I came not to send peace, but the sword" (Matt. x. 34).

When Bishop Colenso propounded the new heresy, that the natives of South Africa were not to be disturbed in their gross habits of polygamy, and pushed the *argumentum ad hominem* to the utmost by arguing that we were not to shock the feelings of the natives, by requiring from them an act of injustice, according to their ideas, in compelling them to put away all their wives but one, he forgot here, as in many of his other natural views of Religion, that the Divine message, and not a human interpretation of it, is necessary to salvation. When he pleaded for his protegés, with more than his ordinary eloquence and persuasive powers, he seemed not to bear in mind, that our Divine Lord had declared "that a man's enemies should, under His law, be they of his own household" (Matt. x. 36), and that sacrifices far greater, than separation from many wives, were actually made by the two and a half millions, who in the first three centuries of persecution, in Rome alone, sealed their violent rending from worldly honor and distinction, and home and all its endearments, by the testimony of their blood.

The subjects treated of in this chapter seem to me to require as full an account of the Catholic doctrine of justification, as can be given in a work of this kind; it will therefore form the subject of the next chapter.

CHAPTER XI.

Catholic Christianity, Justification and Sanctity.

IN the last chapter, I endeavored, as briefly as possible, to combat that false notion of unbelief, which assumes that Catholic Christianity teaches, that the greatest reprobates may, in a moment, by an inward sensible conviction, be transformed into "children of light." This involves a grave error not unmixed with truth, and requires that I should, plainly and in simple language, unfold the Catholic doctrine of justification. My best efforts will be directed to avoid theological technicalities, and to popularize, as far as I can, this profound and mysterious subject, which, for the last three hundred years, has exercised the minds of the most able scholars in Divinity, both Catholic and Protestant.

There is something shocking to natural reason in the notion, that a vile ruffian, steeped in crime, may be suddenly transformed into a saint; that the murderer, robber, and adulterer may, in a moment, shine before men like the perfection of angelic purity; that, to quote Dickens again, the Fagins, and Heeps, and Pecksniffs of society, may, suddenly and without any external signs of repentance and change of heart, rise to the moral dignity of self-sacrificing, simple, candid natures, like Nelly or Little Dorrit.

Yet there have been such transformations. The sinful woman of the city looked into the face of our Divine Lord, wept, and was forgiven. The robber on the cross was no sooner touched with pity for the suffering Saviour beside him, than he heard words of comfort, seldom vouchsafed to the most holy on earth. Paul, while thirsting for the blood of the disciples of Jesus, was changed into "a vessel of election." David, burdened with sins that cry to heaven for vengeance, said, in the sincerity of his heart, "I have sinned," and forthwith became dear to the heart of God, and the model of all true penitents. Nay more than this, for these are extraordinary cases, an act of perfect contrition will, according to Catholic theology, secure, through the superabundant merits of Christ, the immediate pardon of the greatest sinner.

Where then is the difference between Catholic teaching on this point of justification, and that instantaneous change of a reprobate into a fully developed rose of sanctity, that excites the disgust and scorn of the children of unbelief? It is to be found mainly in that plain teaching of St. Peter (2 Pet. i.) already quoted in the last chapter. We are changed indeed in a moment—"made partakers of the Divine nature;" for the communication of a vital principle cannot be considered other than as consummated in a single moment.

Grievous sin is called mortal, because it kills the soul; and the change from death to life, when one is really converted by the grace of God, must be, from the very nature of the case, an instantaneous change. One cannot be dead and living at the same moment. But there is a vast difference between the first germ of life, and that further development in virtue, knowledge, abstinence, patience, piety, and brotherly love and charity, of which the Apostle speaks, before there can be an entire transition from the life of the flesh to the life of the spirit.

It is something monstrous, not only to the view of

natural intelligence, but to sound Christian theology, to behold the scandalous sinner of to-day, a full-fledged saint to-morrow, to hear the brawler, or the drunkard, or the profligate, become at once, not a mere "babe of grace," but a preacher, and a teacher, and an exhorter, "forgetting his being purged from his old sins," and, like Uriah Heep, only anxious about the sins of others. There is something sickening and revolting in the spectacle of a wretch, who should, like Magdalene, be bathing the feet of the merciful Saviour with the tears of compunction, or, like David, supplicating the Divine mercy from the depths of his humiliation, standing boldly forward on a platform, and in the presence of his late associates in every enormity, recounting "his experiences," and deploring their blindness.

Such a disgusting spectacle is altogether unknown in the Catholic Church. He who has given scandal, should indeed repair the scandal, by suffering, under wise direction, the light of his altered life to shine, in modesty, and gravity, and persevering prayer, and the avoidance of the occasions of his former sins, so that they, who had been witnesses of his folly, may glorify God, in his change of heart. But the less he has to say about himself the better. The public confession of his evil deeds is unnecessary; and would, even if they were not detailed in all their enormity, be scarcely edifying; and the manifestation of "the very great and precious" favor accorded to him by the Divine mercy, might flatter a secret pride, that would soon extinguish the small ray of Divine light, which had communicated a feeble life to his guilty conscience.

In the early days of the Church, penitents often confessed their sins in public; but this was only under the

JUSTIFICATION AND SANCTITY. 231

direction of a prudent priest, duly appointed to the office of determining when this part of the satisfaction for sin was likely to conduce to the spiritual benefit of the public penitents in the congregation. We know, from Socrates and Sozomen, the historians of the primitive ages of the Church, that, through scandals, the practice was discontinued. What I have said will enable my readers more clearly to understand the difference between Catholic belief and practice concerning justification, and the notions prevalent amongst certain Christian sects, which excite the bitter hostility of unbelievers.

The Council of Trent describes justification to be an exaltation from the state of sinfulness to that of grace, and of adoption of the children of God—"A state, which," as Dr. Moehler says (Symbolism, p. 146), "is in a negative sense, that of remission of sin, and in a positive sense, that of sanctification."

These two states are often confounded by Christians, who do not accept the teaching of the Catholic Church: and this confusion has led to the misconception by unbelievers, and abuse of Catholic doctrine. By the grace of God, purchased for us through the sufferings and death of our Divine Redeemer, the truly penitent obtain pardon, are made just, and this instantaneously, so the light is admitted in the room of darkness, and death gives way before life. But something more takes place, that, ordinarily speaking, requires time; and this is the transfusion of the Spirit of Christ into the soul of the penitent, in other words, the development of the germ of the new life, communicated instantaneously by the act of justification.

To express this more plainly, and in a way in which the sense will be obvious to a passing reader, I would say, that, by justification, life is communicated to one that was dead: but this little spark of life, like the first faint indications of breathing in one recovering from a trance, or rescued, at the last moment, from a watery grave, must be carefully nursed into vigorous life, before it is capable of anything that can indicate sanctification. If, in addition to this, we picture to ourselves a certain state of soul that precedes the instantaneous act of communicating spiritual life, a certain "susceptibility," as Dr. Moehler expresses it, "dependent on a series of preliminary, mutually qualifying emotions in the inner man," we shall then fully understand justification in the Catholic sense, and as opposed to that extraordinary transition from turpitude to sanctity, which excites the ridicule and contempt of unbelievers.

Before man can be adopted as a child of God, there must be a gradual preparation, a certain disposition on the part of the sinner to avail himself of the great gift, when it is offered. "From the period," says the learned Doctor, already quoted, "wherein our faculties of discernment have clung with undoubting firmness to revealed truths, the struggling soul moves on through fear and hope, through grief and intuitive love, through struggle and victory, up to that happy moment, when all its better energies, hitherto dissipated, unite under the impulse of a higher power, for obtaining a decisive conquest; where, by the full infusion of the Holy Spirit, the union with Christ is consummated, and we belong wholly to Him, and He again joyfully recognizes Himself in us" (Symbolism, p. 149).

It is not that, by this mental process, and this gradually developed susceptibility, we *merit* the grace of justification. That would be Pelagianism, a rank heresy condemned in the days of St. Augustine, by the Catholic Church.

Perhaps what I have said about the sudden raising from death to life, may render what I have just explained, somewhat obscure. But the meaning is soon clear. Though the soul be dead in a spiritual sense, yet the grace of God may be active within it; moving and exciting the tardy death-like will to something like exertion. God can do nothing in the soul of the sinner, till the human will, under the influence of preventing grace, begins to believe, and fear, and then hope, and love, and thus co-operate with the impulses that indicate the advent of returning life. This is what we understand by that susceptibility or fitness for the precious gift of justification.

But, at the same time, this crowning of the good work, begun by Grace, is purely gratuitous on the part of God. Man, however readily he may co-operate with these first impressions of Grace, cannot, *on this account*, be said to merit or deserve this grace: a certain state of preparation for a thing must not be confounded with the cause of that thing itself. The signal-man, and others preparing actively for the arrival of the train, have no influence whatever in causing its approach.

If what I have explained be clearly understood, there will be so much the less difficulty for any one of ordinary intelligence in mastering what is further necessary to be said, in order to show the difference between Catholic justification, and the notions of Christian sects, which are wrongly ascribed by unbelievers to the Church of God. The work of justification proceeds gradually in the soul of the converted and justified; because, after sin is forgiven, there remains a perverse sensuality. This concupiscence, as it is called, or stimulus to sin, is not by any means a sin in itself. It will no doubt lead us to sin, if we follow its suggestions; but as long as we resist, it cannot injure us; nor separate us from the new life obtained in justification. On the contrary, if we resist it victoriously, by co-operating with the grace of God, it will render us more pleasing in His sight, and add to our crown hereafter.

But it is only by determined and persevering conflict with this temptation to evil, that the fruits of sanctification begin to manifest themselves. These happy effects are seen and felt in the sincere and earnest Christian; first by himself, in the gradual decrease of the influence of this concupiscence; and, in course of time, by those about him, in the steady calmness, and absence of anything like singularity in the service of God. The more his soul is at peace with God, the stronger does the penitent feel, by God's sanctifying grace, in the possession of his new life; the more instinctively does he shrink from public notice; and the less does he estimate, as something to be exhibited, his newly acquired virtue. "By the grace of God," he says with the Apostle, "I am what I am."—" I am not conscious to myself of any fault, but in that I am not justified."

There is a prevalent idea among unbelievers, not exactly that pious Catholics do not trust in the merits of their Redeemer, and that they confide solely in their own good works (it is reserved for our separated brethren to entertain these charitable views), but that these pious Catholics must necessarily be proud and Pharisaical, and always thanking God "that they are not like the rest of men."

How little they know of true sanctity, who fancy that

the Holy Catholic Church can reverence the blatant egotism and effusive piety of these "brands saved from the fire," that love to make their sentimental piety fizz and blaze before the public; and attribute to her the development of such specimens of outrageous hypocrisy?

Cardinal Manning gives a far different notion of such sanctity, when he says—"All our conformity to the Sacred Heart is the work of God in us: and He perfects it in measure and degree, as He sees it to be for our good. He humbles us by making us wait. We desire to be sanctified with great speed, that we may be delivered from the bondage of our temptations. We pray to be saints out of love to ourselves; and if we were made saints to-day, we might fall to-morrow, as the angels did by self-contemplation. . . . Neither you nor I are saints now, nor, in this world perhaps, ever will be. And yet some of you may be. There may be some poor humble soul who hears me who thinks that he is the worst of sinners; there may be some poor woman, who says that 'no soul was ever farther from being a saint than I am;' and yet it may be that these two are nearer than we are in their conformity to the humility of Jesus, for 'the last shall be first and the first last.' But of one thing I am sure—that if there be such they will be the least conscious of it; and if anybody here thinks well of himself, and that he is in the way to be a saint, he is far —perhaps the farthest—from it."

To mark more distinctly the essential difference between the Catholic doctrine of justification, and that which is often mistaken for it, I may be allowed briefly to go to the very root of the matter.

According to the Formulary of Concord, in which Lutherans and Calvinists coincide,—"Justification signifies the declaring any one just, on account of the justice of Christ, which is by God imputed to Faith; and it expressly declares our justice *is not of us*. So that while, according to Catholic doctrine, Christ, by justification stamps inwardly and outwardly His living impress on the believer, in such a way that the latter, though feeble and imperfect, becomes gradually a real copy of the type, on the other hand, according to the Protestant doctrine, Christ casts on the believer His shadow only, under which his continued sinfulness is merely not observed by God.

There is in this view no real change; the sinner remains truly a sinner unto death. Only in some extraordinary way, the Omniscient is deceived, and regards the sinner, whose heart is unchanged, as if he were a saint. Faith, according to them, constitutes the only decisive distinction between sinners in the eyes of God. When the sinner believes, and as long as he believes that the merits of Christ are imputed to him, he is at once all holy.

There is therefore, in this view, no essential difference between the converted and the unconverted; the same moral being remains; and the effects of penance, restitution, avoidance of the occasion of sin, unfeigned humility are all self-delusion.

This of course explains how in a moment, the greatest reprobate becomes a saint, and may show off, before admiring crowds, the bright garment which hides all his iniquity. It is almost amusing, if the subject were not in itself so serious, to note how far even the most distinguished among the so-called Reformers, pushed this point. Melancthon, wishing to prove that a Saint Francis, or some other of the most exalted servants of God is not in reality holy, triumphantly puts the question—" Do not they all seek their own interest?" As if there were no meaning in the words of the Apostle, that " Charity"— the chief test of true sanctity—" seeketh not her own ;" and that a perfect follower of Our Divine Lord, always seeks his own interest, and not the glory of his Divine Master!

Men of this school see nothing but sin in concupiscence. But if concupiscence be bravely resisted, where is the sin? And, if it be successful in its assaults, what becomes of the saint? It must never be forgotten by the Infidels who assail the Catholic doctrine on this point, and fancy that we Catholics are no better than those who believe in instantaneous sanctification, that the Catholic Church, above all things, insists on a radical internal change. Here, in the words of Dr. Moehler, is the essential difference, so clear and distinct, that it cannot possibly be mistaken. When the Protestant believes that the merits of Christ are imputed to him, "at this point of his spiritual life, he can calmly sit down, and without advancing a step farther, be assured of eternal felicity,— while the Catholic can obtain the forgiveness of his sins, only when he abandons them."

I would not care to be obliged to defend the Protestant position against the assaults of unbelief; for however potently, if I were a Protestant, I might urge abstract principles, and attempt to overwhelm my opponents with scholastic reasoning, founded on the effects of original sin, I should feel at once, that the reasoning of common-sense was decidedly against me, in attempting to maintain that a reprobate might become a saint, without a real change of heart and a complete reformation. I might as well hope to convince a sober-minded reasoner of the existence of such a phenomenon in the moral world, as a flying ox or a conscientious parrot.

The chief cause of this great difference between Catholics and Protestants, may be traced to the erroneous notions of the latter concerning original sin and its consequences. According to them, the ravages of the sin of our first parents are so frightful in their posterity, that they cannot be cured even in the regenerated. Instead of holding the belief of the Catholic Church, that the inclination of the will to evil, left in us by the disturbing influence of the primeval act of disobedience, is not sin, except where this inclination or solicitation is entertained with full consciousness, and consented to by the will, Lutherans and Calvinists assert, that this solicitation, even when resisted, is in itself sinful.

This appears so monstrous to unbelievers, that if with Ingersoll, they do not cry out against "the infamy of the Atonement," they express the notion of the injustice involved in this inheritance of evil, independent of individual will, in the strongest terms. "The visiting on Adam's descendants," says Herbert Spencer, in the January, 1884, number of the *Nineteenth Century*, "through hundreds of generations, dreadful penalties for a small transgression, which they did not commit; and the effecting a reconciliation by sacrificing a son who was perfectly innocent, to satisfy the assumed necessity for a propitiatory victim; are modes of action, which, ascribed to a human ruler, would call forth expressions of abhorrence."

Strong as this language is, it seems in some sort justified, if real Catholic Christianity maintains, with the leading Reformers, that personal sinfulness does not consist in a deliberate perversion of the will, but in something positively evil in itself outside the will, that is transmitted. If the consequence of original sin, as a positive evil, be in the soul, notwithstanding the determined action of the will in resisting it, and this evil, thus sternly combated by the will of the individual, exposes him to certain damnation, then we must say, that he is condemned without just cause ; and that he is lost, not through his own fault, but by a fatal necessity.

But Catholic Christianity has never imagined, or taught anything of this kind.·* The doctrine of the Church on original sin is simply this. Adam by his sin lost the supernatural gifts of holiness and original justice, which God, in pure gratuitous mercy, had bestowed upon him for transmission to his posterity.

In other words, the father of the human race, by his sin of disobedience, rejected that original justice, which involved privileges of the highest order, to which he had no natural claim : and we, as members of the human family, of which he was the head, bear the consequences of that rejection. We are not implicated in his personal sin, in his ambition, pride, and disobedience ; but we are implicated in that special guilt of his sin, in which he could, and did act as head of the human family. He sinfully rejected the supernatural gifts, to which his nature had no claim : and we, as united to him, have shared in this rejection of original grace. Original sin in us does not simply mean the loss of what was so precious, but it means self-rejection of these gifts, in as much as this rejection was willed by our human nature in Adam, with the will of Adam. It is not a personal sin, for our personal will had no part in it ; it is the sin of our nature, as our nature is one with that of Adam. It is a necessary consequence of the sinful breaking of the supernatural order established by God, in which sin we share, inasmuch as we form one moral body, that is one family with him.

Of course no illustration can make clear a mystery, and this transmission of original sin is one of these incomprehensible truths, which form the entirety of our heaven-born and mysterious Religion. But, to a certain extent, it may be illustrated thus. A subject of a great monarch finds favor in the eyes of his master, and is in consequence raised to a Lordship and privileges of the highest rank. Had he persevered in his fidelity, he would have transmitted these honors to his children. But he rebelled, and they, disinherited like himself, bore the consequences of his guilt. The illustration fails however, because under original sin, the children of Adam share, not only in his misfortune, but his guilt. That guilt consists in this, that they have lost favor in the eyes of God. He loves them, it is true, as His intelligent creatures, made to His image: but He does not love them as beings worthy of His gratuitous love and supernatural blessedness; for they have lost in losing original justice, the likeness to Him, in which their nature was created.

It is not true to say, with Spencer and his school, that God imputes to us the personal sin of another; it is rather the effect of this sin, the wilful rejection, made by human nature, in its representative, of original justice and its glorious privileges. There is no injustice here; men do not lose anything which their nature requires. As Dr. Moehler says, "What nature without supernatural grace, would have been, it is now, in consequence of the self-incurred loss of that Divine light."

The great difficulty, in the whole question, is this, to explain how the wound inflicted on human nature, has reached the immortal spirit: how the souls of each of us, created by God, at their union with the germ of the body transmitted by nature, feel the noble faculty of the will weakened and perverted. This is of Catholic and Divine Faith, for the Council of Trent has declared, under the infallible guidance of the Holy Ghost, that by original sin and its transmission, the will of every human being is weakened, and inclined to evil "*viribus attenuatum et inclinatum*" (Concil. Trid., sess. vi. cap. v.). But the same council has also defined it, as a dogma of Faith, that Free-will is by no means extinguished in us—"*liberum arbitrium minime extinctum.*" Hence it follows, that although we cannot, without the grace, communicated to us through Jesus Christ, produce any act in itself, and by itself acceptable to God, and anywise perfect, every moral act of ours is not necessarily sinful.

This doctrine differs *toto coelo* from the notions of the Reformers, that a positive evil power, independent of our will, has been transmitted to us, and that a fallen man is all evil.

There is something good in human nature, no matter how fallen, corrupted even by actual and personal sin: and there is nothing, in Catholic doctrine, which does not cheer and encourage every benevolent and noble-minded Christian, who, through many self-sacrifices, devotes his best energies to find out the latent spark of natural goodness, and to endeavor, by kind words and generous deeds to fan it into vigorous activity.

Those who, like Ingersoll and Spencer, seek to drag down the justice of God as shown in Catholic teaching, below the level of that which is human, only exhibit, in their showy theories, the littleness and short-sightedness of even great minds, when they attempt, without the aid of revealed Religion, to speculate on the infinite attributes of God. The great being "who has made all things well," is the Master of His own gifts; so that not even His goodness, not to speak of His justice, can be impugned; since the gifts He confided to the keeping of Free-will enlightened by Grace, were infinitely beyond what human nature at its best, could have ever merited.

How completely ignorant are they of the loving condescension of our Divine Saviour, who see in His self-imposed sacrifice for our sakes, and Infinite pity for a fallen race, nothing but an "infamy," and consequences abhorrent to our natural ideas of justice! Verily the poor ignorant Catholic, who cannot read, but has learned to say his beads, while thinking over the sufferings and death of his Saviour, and has thereby trained himself to bear poverty and afflictions of every kind, not only with patience, but with joy for Christ's sake, is before God and His angels, far higher in the scale of humanity, than the proud philosopher, who exclaims against the folly of the Divine appointments. Those Christians who will not hear the Church, and are doomed to follow the first rebels to her authority, through all the weary mazes of error, and doubt, and inconsistency, have inherited something far worse, in its personal effects, than Original sin: for their obstinacy in clinging to these wearying by-roads and circuitous paths, and so wasting their lives in wandering round and round in endless perplexity, deprives them of anything like real Faith and peace of mind. It may be a sort of diversion to them, when they have abandoned the narrow way that leads to life, with its modes of worship adapted to our needs, and its sacraments, like so many refreshing fountains, and its "Bread of life" to sustain them, to forget for a moment their anxieties in exhilarating sentimentalism and emotional fervor.

But if they prefer these enjoyments of mistaken piety, to the path trod by our Divine Lord Himself, because it is steep and arduous, rough and thorny, and irritating to human pride and sensuality, in the very simplicity of its refreshments, and its occasional austerities, they may hear one day the saddening words,—" Amen I say to you, you have received your reward " (Matt. vi. 2). Yes, they may well imagine it said to them: you experienced much satisfaction in your own ways of devotion; you were raised above the earth, when certain chords of feeling were touched that gratified self-love; in the delightful fervor, that thrilled sensibly through your whole being, as you joined in the gushing prayer, you felt the touch of the spirit that pleased you with its whisperings of false peace. But in all this "you have not walked according to the will of God" (Wisdom vi. 5). In these exercises of seeming piety, as in the fasts of the Jewish people, "your own will is found" (Isaias lviii. 3). There was another way—" the holy way"—a straight way so adapted to the wants of humanity, that "fools could not err therein" (Isaias xxxv. 8); but this you abandoned to please your own caprice, "therefore you have erred." No doubt it does seem more delightful, "nicer" to use a common expression, to certain individuals of the sentimental class, to revel in various forms of new-fangled piety, than to adhere to the ways sanctioned by the practice of primitive Christianity.

There is, beyond question, a more highly spiced charm in listening to one's self, or dear friends, pouring out the thoughts and feelings of passionate excitement, than joining with the poor round the altar or kneeling humbly and alone at the tribunal of penance. But the great question is what is the form of worship with which God is pleased.

These considerations however will probably have less effect than mere human considerations, on the admirers of emotional Christianity. If they heard what calm and sensible men think and say of extempore prayer, and its accompaniments, their intense admiration for these spiritual enjoyments might be rudely chilled.

I have heard it said myself, and from my knowledge and experience of human nature, I believe there is a deal of sound truth in the observation,—" These people, who are ready at any moment to engage in public extempore prayer, must be rarely gifted, if this exuberance of gushing piety is real; and if, on the other hand, they are only acting, they must be the most consummate hypocrites."

I know that it is hard at all times to fix the thoughts on God. As Father Faber says, "Often when we place ourselves in the Divine presence, and try to pray with attention and devotion, it seems as if a fountain of distracting thoughts began to play in the centre of our being." Those who disdain to use prayers carefully prepared in humble and respectful language, and sanctioned by long and general use, must often commit themselves, under the influence of excitement, to words that are hardly wise. It is to be feared too, that in "wrestling with the Spirit of God" they may betray a boldness and irreverence, which they would not dare to use in addressing an equal or a superior among their fellow-men. And suppose the feelings of fervor and the unction will not come at the precise moment that they are wanted, must they be worked up for the occasion? With what a sense of unreality does not the bare thought of such acting affect our judgment of the pious practices of those, who are supposed to be superior "to the rest of men," in the earnestness of their devotions! "Sing praises to our

God,"—says the fervent Psalmist, but he adds—"Sing ye wisely."

I have touched on this matter, because in pointing out the difference between Catholic Christianity and the Religion of sentimental emotion, I thought it necessary to indicate a remarkable feature in the latter, which is abhorrent to Catholic piety. If unbelievers are tempted to use very strong words, in their denunciation of the language used at Camp-meetings, and Revivals, and public prayer-meetings; and not from what they believe themselves about our Divine Lord, but from what they know of Christian belief in His Divinity, express their horror at what Dickens has called "the most impious and awful familiarity" of those, who often rant on these occasions, they should not charge the Catholic Church with these excesses.

While Catholics respect the motives and intentions of those who piously join in this kind of popular devotion, they are grieved and pained at the mockery, and ridicule, and contempt, which exhibitions of this sort excite in the minds of the enemies of the Christian religion, for every worship that bears the name of Christian.

In the next chapter, I will say something about the gloominess and misery supposed by unbelievers to be intimately and necessarily connected with Catholic Christianity. .

CHAPTER XII.

Catholic Christianity Untinged by the Gloom of Predestination.

ONE of the most common arguments of Infidels against revealed Religion is that it casts a gloom over the innocent enjoyments of the present life; and discourages men from the discharge of the duties which they owe to society. "If," they say, "happiness in a future state is 'the one thing necessary,' and this happiness is to be secured only by self-denial, and making ourselves miserable, what interest can a thorough believer take in the affairs of the world? And, as it is quite certain, that men are irresistibly impelled by their reason, and the noblest and most elevating feelings of human nature, to seek their own happiness, and promote that of their fellows, whatever opposes these principles is evidently beneath the notice of cultured humanity."

In this respect, Catholic Christianity is the chief object of attack. Other Christian systems establish a friendly alliance with the ordinary pursuits of the world. There is nothing in the most rigid forms of Protestantism, that hinders one from seeking wealth, and honor, and the prizes set before us, in the beautiful dwelling where we find ourselves. Whereas "the strict Catholic," they say, "is impelled, by the rule of his Church, to fast and pray, and wear himself out in acts of penance and mortification; and, if he happens to have a fair share of the good things of this world, he is bound to sacrifice them to the objects of doubtful charity, which surround him on every side." And, pressing the argument to its extreme point, they urge—" Look at Catholics who aim at what they foolishly call the perfect life, and you will find that, wherever they find it possible, they shut themselves up in Religious houses, and pass their days in wretched silence and seclusion, wear poor clothes, use the plainest food, and submit to the drudgery of a Rule, that must, after a time, become intolerable, in the strictness of its minute observances. What fools these Catholics must be, who allow themselves to labor under such stupid delusions!"

I remember once, when I was a boy, hearing of an English Protestant traveller in Ireland, who was strong in these views, and who fairly nonplussed the poor driver of the jaunting-car, by his stern dogmatism on the Religious life. They were passing a celebrated Carthusian monastery, and the driver, hoping to entertain, and perhaps edify his rather taciturn " fare," began to detail to him the privations and austerities of the monks—" They are wonderful people, sir; they rise at midnight to sing their prayers."—" More fools they."—" They never touch meat."—" More fools they."—" They fast two Lents in the year."—" More fools they." And so it went on, till the driver, at last, aggravated beyond measure, by what he considered the want of religion of the other, exclaimed —" Why then, sir, do you mean to go to Heaven at all ?" " Yes, my good fellow, certainly," replied the other, "but not by making myself a ridiculous fool." I could not help thinking even then, that it was no sign of folly, to renounce all things and to follow Christ for the sake of Heaven. I have long ago learned, as a truth beyond doubt, that they are the wisest and best of the human family, "to whom it is given" to correspond with the grace of a Divine vocation.

It does not follow that, because there are many who heed the Divine call addressed to the young man who had large possessions,—"leave all and follow me," and who thus enter on the rough and narrow way of perfection, that this mode of life is set before the great body of earnest and thoughtful Catholics.

I have already pointed out, in the fifth chapter, what is meant by a vocation to the perfect life, how rare it is, and how severely it is tested. This at once cuts away the very root of that fallacy, so constantly urged by the leaders of "progress," that, if the Catholic religion had its full way, this fair world would soon be changed into a gloomy waste, and that the human race would perish.

But let it be observed, Marriage is "a great sacrament," honored by Christ's first miracle, and a figure of the admirable union that exists between our Divine Lord and His mystic spouse, the Church. The great majority of Catholic Christians—a majority so immeasurably beyond the number of those who are called to the higher life, that the latter, though a numerous class, is scarcely perceptible in the multitude of believers—the many, can not only save their souls by gratifying a taste for wide intercourse by living in society, and mixing in the busy pursuits of the world; but they could not, in the ordinary ways of Providence, be saved at all, unless they followed the bent of this inclination. Very many who have lived happily in the married state, brought up children in the fear and love of God, are now, according to the belief of the Church, brightly conspicuous in the mighty host of the white-robed, who enjoy the beatific vision. Every treasure born of them, which they have carefully preserved in innocence and purity, or which, like the mother of St. Augustine, they have, by their prayers and good example, rescued from the fangs of the wicked serpent, is another fair gem in their crown of everlasting glory. God often blesses them here below with happiness, far beyond the luxurious dreams of pleasure, which mock the desires of the ungodly; and fills their souls with comfort, in proportion to their fidelity in dispensing His bounty, a comfort which is altogether unknown to the weary pursuers of sensuous gratification.

What folly it is for worldly-minded men and women, the wretched slaves of ever-changing fashions, and tyrannous obligations of human respect, to sneer at the delights of generous, and unaffected, and simple-minded virtue! What do they know of the pure and unadulterated and ever fresh enjoyments of self-sacrifice, who shrink with terror from every work of charity that necessitates discomfort, and scatters their largesses, not for God's sake, but to ward off vexatious importunity, or to gratify the suggestions of ever-craving pride? If they could only for a moment pierce, with steady glance, the mists of prejudice, and obtain one view of that joy, which a merciful God often bestows, even in this life, on those who love Him above all things, and their neighbor for His sake, they would be impelled to tear from their brows the fading flowers of earthly pleasure, and trample in the dust those perishable nothings, for which they have bartered their eternal welfare.

When pious Catholics, who have learned betimes to walk with God, either in the Religious state, or abroad among men, are faithful to the graces so lavishly bestowed upon them, they realize something of that pure happiness, which must have flooded the souls of our first parents, when they heard the voice of God speaking gently to them "in the paradise of pleasure."

But these things are foolishness to those who have blunted their appetites on the gross things of earth, and are filled and surfeited with this unwholesome food. They do not understand the ways of God, and it is therefore useless to dwell further on this point in attempting to reason with them. I will only say that there is no place in this weary world more like Heaven, than those happy homes, where God, and all that concerns His service, honor, and glory, are the main objects of daily life. "Be not solicitous," says our Divine Lord, "about what you shall eat or drink, or wherewith shall you be clothed. For after all these do the heathens seek. Seek first the kingdom of God and His justice, and all these things shall be added unto you" (Matt. vi. 31-33).

It is a great mistake to imagine that they who set their hearts on "the one thing necessary," and "place their treasure in heaven," are thereby unfitted to attend to their duties in society. Every state has its fixed duties. Those of the professional man, of the merchant, of the landed proprietor, and of the laborer,—of the poor as well as the rich, are clearly laid down in our books of instruction, and form the subject of continual sermons.

Idleness has ever been regarded as a crime in the Church of God. All Catholics must labor diligently to fit themselves, to the best of their abilities, for the faithful discharge of their several employments. It was always a maxim, even amongst the Contemplative Religious orders, that "he who works, prays." It is only solicitude, over-anxiety, heathenish forgetfulness of God and His Providence, that is condemned. If men will neglect God, and trust entirely in the power of their own hands, and never ask His blessing on their labors, who alone can give the increase, they are, according to the teaching of the Catholic Church, the real "fools," who despise "the one thing necessary," and are entirely taken up with those worthless trifles, that must soon be abandoned forever. There is no such thing, in Catholic teaching or practice, as sitting down on the road that leads to heaven, and abandoning one's self to blind fate and the gloomy horrors of Predestination.

The Catholic who would say to himself "Either I am one of the Elect, or of the Reprobate ; God who knows all things knows with absolute certainty whether I shall be saved or lost, and therefore it is useless for me to trouble myself about doing good or avoiding evil," would, he fully understands, be acting as foolishly as the fanatic Turk, or the man perishing with hunger, who would not stretch forth his hand to take the food that lay within his reach. "Allah sees my fate," says the blind zealot, who rushes madly upon the bayonet of his adversary: "God must feed me or I die," may say indeed, according to the principles of his creed, many a misguided Christian ; but the least instructed Catholic cannot entertain, for an instant, the thought of so great an absurdity. He has been taught, it is true, that "whether he eats or drinks, or whatever else he does, he must do all things for the glory of God" (1 Cor. x. 31); but while he thus puts himself in the way of receiving the Divine blessing, on even the most ordinary of his actions, he must attend to what he is about; and use his best efforts to be a faithful servant. "He who soweth in blessings, shall also reap of blessings" (2. Cor. ix. 6). And therefore he is bound to do the work before him, "not with sadness, or of necessity," like those who have no hope in a kind and ever-watchful Providence; but cheerfully, because he is assured that the duty, be it ever so difficult, and surrounded with vexatious trials, has been appointed for him by one, who loves the cheerful giver and the contented mind, and who has chosen, by this path, to lead him to his eternal rest.

I never yet knew a pious Catholic who was not, as a rule, bright and cheery. The expression, so familiar to all Catholics, ignorant as well as learned—"It is the will of God" is never associated with gloomy thoughts. On the contrary, this outburst of consoling Faith and Hope, which springing from the heart, finds utterance on the faltering tongue, lightens the load that presses heavy upon us at times.

God be praised! in long-suffering and afflicted Ireland, the Faith of which the words "Blessed be the Holy will of God" is the natural outcome, is too deeply fixed, by pious mothers in the hearts of their children, ever to be eradicated. Nay rather, it seems to sink deeper with every blow to long-cherished hopes, till it has grown into the very instincts of the people. We Irish are never gloomy; and we have to thank Faith, as well as natural temperament, for so great a blessing. Our priests and Religious, when the hard work of the Confessional, or ministering to the sick, or the works of mercy in the school, or the homes of the poor, is finished for the day, can be as joyous, and as free from care as the children who cried out, in the presence of the Saviour,—"Hosannah in the highest."

We Catholics know nothing practically of the grim Calvinistic piety, which, instead of finding in the belief of God's Providence, a cheering light in the midst of darkness and sorrow—

> "Like moonlight on a troubled sea
> Brightening the storm it cannot calm"

invites rather in the soul of the puritan a religious gloom, like the dark mist, as Homer describes it, "brooding on the abyss and hatching the tempest," of rebellious excitement and passionate resistance to the Divine appointments. We are happily ignorant, as well in doctrine, as in practice, of anything like dismal forebodings of this kind. This *bête noire* of sectarian Christianity, so well depicted by Dickens in the character of Mrs. Clenham,— this nightmare of Calvinism, never disturbs even our dreams.

"The world," says this wretched incarnation of ultra-puritanism, shut up in the airless room, with its bier-like sofa, and other funereal details, "has narrowed to these dimensions"—this to one who felt he was her only son, and who had just returned after a long absence. "It is well for me that I never set heart upon its hollow vanities. I know nothing of summer and winter, shut up here. The Lord has been pleased to put me beyond all that." "Great need," continues the clever and observant writer, "had this rigid woman of her mystical religion, veiled in gloom and darkness, with lightnings of cursing, vengeance, and destruction, floating through the sable clouds. Forgive us our debts as we forgive our debtors was a prayer too poor in spirit for her. 'Smite Thou my debtors, Lord, wither them, crush them: do Thou, as I would do, and Thou shalt have my worship;' this was the impious tower of stone she built up to scale Heaven."

Such sentiments actually make one's blood run cold;

and I am sure Catholics must marvel whence such a picture of mistaken religion could possibly be drawn. This keen observer of the stage of life had however distinct visions of actors like Mrs. Clenham. They grow, by a sort of necessity, from the incubus of Predestination.

Damned for all eternity, hopelessly crushed forever under the heel of pitiless destiny, is the stern decree which, creeping out of the dark mists of error, weighs down every joyous impulse in the soul of the believer in such monstrous aberrations. Natural religion, if it has done much evil to Faith, has at least almost banished this hideous phantom from any practical influence over the affairs of life. Puritans now, exultingly quote the words commonly attributed to their pet-idol, Cromwell, and sing, "Put your trust in God, my boys; but keep your powder dry." Still the principles of Calvin are so intimately involved in the belief, that Christ died only for the elect, and that the mass of humanity are foredoomed to eternal misery, despite their best efforts, that it is no wonder, unbelievers, deriving their knowledge of Christianity only from formulas, and confessions, and other authentic documents, take the information obtained from these sources, as the firm ground of their worst assaults on the Christian religion.

According to Calvin, "Predestination is that eternal decree of God, whereby He hath determined what the fate of every man should be. For not to the same destiny are all created: for to some is allotted eternal life; to others eternal damnation. According as a man is made for one end or the other, we call him predestined to life or death" (Calvin Instit., lib. iii. c. 21, n. 5, p. 337). "We assert that by an eternal and unchangeable decree, God hath determined whom He shall one day permit to have a share in eternal felicity, and whom He shall doom to destruction. In respect to the elect, this decree is founded on His unmerited mercy, without any regard to human weakness; but those whom He delivers up to damnation, are, by a just and irreprehensible judgment, excluded from all access to eternal life" (L. C., n. 7, p. 339).

Is it any wonder that, on the suppostion that this appalling doctrine is that of the Catholic Church, Infidels should rave against Christianity, and that Ingersoll and others of his school, should have expressed their hatred of the God of the Bible?

It must be remembered, in connection with these stern decrees, that he who propounded them, and his followers hold, as a fixed principle, that there is no such thing as free-will; and consequently, that they who are doomed by the eternal and inexorable decree, are lost forever, without any fault that can in justice be attributed to them.

But Calvin went farther than this, and maintained that, though Faith is a gift of God's mercy, yet believers who are lost, are condemned, because God did not give them a real Faith. "He insinuated Himself into their souls under an apparent Faith, that He might render them more inexcusable" (p. 195). That is to say, he charges the Almighty with intentional deceit, that He may gratify the more thoroughly His awful vengeance.

It would be altogether wonderful that a doctrine like this could have perverted the sound sense of Christians, did we not know, to what extremities men are driven, when they will not hear the great teacher, whom our Divine Lord has left to guide us in our perplexities, but are obliged, through some false principle or other, to adopt new and strange doctrines.

Astute, as was this leader of error, and warily on his guard to keep clear of the monstrous extremes of Luther, who maintained that Free-will, by the fall of man, was utterly destroyed, he is yet irresistibly led into the same abyss of blasphemy, when he asserts, that the faint modicum of co-operative power is completely overwhelmed by the invincible action of Divine grace. " When Divine grace knocks, the door *must* be opened: it works quite *invincibly*, and those who enter into life, are never so touched by it, as to yield voluntarily to its suggestions: it simply never touches them, but saves them in spite of themselves."

How bright and clear and cheering is the Catholic doctrine compared with these wretched principles of despair, which trample out of the heart of man, the bare conception of anything like hope! According to the Church, Divine grace, the seed of any merit worthy of the Divine acceptance, is indeed unmerited by man; but it is freely offered, through the merits of Christ, to all men without exception; and none are lost but those who freely or wilfully reject this redeeming aid (Concil. Trident., sess. vi. c. 2). If any one is lost, notwithstanding the means of salvation that God affords to every one, such a one cannot justly blame God, but only himself and his sins. Sin alone, voluntary sin, sin committed wilfully and knowingly in the light of God's grace, is the only cause of exclusion from Heaven. No one is a reprobate, but by his own most grievous fault. According to the Catholic Church, the goodness of God precedes any hopeful movement of the soul, and gives to it a first grace, a purely gratuitous and unmerited supernatural impulse.

This is called an *actual* grace. It does not justify the sinner; but it will help him to perform good works, and obtain further grace. He may reject it if he will; if he does, it will be no benefit to him. If he turn it to good account, by his free co-operation, it will obtain more grace, and dispose him to obtain the free gift of justification; and by co-operating and working with this, rising from virtue to virtue, repairing the evil effects of sin, avoiding its occasions, and the like, the penitent will at last arrive, by a gradual process, to sanctification, and life everlasting. Here all is hopeful; there is no place for desponding gloom.

The sinner who is moved to say, like the publican, " God be merciful to me," who, like the prodigal, feels weary of sin, and thinks of returning to the kindest and best of fathers, or like the man who, on the brink of an abyss, is warned in time by some hairbreadth escape, and the nearness of some terrible accident, already feels in these impulses, the voice of God inviting him to repentance. Let him only freely yield to the impulse, and he has already made the first step towards salvation.

But it may be asked is there not in the Catholic Church also a doctrine of Predestination? Yes, truly there is of the good who are saved. God foresees their co-operation, and final perseverance, and because it is His grace alone that has wrought this mercy, because, although they could have resisted, He foresaw that they would not resist, their salvation may be said to have been predestined; for God not only foresaw this happiness in store for them, but actually effected it without constraining their liberty.

But, according to Catholic theology, God cannot be rightly said to have predestined the Reprobate. He foresees indeed their doom; but, instead of effecting it, He does everything, consistent with the free-will of the sinner, to avert it. He cannot be said therefore to will their condemnation, and, by willing, to bring it about, because He does not produce their evil works; on the contrary He gives them every help to avoid prevarications. If they are lost, they are lost through their own fault, and not by virtue of God's eternal fore-knowledge and predestination.

It may easily be inferred, from this explanation of the Catholic doctrine of Predestination, how wide of the mark are all the shafts directed by the sneers, and wit, and ridicule of unbelief against the justice and goodness of God, as represented to us in revealed Religion. Catholics do not believe that any soul is predestined to be lost, or that God causes any man to fall into sin; such notions we condemn as impious and blasphemous. God indeed foresees that certain men will abuse His graces, and their own free-will. He cannot consistently, with man's noble gift of freedom, *force* any one to do what is right; but "God tempteth no man" (James i. 13). He saves those whom He pleases; and those who, in His infinite mercy, are saved, must attribute this crowning grace to His gratuitous goodness, more than to any merit of theirs. But condemnation is a punishment, and can only be inflicted on one who is guilty; and therefore it cannot be said, with anything like a shadow of truth, that He predestines the Reprobate to Hell. His foreknowledge has no influence whatever on their free choice. The unfortunate wretch who, in the misery of despair, is about to take his own life, knows well, that he may, if he pleases, cast away from him the weapon of destruction, and not seal his fate forever like the unhappy Judas. "God will render to every one according to his works" (Rom. ii. 6). None will be lost but the wicked; and the wicked may, even "at the eleventh hour," repair the follies and idleness and utter worthlessness of a life of sin, by turning with all their heart to Him who is not willing "that ANY should perish," but desires that ALL should return to penance (2 Pet. iii. 9).

Here, as I have said, there is no place for gloom or despair; and the unfortunate Catholic, who would abandon hope, and consider himself predestined to eternal misery, must close his eyes to the light of truth, and be guilty of that terrible sin, which is but the coping-stone of his tower of iniquity, and invites the Divine wrath to burst upon it, like the dread lightning,—the sin against Hope, or distrust in the mercy of God, the greatest of all the Divine attributes.

When Herbert Spencer says, in that article to which I have already alluded, that "a deity who, in early times, is represented as hardening men's hearts, so that they may commit punishable acts, and as employing a lying spirit to deceive them, comes, through a convenient obliviousness, to be thought of as an embodiment of the highest virtues," he is riding the hobby of religious Evolution to the last gasp.

A child, well instructed in the Catechism, could tell this profound Philosopher, that there can be no contradiction in the word of God. This child could further explain, to this eminent leader of Free-thought, that whatever seems to jar with the plain doctrine of God's love for the whole human race, and "who will have ALL MEN to be saved" (1 Tim. ii. 4), must be understood in a sense consistent with this frequently repeated declaration of the Divine goodness. When God is said to darken the mind, and harden the heart of the obstinate sinner,

He does so, not by acting *directly*, but *indirectly*, by permitting and not stopping those evils, which the willfully obdurate sinner rashly courts, and from the fatal embrace of which, God is bound, neither in justice nor in mercy, to tear him forcibly away.

So much then for "the gloominess, and savage harshness of revealed Religion," as it appears to its enemies. When men, like Ingersoll, heap up all the terrible things which are recorded in the Old Testament, as the means which God found necessary to check a perverse people, ever sliding back into the worst depths of corrupt Idolatry, and sums up, by calling the God of the Bible, "a fiend," and in the extremity of his hatred for the Being who has made him, turns lovingly to the God he imagines he finds in unconscious nature, he seems to forget that this Personification of amiability can be very wrathful at times.

There are such things as earthquakes, and plagues, and inundations, suddenly sweeping away thousands of innocent with the guilty, and dreadful shipwrecks, wherein helpless infancy, and fond mothers, and brave men perish, with the ungodly, beneath the cruel waters.

These cataclysms are of course, in his view, only the freaks of his charming and idolized mistress. And if she indulges in these sports, which he denounces as savage and undiscriminating, she cannot be "all his fancy painted her." How much more wise it would be for him, instead of stupidly fondling with a thing without feeling or intelligence, to turn to the great Being "who has made all things well," and who " is gracious, and true, and patient, and ordering all things in mercy" (Wisdom xv. 1), "*because He considereth the end of all things*" (Job xxviii. 3).

Perhaps with this key of the far-reaching knowledge of

God, he might, notwithstanding his bitter prejudices, the offspring of narrow and short-sighted views of Providence, be brought, like Voltaire, to see that there is something after all in the consideration of final results.

Men of the school of thought of the American Freethinkers, are always harping on that newly-discovered principle of ethics,—that "Consequences determine the quality of an action." Of course this is senseless as regards man's limited experience: as no individual can form the least idea of the ultimate consequences of his own acts. But applied to Him—in whose infinite knowledge the past, present, and future are as one, the consequences of what seem to us unmitigated afflictions, may be, as no doubt they are in the Christian view—sovereign acts dictated by Infinite mercy. He who has created all men, not merely to be rich, or happy, or prosperous in this world, but to be happy with Him for all eternity, and is Lord and Master of all things, knows how to dispose of His creatures, as will best accord with "the one thing necessary."

If unbelievers would only carefully examine the history of their own lives, they would find, in their experience, much reason to admire the Infinite mercy of the Great God, "Who endures with much patience vessels of wrath, fitted to destruction" (Rom. ix. 22). If the troubles and misfortunes, under which they may have groaned, and which probably excited much of their bitterness against God and His revealed Religion, have opened their eyes ever so little to the vanity of those things which so quickly pass away: they might recognize, in these afflictions, not stern wrath, but gentle mercy.

The subjects treated of in the last two chapters are of so much importance, to enable strangers to Catholic

Christianity to understand the spirit of this venerable creed, that I feel it almost necessary to add to them a short exposition of Divine grace, or that supernatural aid given to all men, through Jesus Christ, to enable them to attain to the end of their being.

CHAPTER XIII.

Catholic Christianity and Divine Grace.

THERE are certain lines laid down by Catholic teaching on the subject of Grace, which, when they are once distinguished, enable a fairly instructed Christian to move safely, through the mazes and obscurities, which Theological discussion has heaped up around this important doctrine.

In the first place, it must be always borne in mind, that Grace is not *merited* by any individual. It is a supernatural gift which God grants gratuitously, and in view of the merits of Jesus Christ, to intelligent creatures, in order to conduct them towards their eternal salvation.

Natural endowments, such as good qualities of soul and body, an attractive exterior, winning manners, a just mind, a natural taste for virtue, an even temperament superior to blind passion, a fund of uprightness, and love for honesty and fair dealing, these are also gifts of God. For "every best and perfect gift is from above, coming down from the Father of lights" (James i. 17).

But these good qualities are not, properly speaking, what we understand by Graces. These gifts of nature are enjoyed by individuals, not because Jesus Christ has merited them for us, or because they have a necessary connection with the great end of our being. The helps which, for Christ's sake, are given us by God, to enable us to merit Heaven,—these divine impulses, or desires, or affections, which stir up the soul, and excite a real interest in the better life beyond the grave, these are the gifts which we call by the name of Divine Grace.

They are called Interior graces, to distinguish them from the Exterior aids which we derive from the lessons of the Gospel, from the preaching of these heavenly truths, and the example of those who make them the rule of their lives.

It may be well to remark here, that Exterior Graces and natural gifts, such as those mentioned above, are the only Graces recognized by the Pelagian heretics, whose opinions on this subject were confuted by the great St. Augustine. I notice this particularly because, as we shall see presently, these errors lie at the root of all the misconceptions of the Catholic doctrine, which prevail at the present day.

We know from our own experience, that Interior Graces, which inspire us with good thoughts, holy desires, and pious resolutions, do not come from ourselves; the Catholic Church teaches that they come from God, and that they are antecedent to all merit on our part. When we say with regard to an individual, that he is so good, that he ought to be a member of the true Church, we are, perhaps unconsciously, expressing opinions, at variance with Catholic teaching. No one, however naturally gifted, however amiable, however admirable in natural goodness, can have the least right to the Interior Graces, which our Divine Lord has merited for us. A good Pagan, or a bad Christian, as far as strict rights are concerned, has just as much claim on the Divine bounty, for these interior movements inclining to holiness, as a dumb animal has to the gift of intelligence and speech. He might deserve from his fellow-men, like Aristides, the title of "the just," and yet not deserve, as something due to him, the least tittle of any supernatural recognition or reward of his apparent rectitude.

To bring out more distinctly how decidedly the Catholic doctrine shows our absolute dependence on the gratuitous mercy of God, I need only mention that it is defined, as an article of Faith, that the first movements towards repentance, and the very thought and desire of this blessing, come to us from the impulse of Divine Grace (Concil. Trident. sess. vi., de justificatione, C. 5, Can. 3). This is in fact only the development of the truth taught by the Apostle, "No man can say the Lord Jesus, but by the Holy Ghost" (1. Cor. xii. 3); and "We are not sufficient to think anything of ourselves, as of ourselves; but our sufficiency is from God" (2. Cor. iii. 5).

From the rigor with which the Catholic Church maintains this doctrine of St. Paul, Infidels argue, that there is no encouragement given to those, who, by a naturally good disposition, or the effects of early training, are disposed to rise from the depths of sin.

If they would only recognize, in these interior promptings to good, the preventing grace of a compassionate God, they would easily comprehend, that there is no ground whatever for a charge of this kind. There is, on the contrary, in Catholic theology, the very highest encouragement to a change of life. Every one who comes into this world receives this preventing grace. It is called also Actual Grace, as distinguished from Habitual or sanctifying Grace. It does not, like this latter, render those who receive it, acceptable to God, and worthy of eternal happiness; but it prevents, or leads them on, by its inspirations before their thoughts are naturally inclined to virtue, to this happy determination.

This common grace, given abundantly to every one

for Christ's sake, is not the result of early training or good natural dispositions; it is a real operation of God, whereby He enlightens our mind, and moves our will to break the bonds of Satan, to overcome a temptation, or to accomplish a duty long neglected. It is, in all probability, the Grace of prayer.

God has, in His Infinite mercy, made prayer a sort of instinct of our weak and fallen nature. At times it is felt so strongly that, without positive resistance, the erring soul is impelled to cry out to its Creator for help. When danger to life is imminent, and human aid is out of the question, and self-exertion is utterly powerless, man is, in a manner, irresistibly moved to appeal to some power superior to himself, or his fellow-creatures. He may not have any determinate notion of a God; he may be, not only a Pagan, but a wild savage destitute of any knowledge, save that feeling immediately connected with the sense of self-preservation; yet if he yields to this impulse, though it may be only to send forth a cry for help,—an almost involuntary cry, wrung from him by the agony of pain, or the misery of helpless desolation, that cry is in itself a prayer, and will be heard by Him who has inspired it. It is a first Grace, and if the unfortunate being who utters it, accompanies the appeal with a corresponding movement of the heart, and thus co-operates with the supernatural movement within him, it will be followed by other Grace, which will bring either the relief desired, or, better still, will rescue the almost perishing soul from blank despair.

It is the distinctive doctrine of the Catholic Church, as opposed to every shade of Calvinism or Lutheranism, that no matter how deeply fallen man may be, he still possesses the power of co-operating with the Divine im-

CATHOLIC CHRISTIANITY AND DIVINE GRACE. 267

pulse. He may, if he pleases, stifle the impulse; but he may also, with perfect freedom, yield to its suggestions.

It would be contrary to Catholic doctrine to believe, that an impulse like this, which is in reality an interior grace, is reserved only to believers. As Dr. Moëhler observes, "Catholics not only demonstrate, from the examples of illustrious Pagans, the moral freedom enjoyed by heathens, and the remnants of good to be found among them, but they defend moreover the proposition that God's special Grace, communicated for the sake of Christ's merits, working retrospectively, and confirming the better surviving sentiments in the human breast, is undeniably to be traced in many phenomena" (Symbolism, p. 106).

That there are no Graces given except through faith in Christ, and that, outside the Catholic Church, there is given no Grace, are propositions condemned by the Church as heretical (Constitut. Unigenitus, Prop. 26 and 29).

It was the peculiar teaching of the early Reformers on Original sin, that led them into those grave errors, which shock the common-sense of unbelievers, and cause them to declaim against the degradation of humanity, which they wrongly believe is attributable to the teaching of the Catholic Church. How beautiful is the real Catholic doctrine, when compared with these foolish fancies of Luther and Calvin!—"that man under the influence of Divine Grace is as a saw that passively lets itself be moved by the hand of the workman"—or "a pillar of salt, a block, a clod of earth, incapable of working with God" (Luther in Genes. c. xix.).

The following is the true doctrine of the Catholic Church, as expressed by Moëhler, quoting from the

Council of Trent,—" This Divine call, sent to the sinner for Christ's sake, is expressed not only in an outward invitation, through the preaching of the Gospel, but also in an interior action of the Holy Spirit, which rouses the slumbering energies of man, more or less sunk in the sleep of spiritual death, and urges him to unite himself with the power from above, in order to enter upon a new course of life. If the sinner hearkens to this call, then faith in God's word is the first effect of Divine and human activity, co-operating in the way described. The sinner perceives the existence of a higher order of things, and with entire, and till then unimagined, certainty, possesses the conviction of the same. The higher truths and promises which he hears, especially the tidings that God so loved the world, as to give up His only begotten Son for it, and offered to all, forgiveness of sins, for the sake of Christ's merits, shake the sinner. While he compares what he is, with what, according to the revealed will of God, he ought to be; while he learns, that so grievous is sin, and the world's corruption, that it is only through the mediation of the Son of God, it can be extirpated, he attains to true self-knowledge, and is filled with the fear of God's judgments. He now turns to the Divine Compassion in Christ Jesus, and conceives the confiding hope, that, for the sake of his Redeemer's merits, God may graciously vouchsafe to him, the forgiveness of his sins. From this contemplation of God's love for man, a spark of Divine love is enkindled in the human breast—hatred and detestation for sin arise, and man doth penance" (Moëhler, Symbolism, p. 117, quoting Conc. Trident, sess. vi. c. 6).

This is the doctrine of free co-operation, without which, God's Grace, though omnipotent in itself, can by the order established by Him, effect nothing in the heart of man. God has made us free, and while He would again, if it were necessary, give up His Divine Son for us all, so that none should perish, He will not in any way deface the image of Himself, stamped on man, by overruling the glorious privilege of human liberty.

The immense difference between the Catholic doctrine and that of the Reformers, the latter teaching, as it does, the total annihilation of free-will, clearly demonstrates how intimately all revealed truths are knit together: and that one cannot be disturbed, without throwing the whole into confusion,—a confusion that affects not only abstract principles, but extends to the most practical consequences.

Christians who reject the teaching of the infallible guide, point with satisfaction to the serious disputes, and heart-rendings, and bitter persecutions, that arose in the times of the Council of Nice, from the change of a letter in the expression of orthodox faith. "See," they exclaim, "the folly of extreme dogmatic teaching. Can anything be conceived more pitiful than the fierce contentions about the spelling of a word applied to the Redeemer, and whether one single vowel should be omitted —whether the word should be *omousios* or *omoiousios !*" Yes, but the great fact of the Atonement, and therefore the whole foundation of Christianity, in the faith of believers, rested on the very point indicated by the single letter. It was a matter of sovereign importance whether Christians should believe, that Christ was really God, or only a Being, in some sort like to God; the first Greek word clearly expressing His Divinity—the second only indefinitely something like unto God.

Those who applaud the "broad" interpretation of a

mystery, see with indifference the whole Athanasian Creed crumble into nothingness;—while the Catholic Church, to-day, as ever, and until the end of time will proclaim that Mary is the Mother of God, and that Jesus Christ our Lord is "the Word made flesh," and " the glory of the only begotten Son of the Father,"—consubstantial with Him— " and full of Grace and truth" (John i. 14).

The second grand principle, that man can co-operate with, or resist Divine Grace, taken with the truth explained in the beginning of this chapter, that Grace is beyond all human merit constitute the unmistakable lines, on which orthodox Faith moves safely, through the mists and shadows, which obscure the whole subject.

The main difficulty consists in reconciling the freedom of the will with the efficiency of the Divine impulse; and though Theologians differ, and probably will differ to the end of time, all Catholics are agreed in this, that Divine Grace is given to us *gratis*, or without merit on our part, and that, in determining us to good, it leaves us perfectly free to accept or resist its influence. It will be sufficient merely to note that the dispute runs on the points whether Grace acts physically or morally, in producing meritorious human acts; whether it works directly or indirectly; immediately, or by rendering the object before the choice of the soul, pleasing and delectable.

There are different systems which undertake to explain these apparently insoluble questions, but they could scarcely interest the general reader. It is in truth a mystery, and all the explanations go to establish the conclusion, that the efficiency of Divine Grace depends practically on the free acceptance, or resistance of the will. Our Father who is in Heaven, may urge us to do good, or to avoid evil, by exciting within us certain feelings, that ordinarily affect human beings, or a special congruous feeling, that falls in with the peculiar tendencies of each individual, or Grace itself—may mould and fashion, directly and immediately, the will; but He will never move us to act by the exercise of an omnipotent force, that *necessitates* our determination. If He did, He would, by this exercise of His sovereign power, destroy in the individual, thus moved to any particular act, so far the grand distinction by which, notwithstanding all our unworthiness, He has been pleased to exalt us above all His creatures, and stamped on our souls the image and likeness of Himself.

When the Reformers taught that Free-will was so fatally wounded by the Fall, that it perished altogether, and that, consequently, man had no power to co-operate with, or to resist the supernatural influence of Grace, they were driven, by the necessity of this position, to deny the existence of moral responsibility. Whether they wished it or not, they found themselves fixed, as immovably as Stoics, on the suicidal, and revolting weapon of absolute fatality. Their disciples may do all they can to soften down the terrible consequences of this fatal error; but in the judgment of common-sense and sound morality, they stand before the world convicted of a fearful mistake, which, more than any exaggerated calumny, invented to injure the fair name of the Spouse of Christ, has covered Christianity, as interpreted by them, with hopeless confusion and disgrace.

I said, in the beginning, that the errors of the Pelagians lie at the root of all the misconceptions of Catholic doctrine on this subject, which prevail at the present time; and hence, it may be interesting to know, in a few words, what these errors mainly were.

The Pelagian heresy is the exaltation of humanity, at

the expense of the Divine government. Under pretence of defending Free-will, the Pelagians, with their upholders, semi-Pelagians, Armenians and Socinians, deny the influence of Divine Grace. They deny the transmission of original sin, and therefore, maintain that the descendants of Adam are able, without any supernatural help, to attain the end of their being. According to them, Free-will consists in a perfect balance between good and evil. Grace, or what is properly called Grace, the interior emotions excited in the soul by God's Holy Spirit, overturns, in their view, this balance, and thereby destroys Free-will.

Of course their notion of Free-will being a perfect balance, between good and evil, is a mistaken premise; for it is evident, on this explanation of human liberty, the really virtuous man would, in proportion as he advanced in holiness, lose his liberty. The balance, inclining more and more to the side of good, by the force of habit even, not to speak of inclination and conviction, would leave him the slave of goodness.

They got over the difficulties of numerous texts in the Bible, by explaining that, where the Sacred Scriptures insisted on the necessity of supernatural help, the meaning was, only exterior help, such as reading the Scriptures, or listening to sermons and expositions of the Law of God.

They never would admit the necessity of Interior Grace. When they say, that God does not refuse Grace to the man who does all he can to live well, they mean that He gives knowledge of Jesus Christ, or of the precepts of the Gospel, or the moral excellence of the Divine law.

The semi-Pelagians did not deny altogether the necessity of Interior Grace; but they maintained that what we call "preventing Grace," or the first impulses to serve God, the desire and love of virtue, disgust for sin, and similar movements, were not supernatural; but proceeded from man's own natural feelings; and that, only when man disposed himself naturally to merit and receive the supernatural interior help, did he really receive it. They held, moreover, that having once received this interior help, he had no need of its continuance, to enable him to persevere.

The Catholic Church declares that actual interior grace is absolutely necessary to man, not only to enable him to perform a work meritorious in the sight of God, but even to desire to do it. The simple desire of Grace is, in itself, a Grace; consequently Grace is always gratuitous, and never the recompense of natural good dispositions; and moreover to enable man to persevere in doing good, and avoiding evil, he always needs a special supernatural help, without which, however strong his determination, he will certainly fall away again. Hence it follows that God gives to those who are saved, first justifying Grace, and then final perseverance, not because He foresees in them good dispositions, which will lead them to correspond with these gifts; but because, in His infinite wisdom and goodness, He judges fit to bestow these gifts gratuitously.

This doctrine is, of course, most offensive to human pride; and is as much hated by the spirit of unbelief, as any of the misapprehensions of Catholic Christianity, that shock human reason.

It is particularly odious in these days; for the popular religion of the present time is, not so much the worship of nature, as the worship of humanity. To quote the words of Frederic Harrison, in a remarkable article in the number of the *Nineteenth Century* for March, 1884— " The religion of men, in the vast cycle of primitive ages, was reverence for Nature, as influencing man. The religion of man, in the vast cycles that are to come, will be reverence for Humanity supported by Nature. . . . The final religion of enlightened man is the systematized and scientific form of the spontaneous religion of natural man. Both rest on the same elements,—belief in the Power which controls his life, and grateful reverence for the power so acknowledged. The primitive man thought that Power to be the object of Nature affecting man. The cultured man knows that Power to be Humanity itself, controlling and controlled by nature according to natural law."

How this new religion will, as the clever essayist believes, make good men and women, is more than one of practical common-sense can see. Mr. Harrison does not believe in the immortality of the soul,—this dogma is, according to him, "a vapid figment." The humanity of the past is therefore, according to his views, resolved into nothingism. The poor, and afflicted, who most of all, need sympathy between them and the object of their belief, will hardly give their veneration, and service, and love, to that thing called Humanity, which, in the pride of its Egoism, as manifested in the enlightened individuals, who are supposed by Progress to personate this unknowable abstraction, is rapidly freezing up the hearts of all, who have been taught by it, to forget the Sovereign Lord of all things, and the Father, and Protector, and Rewarder, of those who place their trust in Him.

But when the Catholic doctrine of Grace is separated from all the dross and impurity, with which error and heresy have confused it, how beautifully it falls in with all that we know, by Revelation, of God's infinite goodness! When it is considered, in its simple truth, apart alike from the gloom of Puritanism, and the sickly garb of emotional and sentimental religious fancies; and contrasted with "the concupiscence of the flesh, and the concupiscence of the eyes, and the pride of life," which form the true character of the idol of the day; "men of good-will" are sure to cling, with fonder love and more confidence than ever, to the blessed God, " from whom every good gift comes;" and who is the real Father of His children in every age.

For, what does the consoling Catholic doctrine of Grace emphatically teach us? Is it not, first of all, that the Great God "is no respecter of persons" (Acts x. 34); but One "Who, without respect of persons, judgeth according to every one's work" (1 Pet. i. 17); "Who maketh His sun to rise upon the good and the bad, and raineth upon the just and the unjust" (Matt. v. 45). We are all His children; and to the poorest, the lowliest, and the most degraded, is given, according to the measure of His bounty, a gift beyond all price, that supernatural gift, which will enable every one to merit Heaven. To some He gives more, to some less, but to all, sufficient. He gives to every one a treasure of infinite value; for if it is only well employed, it will be the price of that glory, which is the happiness of God Himself.

More than this, He gives it again and again, when, through our own most grievous fault, it has been squandered and lost. Not seven times, but "seventy times seven times," He is ready to renew His gift. Nay more, though during a long life, we may have set our hearts on perishable objects, and preferred them to Him;

even, "in the eleventh hour," when the dawning of eternity shall exhibit to us the awful precipice, to the brink of which our blind folly has conducted us, and fill us with terror, He will still be near us, with His merciful arms stretched out to save us. If, even in that last hour, we will only yield to the pressing influence of that common grace of prayer, and cry to Him for help, He will so surely give us that abundant aid which alone can save us from destruction, that a deliberate doubt of His mercy, and the wilfulness of despair, would, in the injury it offers to His promise of loving patience, surpass in perverse wickedness the iniquities of a sinful life.

Such thoughts as these help us to understand something of the consolation afforded to the worst sinner in the world, by the Catholic doctrine of Grace.

CHAPTER XIV.

Catholic Christianity and Material Prosperity.

THE thoughts naturally suggested by the passage from Mr. Frederic Harrison, quoted towards the close of the last chapter, that Humanity is to be the sole Deity of cultured and enlightened man in the future, lead me to consider another popular argument against revealed Religion which is intimately connected with this new object of deification.

I do not question the truth of the statement of this apostle of Free-thought, as regards those whom he considers enlightened; nay I will go further, and express my conviction, that "Humanity," which can mean nothing else, than all that is dear to the natural man,—his comfort, and ease and happiness in this life, is already enthroned, as the object of adoration, by ever-increasing crowds of silly votaries.

Perhaps it would be more intelligible to substitute for the abstraction, something more akin to Realism; and say that Riches or Wealth, which enable man to be happy, as they understand happiness, here below,—is the actual Deity of the unbelieving world. Our Divine Lord calls this Deity—Mammon: our practical friends beyond the Atlantic, call it profanely, "the Almighty Dollar."

There can be no doubt upon the matter; those who reject the hopes held out to us by Revelation, worship the great enemy of Christ, whose service is absolutely incompatible with that which we owe to the Son of God.

"You cannot serve God and Mammon" (Matt. vi. 24). All the fashionable "isms" of the present day only amuse the intellect; but the heart clings to its treasure, and loving it, must hate the other master who demands its affections.

Of course, I do not mean Wealth for its own sake; but that which worldly men treasure as their chief good as a means and opportunity of satisfying the various forms of desire. Neither do I mean for a moment to insinuate, that the majority of the worshippers of Mammon seek their happiness in the gratification of low animal passions. They are far too wise, and too fond of their comfort, to plunge into excesses, that soon bring their own punishment. What the votaries of the new Deity call virtue, is not so much "irrational self-denial," as that keen-sighted prudence, which guards against excess, and those refined tastes, which afford exquisite enjoyment and gratification to the sensual appetite. This naturally involves the highest degrees of quasi-intellectual and æsthetic culture.

But all the pleasures of life, the most refined, as well as the most animal, depend on wealth, as the means of enjoying them. The deity of wealth is devoutly worshipped, not only by unbelievers, but also, covertly perhaps, by many Christians. Hence comes the objection which I mean to answer, and which is urged fiercely, and with entire conviction of its truth, against Catholic Christianity by all its enemies.

"The Catholic teaching is," they say, "the enemy of social happiness, because Catholic countries are always poor, and behind all others in the race for worldly prosperity, and wealth, and influence. There is something in this old creed, which weighs down on the nations, that put faith in its teaching, and leaves them broken down and distanced, and without life and energy, in the midst of general prosperity." "Look," they triumphantly exclaim, in every record of public opinion devoted to their interests, "the old Church is manifestly behind the times, wherever it exercises its baneful influence. Where are now the nations that still profess the Catholic faith? Where is Catholic Spain, and Austria and Italy and France?"

Or, to bring things nearer home to those who speak the English language, mark the state of Ireland. Compare it with Protestant Scotland, or note the fatal degeneracy, that invariably exists in the same country, amongst the Catholic part of the population, in comparison with those Provinces or districts that are enlivened by the Protestant element. The difference is so great, for example, between the Protestant and Catholic Cantons of Switzerland, or Ulster with its sturdy Presbyterians, and Connaught with its miserable and starving cottiers, that a stranger, merely passing through these different parts of the same country, will at once perceive the wretched decay, which follows necessarily from clinging to the musty traditions of old-fashioned ideas."

I cannot help noticing, before I answer this popular objection, how strange it is, that Protestants, who are ever boasting of their purer and more spiritual worship, should give their attention, almost exclusively, to this worldly and temporal view of Religion. Admitting for a moment, that the facts are not to be questioned or denied, does it follow that worldly prosperity, and the active and successful pursuit of wealth and power and distinction of this kind, is a proof of the truth of Protestantism? If so, the nature of the Religion preached by our Divine Lord, and exemplified in His whole life, must have completely changed its character. He not only declared expressly, that no man, and therefore no body of men, can at the same time serve God and Mammon; but He denounced riches, as one of the greatest obstacles to the attainment of the eternal happiness, He promised His disciples. "And I say to you, it is easier for a camel to pass through the eye of a needle, than for a rich man to enter into the kingdom of heaven" (Matt. xix. 24). And again—" Wo to you that are rich: for you have received your consolation" (Luke vi. 24). He sternly repressed the earthly ambitions of His disciples; and told them, that they would be outcasts, and persecuted, and the most miserable of men: and as far as He could, impressed it upon their minds, that worldly prosperity is no evidence of Divine favor.

What has changed all this? Is it the "progressive" spirit of the world? But the world and its false principles will perish, while His words will never pass away.

However I do not care to press this point farther with those who look down on us Catholics, as being so far beneath them, in our appreciation of Gospel lessons, and esteem it their peculiar privilege to hold fast to "the truth as it is in Jesus." It is only one of these numerous inconsistencies, that reveal themselves constantly in the ways of thinking and acting of those who will not "hear the Church."

Those who openly worship Humanity, and all that pleases human nature, and ridicule the maxims and counsels of Christ, wherever they clash most forcibly with ideas of "progress," have a right to press the objection to its fullest consequences. If they are perfectly satisfied that the only true wisdom and practical common-sense, is "to love the world, and the things that are in the world," as the chief good, they may fairly and consistently urge this point against Catholic Christianity. Let us briefly see if the objection is founded on facts: it is common enough, but not on this account more true.

I will admit at once, that pauperism, bringing with it physical and moral evils of the worst kind, is one of the greatest plague spots of modern civilization.

But it cannot be doubted, that Catholicity, in all ages, has devoted its most earnest attention to assuage these evils. The existence of numerous Religious orders, founded mainly to keep alive the spirit of real Christian charity, in the performance, according to solemn vow, of the works of mercy, spiritual and corporal, settles that question. However great national wealth may be, there must exist, in spite of this wealth, an immense amount of real poverty. "The poor," says our Divine Lord, "you have always with you" (Matt. xxvi. 11).

Wealthy London, it is well known, has its tens of thousands of wretched human beings, who, when they rise from the bare earth, or from crowded dens, worse by far, in their squalid misery than the caves and earth-homes of our Bushmen, know not where to turn for the bare necessaries of life. It is the same more or less in all the great cities of Europe and America.

All that can be done for these victims of extreme want is to endeavor, as far as possible, to alleviate their sufferings: and the most blind and bigoted enemy of the Catholic Church must admit, that, in proportion to the means at her disposal, and to the liberty of action allowed her by civil governments, she has always made the most strenuous exertions to provide for the suffering poor. In this respect, she has so far surpassed other creeds, that she has been charged with an excess of liberality, which fosters and encourages the evil.

I need not say any more on this point, but come at once to the main charge, urged against her by the abettors of material progress,—that she is the chief obstruction to national prosperity.

The case of Scotland, as compared with Ireland, is most frequently quoted, as a clear and convincing proof, that Protestantism favors the development of national wealth, while Catholicity prevents it.

"Catholics," say the Infidel and the upholders of ultra-liberalism and Free-thought, "are so ground down by dogmatic teaching, and senile submission to authority, that they dare not cherish the aspirations of a free and enlightened people. They must obey their priests, and as it is the interest of the clergy to keep them in bondage, the people have no chance of breaking their fetters, and rising to the sense of manly feelings.

"Sectarian passions," says M. de Laveleye, a leader of this school of thought, "have been too often imported into the study of these questions. It is time that we should apply to it the method of observation, and the scientific impartiality of the physiologist and the naturalist. When the facts are established, irrefragable conclusions will follow. It is admitted, that the Scotch and Irish are of the same origin. Both have become subject to the English yoke. Until the sixteenth century, Ireland was much more civilized than Scotland. During the first part of the middle ages, Ireland was a focus of civilization, while Scotland was still a den of barbarians. Since the Scotch have embraced the Reformation, they have outrun even the English. . . . Ireland, on the other hand, devoted to Ultramontanism, is poor, miserable, agitated by the spirit of rebellion, and seems incapable of raising herself by her own strength."

And he adds, "More than this, in the very same country, Protestant Ulster is wealthy, while Catholic Connaught is wretchedly poor" ("Protestantism and Catholicity in their Bearing upon the Liberty and Prosperity of Nations," by Emile de Laveleye, p. 12). The comparison is so often made, and is put so distinctly by this writer, that, if as I hope to do, I prove it to be stupid and worthless, it may effect more to enlighten my readers on this point, than whole pages of more general reasoning.

With all his professions of treating the question of fact "with scientific impartiality," this writer makes egregious blunders. The Scotch are not of the same origin as the Irish. This is true only of a small portion of the Scottish race, the Highlanders, and the men of the Isles. Again, the races differ in Ulster and Connaught. In Connaught, we have the descendants of an early Celtic nation; in Ulster, a colony of English and Lowland Scotch. So much for scientific accuracy.

But mistakes like these do not affect the question very much. The causes of the prosperity of Scotland, and the want of prosperity in Ireland, are to be sought in the history of the two countries.

They are thus clearly put by a writer in the *Dublin Review*: "Scotland has been eminently fortunate. She was united with England on equal terms; she preserved her own laws, her own courts, her own local institutions. Her manufacturers competed on equal terms with the English trader; the capital of the richer country was placed freely at her disposal; under her own free laws, her educational system was steadily developed; finally there were no wholesale confiscations of land;

there was no alien colony, no laws passed in the interest of a minority; no state Church established in the interest of a few.

"On the other hand, all the miseries that Scotland escaped, were inflicted on Ireland; of all the advantages that Scotland possessed, Ireland was deliberately and systematically deprived. The English rule was firmly established in Ireland, by the wars of the Tudors; and from the outset, she was governed in the interests of the English Colony. Repeated confiscations ruined the native proprietor, and placed the land of the country in the hands of men who were really foreigners, who spoke not a word of the Irish language, who professed a strange Religion, who, in a word, were an armed garrison, holding Ireland in their own interest. The faith of Ireland was proscribed, and those who held that faith were systematically plundered and persecuted. More than once, they took up arms against this intolerable tyranny, only to be defeated and placed more completely in the power of their Protestant rulers. Their schools were destroyed, the laws were directed as much against the Catholic schoolmaster as the Catholic priest. Their trade was destroyed by laws for the protection of English commerce and English manufactures. An Irishman and a Catholic could not have his children educated in his own country; could only practise his Religion by stealth; could not aspire to any civil or military dignity; could not even have a horse worth more than five pounds in his possession."

There is not a word stated here that cannot be vouched for by English writers who are by no means favorable to Ireland.

Even Mr. Froude's "English in Ireland" will furnish ample evidence, that the worst forms of protection were used to destroy Irish, to the advantage of English trade. Lord Brougham said of the penal code, under which the fathers of the present generation groaned, "It was so ingeniously contrived, that an Irish Catholic could not lift up his hand, without breaking it." Well did Edmund Burke denounce it, as "the most proper machine ever invented by the wit of man to disgrace a realm and degrade a people ?"

Who that knows these facts will attribute the difference between Scotland and Ireland to Religion ? In one sense it is true no doubt, that Religion was the chief cause of Ireland's suffering. The people might have escaped at least the worst of this terrible persecution, had they chosen to purchase immunity from cruel wrong by shameful apostacy. But they preferred to be poor with Christ, rather than to serve Mammon. This is the true reason, that, while Scotland flourished under the smiles of her all-powerful rulers, Ireland became poor and wretched under their hatred and their frown.

The comparison between Ulster and Connaught is most misleading, as far as wealth is concerned. Connaught is naturally a wilderness of bog and mountain, when compared to fertile Ulster. Place the most industrious race on earth in Connaught, and a far inferior people in Ulster, and the latter would, even in a few years, be wealthier and more prosperous in every respect.

People who, like M. de Laveleye, desire to work out pet theories, find it convenient to ignore whatever tells against them. Every reader of history knows what is meant by the expression "to Hell or Connaught." It was the war-cry, but I can hardly call it that, when the defenceless were hunted down like wild beasts: it was the exultant yell of the greedy followers of the pious

Cromwell, borrowed it is said from him, in Ireland, when, after driving out of the country eighty thousand Catholic Irishmen, to be shipped like cattle, and sold as slaves in Barbadoes, the miserable remnant of the five-sixths of the Catholics who had perished, were driven beyond the Shannon into Connaught, there to die of hunger, or survive as they best might, in the wild wastes of this most desolate part of Ireland. When these things are conveniently forgotten, one may venture to say, in spite of the difference of the means of acquiring wealth in the two provinces; Ulster is rich because it is Protestant, and the West of Ireland, poor, because it is Catholic.

"But," it will be said, "look to Switzerland, and there you will find, amongst the very same people, with the same history, and the same country, the most striking difference between the Protestant and Catholic cantons. Here it is not the theory of a light-brained French observer that is to guide us, but the testimony of one thoroughly acquainted with the subject—Mr. Hepworth Dixon."

Mr. Dixon, in his book on Switzerland, tells us that in the very same canton, the canton of Appenzell, the Protestants are industrious and rich, while the Catholics are lazy, poor, ignorant, living in scattered huts, meeting only at Mass, or at their popular sports.

But what are the facts? This canton of Appenzell is divided into the two districts of Inner Rhoden, inhabited by 11,900 Catholics, and Ausser Rhoden, which has a population of 46,726 Protestants. The towns and villages of Ausser Rhoden stand in a fertile low-lying district, while the Catholics of the other district, which is mountainous and unfit for cultivation, are a scattered race of shepherds. M. de Haulleville, who gives us this information, went to the spot, and carefully ascertained the causes of this difference, which has been quoted with conscious triumph, by every tourist who hates the old Church. (*De l'Avenir des Peuples Catholiques*, par le Baron de Haulleville.)

The whole argument, attempting to prove the excellence of Religion by the worldly prosperity of the people professing it, is not only unchristian, but utterly fallacious. If the thrift and industry of the Scotch are due to Protestantism, to what shall we ascribe the enterprise and commerce of the Catholic republics of Venice and Genoa, during the middle ages, before Protestantism was dreamt of?

This is the way in which the point is put by the learned Bishop Spalding, and he presses it thus—" If England's wealth to-day comes from the Reformation, how shall we account for that of Spain in the sixteenth and seventeenth centuries? And if the decline of Spain has been brought about by the Catholic faith, to what cause shall we assign that of Holland, who in the seventeenth century ruled the seas, and did the carrying trade of Europe?"

I remember once hearing a very pious Protestant who had, after spending the greater part of his life in the Colony, paid a short visit to England. He was of course eloquent "in season and out of season," in prayer-meeting, and at the corners of the streets in Grahamstown, on the piety and morality of "the dear little island;" but words failed him, when he attempted to describe her worldly prosperity, the fruit, he said, of her thoroughly Protestant enlightenment and consequent spirit of progress. "England," he used to falter out, is "the—the workshop of the world."

Had he extended his travels beyond the Atlantic, he

might have learned that, in America, where most of the quondam Protestant portion of the population, tired of hearing the praises of "the pure and blessed Reformation," and not finding anything particularly wonderful in it to suit their matter-of-fact notions, have abandoned it for open Infidelity, these people have their workshops too, and possess all the thrift and industry and energy and daring, supposed by the congregation to which this old gentleman belonged, to be the exclusive property of the righteous and the elect.

Thank goodness, all Colonial home-travellers are not of this stamp. I have met with several, who, instead of fanning their devotion to Protestantism and their own particular sect, with the airs of insular conceit, have extended their rambles to the Continent of Europe, and have learned to respect the Catholic people, they were taught to despise. They had their wits about them, and were glad "to pick up notions," wherever they found them.

Such as these have much to say to their friends in the Colony about grand Churches, and Cathedrals, and picture-galleries, and museums, and arts and manufactures, and people gentle and polished in their manners, and refinement and politeness under the rough "blouse;" and other things of the kind, not before "dreamt of in their philosophy."

Foreign travel, in these cases, is not without its value: it expands the mind and enlarges the heart, and disposes men to believe that, after all they have heard to the prejudice of Catholics, there may be something really good, and worth knowing, beyond the narrow compass of their own particular place of worship. They soon learn that there are other matters too, to be learned in the highways of life beyond the shop-keeping and trading Philosophy —that "time is money," and "knowledge is wealth," and all these other "Poor Richard" maxims, which have been dinned into their ears from childhood. There is a lesson to be acquired and one worth retaining, even in a passing visit to the glorious monuments of the ages of Faith.

The grand old Cathedrals, the vast but unpretentious hospitals, and the huge piles consecrated to works of charity, tell of men who believed that there were other treasures to be gained in this life, than mere wealth and riches, which must one day be abandoned. Happy they, who, at the sight of what they might at first be tempted to call prodigality in the Divine honor, begin to reflect, that, after all, we cannot do too much to show reverence and respect to the great Being, who has created us "to know and serve Him here on earth—that we may be happy with Him forever in Heaven."

They cannot fail, under the influence of such thoughts, to respect the motives, and the Religion of those, who make great sacrifices, of what the world most prizes, to testify their ardent love for their merciful Redeemer. And the more they think in this way—the clearer will it appear to them, that worldly prosperity—and luxury, and grand equipages, and gorgeous mansions, and profuse expenditure in the gratification of self—are not certain and positive proofs of the reality and earnestness of the Religion of the people, whose fame for such things is extolled among the nations. Under this outward show of prosperity, the apparent reward of true merit, there are often concealed sins of miserable selfishness, that cry to Heaven for vengeance.

How pregnant with deep meaning is that sublime passage of St. Augustine in "The City of God,"—commencing with the words—"*fecerunt civitates duas amores duo.*" It can scarcely be translated without losing its brilliancy—I can only attempt, feebly to paraphrase it in English. "Two cities have been formed by two different kinds of love,—the earthly city, by the love of self, that reaches even to contempt of God,—the heavenly city, by the love of God, that extends even to contempt of self" (De Civitate Dei, Lib. xiv. c. 17). One that, in a thoughtful mood, amid the rush and roar of the tide of life of wealthy London, recalls the quiet of a continental town, rich in the monuments of the ages of Faith, must make something like the contrast suggested by the words of St. Augustine.

How fallacious is that test of the genuineness of Religion, which is supposed to be found in the prosperity of a people! Apply it to an individual, and can anything equal its absurdity! Sir Gorgius Midas of London is the millionaire of millionaires, therefore he is the most holy of the myriads that throng the vast city!

And is the wealth of a nation an infallible sign of the prosperity of its people? England contains within itself the wealthiest men in the world; are the English people, therefore, the most wealthy? If a few thousand nobles own all its broad acres, while millions grovel in poverty, does this wealth of a few constitute the prosperity of the nation?

"In England," says Bishop Spalding, "the pauper class, compared with the whole population, is as one to twenty-three. In poor Ireland, there is but one pauper to ninety inhabitants. In other words, much as we hear of England's vast superiority in wealth to the sister island, pauperism is four times more common in England than in Ireland."

"But," it is said, "look to the healthy life and vigor of England, and there you will see what sturdy Protestantism has made her,—Protestantism, not so much in itself as a Religion, but as the herald of Free-thought." "The nations subject to Rome," says M. de Lavaleye, "seem stricken with barrenness; they no longer colonize, they have no power of expansion."

Yes, no doubt England is the great colonizer of the day; but is it the national wealth, and her aspirations after Free-thought, that give her this pre-eminence? It is, confessedly, the poverty of the masses in Great Britain, that is filling the emigrant ships, and sending away, yearly, so many thousands from "dear home and country."

"But," continues the objector, "those who are driven out by hard necessity, have in them, thanks to the spirit of freedom, and the right to think for themselves, that comes from the rejection of spiritual bondage, the energy and perseverance which have founded the vast colonial empire of 'Great Britain.'"

But, let it be remembered that the mother country owes much, and by far the greater part of this wide empire, to Catholic enterprise. In the present day, how many of her colonists in Canada, in Australia, Tasmania, New Zealand, and the Cape, are Catholic Irishmen; and in the past, many of her most successful colonies were founded by Catholic France, and fell into the hands of England by the chances of war.

Take Canada for instance, founded by the enterprise and piety of Champlain, and won for England by the valor of Wolfe. The people of Acadia, as painted by Longfellow, thoroughly Catholic in every sense, were not inferior to "the Pilgrim Fathers," of whom we hear so much. Many of the most famous cities of Canada were once humble Catholic mission-stations. The mission-station of Hochelaga, founded by a priest and a few nuns and workmen, in the autumn of 1641, is now the City of Montreal. I quote from the *Dublin Review*.

" The Catholic missionaries have been in the past the pioneers of Catholic colonization, in other places besides Canada. The first white man, who ever looked upon the waters of the Mississippi, was a French Jesuit, the Père Marquette. A few years after, France founded the colony of Louisiana. The colonies of Spain, in the Philippines, belong to the same class. Sir John Bowring has spoken of the Jesuits of the Philippines, as the pioneers and the founders of civilization in the great Eastern Archipelago. India is the chief gem of the Imperial crown of England; but there were days, when only the chance of war decided who should hold it, Protestant England or Catholic France."

Prussia is often pointed to, as a flourishing Protestant country, great in power because of her Protestantism. During the late war with France, it was chiefly the religious feeling that cooled the affection of Englishmen for their faithful allies in the Crimea, and enkindled their sympathy for Prussia. But one-third of the population of Prussia is Catholic; her wealthiest provinces are Catholic. And it must not be forgotten, that Catholic Bavaria, at Woerth, Sedan, and on the battle-fields of the Loire, did much to turn the tide of success against France.

" But look at France, 'the eldest daughter of the Church,' Catholic France, see how she has fallen back in the advance of nations!"

Yes, but is it because she is Catholic? On the contrary, the more she has yielded to the infatuation of Free-thought, the more she has fallen. Let France be again truly Catholic. Let her abjure those silly fancies, which, in the opinion of every one capable of forming a dispassionate judgment on the point, are luring her to destruction, and she will again take her high place in directing the destinies of the world.

But I feel that I have dwelt too long on an objection, which means nothing, when it is thoroughly examined; and has only an apparent force, because it humors the prejudices, and self-love of those who bring it forward. If rapid prosperity, and the accumulation of wealth, are a sign of the true Religion, then the Buddhism of Japan is the true Religion; for where shall we find a nation that has made such wonderful, such rapid, and such substantial progress, in our days, as this empire of Japan?

If it be noticed that I have, in treating this objection, seemed rather to argue with Protestants than unbelievers, the reason is not far to be traced. It is not the mere negative character of Protestantism that is supposed by Free-thinkers to influence the growth of peoples; it is the principle of rebellion against spiritual authority, to which Free-thought owes its existence, that is mainly regarded in this question of material progress.

As Bishop Spalding ably puts it. " The unbelievers make common cause with the Christian sects, against the Catholic Church, because the Church is the only enemy they fear, the only Christian body, which is the faithful and uncompromising guardian of Revelation. They are partial to the sects, because, in their workings, they perceive, as they think, the breaking up and dissolution of the whole Christian system. Protestantism is valuable in their eyes as a stage, in what Herbert Spencer calls 'the universal religious thaw,' which is going on around us" ("Influence of Catholicism and Protestantism on National Prosperity," Spalding's Essays, p. 156).

There is one point, and it is, in my judgment, the most important of all that should be noticed, when we consider the comparative influence of the two Religions on the material prosperity of nations; Religion is most intimately and necessarily connected with the morality of a people; whether it affects their wealth or not, has no weight whatever, in view of this essential element of true civilization and progress. Wealth and progress are transient, and more properly, the accidental accompaniments of national prosperity; but sound morality and manly character are the very heart's blood of a nation's solid greatness.

I have already quoted, in the first chapter of this book, the remarkable words of M. Jules Simon on this point, but they are worth repeating here. "It is not the loss of a battle, and the annihilation of an army, or a province torn away, that begins the fall of a people: a people dies only by the relaxation of its morals, by abandoning its manly habits, by the effacement of its character through the invasion of egoism and scepticism. It dies of its corruption. It does not die of its wounds."

If we apply statistics to that element of morality which constitutes its very "heart of hearts," the purity of its womanhood and the holiness of the family tie, the contrast between Catholic and Protestant countries, as shown by "facts and figures," is positively startling, in its uniformity.

I know it is said that statistics may be brought forward in favor of any theory. But when they are not confined to particular countries, nor subjected to the influence of special causes, when they are extended to all countries, and tested, year after year, under all the varying conditions of social existence, and are found to be unvaryingly constant, they are a demonstration beyond reasonable dispute.

I mean to apply this delicate test very briefly; but viewed however briefly, they are certainly most remarkable in the evidence they furnish of the superior morality of Catholic countries. Take the data, supplied, by the Registrar-General's returns, of the proportions between legitimate and illegitimate births in England, Ireland, and Scotland, and it will be seen that I am not exaggerating, when I say, that the result is marvellously constant. It is, on an average, about the following.

In England, between five and six in every hundred registered births, (every one knows the sort of births that are registered with most regularity, and where the balance of non-registration will incline). In Scotland, the most Protestant of the three kingdoms, nine per cent, and in Ireland between two and three per cent.

And, as I have compared Ulster with Connaught, in the matter of wealth and prosperity, I test them on the ground of morality as well; and find the same constant result. West of Ireland, one and one third per cent; in Ulster between five and six per cent.

From the tables before me, I might show that the proportion is steadily the same throughout Europe; the countries that are Protestant, showing, in this respect, a remarkably higher average than Catholic countries. Thus in Saxony, and Wurtemberg, the average is about sixteen; while, in Catholic Prussia, it scarcely exceeds six.

It is hard to resist the conclusion, that the Religion of the people is the cause of the discrepancy. In Catholic countries, as in France and Ireland, the most Catholic districts stand best in the statistics. Thus, while the rate for all France is 7.8, the rate for the rural districts, which are all Catholic, is 4.2; for La Vendée, which is remarkable for the earnestness of the Faith of its people, 2.2; and for equally Catholic Brittany, 1.2. In England, the rural districts stand lowest in the scale of morality.

The same holds good in Germany, the Catholic districts are the purest; Catholic Westphalia and Rhineland about 3.5; and Protestant Pomerania and Brandenburg 10 to 12. But for the Infidel corruption of Paris, and some of the chief cities of France, "the eldest daughter of the Church" would still hold a high rank in morality.

I believe this evidence is irresistible, as the rule holds good throughout. Hence I conclude, the impartial reader will infer, that the old Church, protecting now as ever, as far as civil Governments will allow her, the virtue of her children, by rigid and unyielding principles, beyond all other Religions, favors the cause of real healthy Progress.

In the next chapter, I mean to treat of a subject, which has been touched on before, the doctrine of "Exclusive Salvation," which perhaps, more than any other, by misapprehension or misrepresentation, has excited bitter feelings against Catholic Christianity.

CHAPTER XV.

Catholic Christianity and Exclusive Salvation.

IF there be one subject more than another that excites hostility against the Catholic Church, it is her doctrine of "Exclusive Salvation." "The Catholic Church," says its enemies of all creeds or of no creed, "is intolerant. She condemns all who differ from her to eternal destruction. This is a patent fact," they continue, "which cannot be denied or glossed over; and this fact alone proves, beyond doubt, that she forfeits every claim to be the true Church of Christ. If there is anything really and unquestionably good in Revelation, it is the spirit of charity and universal brotherhood, which it professes to announce to mankind. All men are irresistibly drawn to admire this noble principle. It is the heart and soul of natural Religion: it covers, with its splendid mantle, the errors and defects of Paganism; it exalts every belief that adopts it, above the contemptible jarrings and inconsistencies of sectarian animosity. They who worship Nature, in her simple grandeur, aim chiefly at uniting all classes of men, in their reverence and affection, for these charms that win without effort their admiration, and the homage of their hearts. The old idolatry, which cherished only the personification of these charms, knew no restrictions over the feelings of its votaries. Whether they worshipped the bright sun, or the gentle moon, or the deities that were imagined to preside over the beauties of earth, or the fascinations of human passion, it was all the same to this bountiful mistress. Christianity even, outside the Church, soon learned to hate the bitter strife, which sprung from the earnestness and intensity of devotion to particular forms; and sought to harmonize all discordant voices in one hymn of praise to the Author of their salvation. The stern voice of Catholic Christianity alone disturbs this universal tendency; and loudly proclaims, now as ever, that there is no peace, either here or hereafter, for those who refuse to bow down, and adore whatever she is pleased to set up as the object of their reverence and belief."

I admit, without any attempt at defence, this sweeping charge. I say it is quite true. The Church does actually teach, now, as ever since her foundation, that there is but one true Religion, one true Faith, and that out of this Religion, and without this Faith, "it is impossible to please God."

But I go further, and declare my solemn conviction to be, that if this were not her teaching, she should cease to be the Church established by our Divine Lord, "as the pillar and ground of truth." If this be stigmatized as intolerance, nevertheless I maintain it is the essential characteristic of unfailing truth, and of "Charity that never falleth away."

Though the thoughts and feelings of the world have associated all sorts of disagreeable and hateful ideas with this word—intolerance, it is, after all, when properly understood, the great law of being for everything that is fixed and stable in this world.

Take that great law of gravitation, which keeps the vast universe together, which reaches, with mathematical precision, to the uttermost bounds of space, and holds, as far as we can see, all created things within its grasp; is it not intolerant? Will it ever, even in the minutest things of earth, allow its principles to be violated without enforcing the destruction of whatever attempts to defy its government, or to rebel against its power? Watch it in the ordinary ways of life, attempt to build a house, to raise the most pigmy of structures with which childhood would amuse itself, not in defiance of this universal law, nor in contempt of what it teaches, but in simple ignorance of its inexorable rules, and the building of brick, or stone, or mud, or sand, or cards, must inevitably fall to pieces.

Every law has its sanction: and this sanction is, that the violation of the law brings, with its violation, the loss of the benefit, which it is meant to confer. The sanction of the law of gravitation is stability: violate it either knowingly or ignorantly, and there is, in the particular instance, ruin and destruction for the object attempted.

It is the same with all human laws. They are meant to secure the protection of those subject to them. If they are violated, society suffers, by the loss of the security provided for in the case: and the individual, or those who combine unlawfully and attempt to carry the object, forfeit the protection, and incur the punishment of the law that has been outraged. It would in fact be impossible to conceive anything like law in nature, or among men, if there were not necessarily involved, in the very notion, what we call intolerance.

It is just the same with truth. Error is opposed to truth, and destroys the very idea of truth; and therefore, truth is intolerant of error. It is silly, in the presence of acknowledged truth, to speak tolerantly of those follies and fancies, with which men have amused themselves in the days of Paganism, or with which they trifle now, in the attractive ways of sentimental conventionalities. They can afford to differ, without bringing on themselves the consequences of outraged truth, when there is no question whatever of truth in reality, but only of conceits that ape the truth and trifle with the imagination.

The old Romans could afford a place in their temples to the Gods of the conquered nations; because they had, in their impiety, and love of sensuous pleasure, and idolatry of self, wandered far away from the source of all truth, and disported themselves amid the turbid waters, which had escaped from the fountain-head. One little streamlet was as good as another, why then should they trouble themselves with endless disputes, when all agreed that none had exclusive possession of the clear water, which alone could satisfy their wants?

If we apply these principles to Religion, it will be evident, that a Religion which is not intolerant, in the sense I have explained, will be no Religion at all. For what is the meaning of Religion, even in its widest extent? Is it not the means by which, the relations, which should exist between the Creator and the creature, are maintained?

Before the advent of Christianity, as taught by our Divine Lord, all thoughtful men knew well, and felt, in their own experience, that these relations had been disturbed, and interrupted. Religion alone could re-establish them.

The most hopeful sign in fallen humanity, before the coming of the true light, was the continual groping in darkness, after these broken and lost links in the great chain of existence, between contingent beings and the centre of their existence. More hopeful still were the precious things that were offered in sacrifice to the source of life, conceived either in its unity or in its manifold attributes, as one God, or as many, in the expectation fondly cherished, that a time would come at last, when, in the dawn of the long-wished-for light, the missing links might be found, and men might be again united with the great Author of their existence.

This is clearly the simplest notion that can be given of Religion. Either there is such a thing in the world, or there is not. If there is not, if man must despair of ever finding a means whereby he may be united to his Maker; then there is no use in discussing what are the necessary and essential qualities of Religion. If there is, it would be worse than absurd to admit in this Religion, a property that is necessarily destructive of its very essence. If it be the way of bringing us to God, then it cannot, at the same time, lead us away from God. The right way cannot be the wrong way. Therefore, from the very nature of the case, true Religion must be exclusive and intolerant.

I do not, of course, mean to say that it must persecute, or punish those who will not submit to its guidance: but it must be intolerant in this sense, that, once it believes itself, beyond all doubt, to be the way that leads to God, it must, as far as it can, point out the misleading characters of every way that diverges from it.

If men can be saved without Religion, or reach God, and the end of their being without any way to guide them, then one Religion is as useless as another; and we may fall back on the nothingness of Atheism and Impiety, as far as any creed or form of worship is concerned.

To adopt the system approved of by the professors of the " new theology," we should, as far as any Religion in the true sense is concerned, give ourselves no concern whatever about it. The simple and the easy way to go through life, is, in this hypothesis, to make the most of this world, while we are in it, and as regards the life to come, to lie down comfortably, on the day of rest, and smoke a quiet pipe, as we gaze listlessly on the bright skies above us, and dream of bliss, as we are borne on imperceptibly to eternity.

I have seen this *dolce far niente* notion of Religion inculcated in some book of the Leyden school, which I was told was largely read on the Frontier. And, though its easy-going thoroughness may provoke a smile, it is, after all, the only reasonable outcome of the fashionable theory, that one Religion is as good as another: and that, without giving ourselves any trouble to find out the right way that leads to God, we may take any path, which the accident of birth, or nationality, or fortune, throws in our way.

I can easily understand that men, who fancy they do not believe in a personal God, and do not consequently trouble themselves with misgivings about the account they are to render after death, or who adopt "the bag of bones" theory—may satisfy their frivolous thoughts about Religion with this notion. But it would seem incredible, if it were not the fact, that Christians could possibly reconcile their consciences to this happy-go-lucky plan of action for securing "the one thing necessary."

There are very many outside the Catholic Church, indeed I might say the majority of those who have no dogmatic faith, and no fixed rule of morality, who affect to reason thus. "All Christians believe that we cannot come to God except through Jesus Christ. We all believe in our Divine Saviour. It may be that one way of realizing the fruits of Redemption is shorter, and more direct than another; but all the highways and by-ways, offered by different forms of Religion, lead to the same goal; and please God, we shall all, Christians of every denomination, and perhaps even Roman Catholics, meet in Heaven."

What seems to give this theory of salvation a peculiar charm, is that it looks large, and open to every one, and has no crooked and sharp ugly twists of intolerance about it.

But this is not Religion, even in its plain and obvious sense; roads that lead in contrary directions, and cross each other at right angles, cannot possibly lead to the one point. Christ has said "I am the way and the truth, and the life;" "No man cometh to the Father but by me" (John xiv. 6). As the pious author of the "Imitation" says on this passage "*sine via non itur, sine veritate non cognoscitur, sine vita non vivitur*"—without *the way*, there is no going; without *the truth*, there is no knowing; without *the life*, there is no living (Imitation, Chap. lvi. Book iii.). Separated as we are from God by the fall, we require a certain way that will lead to Him; a revelation of His truth to know Him, and a participation of the Divine life or Divine Grace, to enable us to profit by this truth, and to sustain us on the long and narrow way, "that leadeth to life" (Matt. vii. 14).

Above all, we require a determined and fixed path, which does not insensibly lead into others, and which always is the right path, and not the wrong one.

To say that one Religion is as good as another, and that the thousand different ways, on which Christians of different denominations are tramping, will all lead to the one eternal life, is the same thing as to say, that all Religions are useless. In this system of general and absolute toleration, which supposes that a man will be saved, whether he turns to the right or to the left, whether he goes forward, or gradually inclines to one side, until he turns his back on the object towards which he meant to travel, all Religion, as a road to God, is completely effaced.

However confidently "the liberal-minded" Protestant may imagine that he has, by this self-destructive system of Religion, shut out from his belief, the notion of anything like intolerance, he has by no means got rid of it. It haunts him, like the ghost of the Religion he has murdered. He must still, unless he has renounced Christianity altogether, maintain, as rigidly as the most exclusive Catholic, that without Jesus Christ, there is no salvation.

Even the Deist too, must be exclusive and intolerant; for unless he holds firmly that natural Religion and the belief in a personal God is necessary to salvation, he would cease to be a Deist. It is a remarkable fact, that Deists join heartily with Protestants, in this extravagant charge of cruel and uncharitable exclusiveness, against the Catholic Church: for it proves conclusively that neither one nor the other, if they believe at all in these principles of general toleration, have anything to distinguish their belief from the nothingness of Atheism. If Atheism is tolerant of all beliefs, it is at least consistent. It is blank nothing in itself; and cannot therefore destroy what never had any real existence.

When will Christians clearly understand that belief in Christ necessarily involves faith in Him, as the *only* way, the *only* truth, the *only* life that leads to life eternal: and if it be said by our Divine Lord, "This is life everlasting, that they may know Thee, the only true God, and Jesus Christ whom Thou hast sent" (John xvii. 3), this knowledge necessarily includes the belief in *all things* He has taught. " Go," He said to His Apostles, "and teach all nations, teaching them to observe all things whatsoever I have commanded you" (Matt. xxviii. 19, 20).

I know it is said, that intolerance of any kind is opposed to human liberty.

But it might as well be argued, that the intolerance of the civil law, which as the embodiment of the natural law, is the very basis of human liberty, is destructive of this liberty. For what is the very essence of this civil liberty ? It is the power which it gives to every member of the community, of doing what he has a right to do. But if this civil law is not inflexible and intolerant, what becomes of this right ? If the civil law is not supreme over all, it is a nullity. If even the ruler of a state, or his representatives, may twist the law at their caprice, there is an end of anything like individual right.

So it would be with the Church, if it were not firm and unyielding, in the maintenance of the conditions of salvation. If Faith in all the doctrines of Christ be necessary to salvation, then all who desire to be saved, must believe, either explicitly or implicitly, these doctrines. If the moral law established by the Founder of the Church is to bind, it must bind all who are capable of obedience. There cannot be one sort of morality for this class, and another for another. The Church, in other words, must be intolerant, or she will forfeit her Divine right to rule us, and make a mockery of our liberties.

The more inflexible she is, in preaching and teaching what is right and true—for it must be understood that, in speaking of intolerance all along, I am contending only for the intolerance of truth and right—the more faithfully and successfully will she protect her children, from the tyranny of error and immorality. This is the meaning of the words of our Divine Lord, addressed to those He calls " His disciples indeed," " You shall know the truth, and the truth shall make you free" (John viii. 32).

Here is a notion of true liberty, in the eloquent words of Cardinal Manning. "Liberty is not license; liberty is not the freedom of madmen; liberty is not the power to do wrong, nor to believe falsehood, nor to err out of the way of justice. Liberty means redemption from sin, from falsehood, from human teachers who may err, and therefore can mislead. It is redemption from all spiritual tyranny of man over man, with all his faculties, his intellect, his heart, his will, his affections; it is redemption of the soul in all its actions towards God, in its obedience, in its faith, in its adoration of the Divine authority of Jesus Christ, who has purchased us with His Precious Blood, and has folded us within a Unity where falsehood cannot enter, under the Divine guidance of a Teacher who can never err. Such is true liberty, and there is no other" ("Temporal Glory of the Sacred Heart," Card. Manning, p. 177).

I have thought it necessary to say so much on the principle of dogmatic or spiritual intolerance, because the subject is so overclouded by the prejudices of unbelief, and a false Christianity; that, without this explanation, the practical doctrine of " Exclusive Salvation" would be misunderstood even by many Catholics.

I come now to the point directly, which excites so much odium against Catholic Christianity, and to bring it out more clearly and distinctly, I will put it before my readers, somewhat in the form of question and answer.

Is it a dogma of the Catholic Church that, outside her pale, there is no salvation ?—I answer distinctly—yes : the Catholic Church believes herself to be the true Church of Christ, and she would stultify herself if she did not maintain now, as she has done all days since her foundation, that those who do not belong to this true Church, cannot possibly expect salvation. The principles already laid down, necessarily, as all intelligent minds can see, lead to this conclusion.

I will put the question more strongly, that there may be no misunderstanding on the point. I will suppose it said to me, Do you believe that none but members of the Roman Catholic Church will be saved ? I answer, If by the Roman Catholic Church you mean, as you ought to mean, the universal Church spread throughout the world, and recognizing the Pope of Rome, as the successor of St. Peter, and the visible representative of Christ, I believe, that none but the members of this Church can expect salvation.

I suppose the question pressed still farther. Do you believe that only those who are known as Roman Catholics, or who are externally united to this body by belief and profession, will obtain salvation ?—I answer, I believe nothing of the kind. As there are many who call themselves Roman Catholics, and are generally regarded as such, who by their disobedience to the Church, by their want of Faith, and immoral conduct, will be lost eternally; so there are many, very many, who, though not united to the Roman Catholic Church, by any external bond of union, are, by their Baptism, their sincere love for God, their earnest desire to know the truth, and their determination to embrace it, when known, at every sacrifice of worldly things,—really members of this true Church. These I believe, if they lead blameless lives, or repent sincerely of their sins, and look for pardon, through the merits of Jesus Christ, will be saved.

But suppose, it may be said, they were not baptized by a Roman Catholic priest, will this prevent their salvation? I answer—no: if they have been duly baptized by any one, a Catholic layman or woman, or a Protestant minister, or a Protestant man not a minister, or a Protestant woman, or even by a Jew, or an Infidel, who, pouring water on the head of the person to be baptized, said at the same time, "I baptize thee in the name of the Father, and of the Son, and of the Holy Ghost," meaning seriously to perform a rite, considered necessary for salvation by the Catholic Church, that baptism is valid. They who are baptized in this way, are made members of the true Church of Christ.

Here I cannot help remarking that the expression "the Church of my baptism" has no meaning whatever, if the Church so referred to, is not the true Church of Christ. It could have no meaning, for Christians who understand the plain signification of the words "One Lord, one Faith, one Baptism" (Ephes. iv. 5).

But suppose there was no Baptism at all? Then the unfortunate individual "could not enter into the Kingdom of God" (John iii. 5). This is of Faith, and cannot be denied without heresy. Only two cases are admitted by the Catholic Church, in which actual Baptism with water is not absolutely necessary to salvation. The Baptism of blood, where one dies a martyr; and the Baptism of desire, where one desires to receive the holy rite, and there is no one near to confer it.

But my supposed questioner, will say, Do you believe that the vast number of persons who have not received Baptism, innocent children, natives of a country not Christian, and millions of others, for some cause or other not baptized, are condemned to eternal torments? I answer, It is of Faith that they cannot enjoy the beatific vision, merited for us by Christ's death, unless they receive actual Baptism of water, or the Baptism of desire, or die for Christ's sake.

I may here mention, a fact known to most Christians, that, in the early days of persecution, many Pagan soldiers, struck by the admirable constancy of the Christian martyrs, or the supernatural signs of Divine approval, so often manifested at their martyrdom, voluntarily offered their lives in testimony of their entire faith in the God of the Christians.

As regards infants, not baptized with water, they are of course incapable of the Baptism of desire; they cannot therefore enter into the Kingdom of God. But, as St. Augustine teaches, and as every Catholic may believe, the fate of these children in the next life is such a one, that it cannot be said of them—"it were better they were never born." We may believe, that, although they can never see the face of God, immortality is in their case a positive boon compared with non-existence.

With regard to the natives of a country not Christian, who have perhaps never heard of Christ or Baptism, if they live according to the law of nature, and are faithful to the common and sufficient grace given to all men, which, as I said, in the chapter on Grace, is most probably the gift of prayer, they by the implicit desire of Baptism, may obtain admittance into the kingdom of

God. Such is the more sound and common opinion of Theologians.

As the learned Bourdaloue says: "It is well known that a pagan, to whom the law of Jesus Christ has never been announced, will not be judged by this law; and that God, Sovereign Master as He is of all things, will observe with him this natural equity, and not condemn him on account of a law which He has never made known to him. This is the doctrine which St. Paul announces in formal terms, when he says, 'Whosoever have sinned without the law, shall perish without the law'" (Rom. ii. 12).

I will propose another question, which will be the last in this delicate matter. What will be the fate, according to Catholic doctrine, of those Christians, who having broken away from the Church by heresy and schism, die in their errors?

The answer is simple, they who wilfully separate from the true Church, and die actually separated from her communion, cannot expect salvation. Their crime is a great one. It is classed by St. Paul with the most grievous sins, with "the works of the flesh, fornication, uncleanness, immodesty, luxury, and idolatry, and even, murder." They who make dissensions and sects . . . "shall not obtain the kingdom of God" (Gal. v. 19, 21). Obstinate heretics are those who refuse to hear the Church; and our Divine Lord said in reference to them, "If such a one will not hear the Church, let him be to thee as the heathen and the publican" (Matt. xviii. 17).

But it must be remembered, that there is a vast difference between those who, by their own act separate from the Church, and obstinately refuse to obey her voice, and those who have the misfortune to be born in a false communion. If through want of diligent inquiry, when they are doubtful of their position; if through attachment to the world, or place in society, or friends, or their own worldly interests, they give themselves no concern about the conditions of salvation; if, in a word, they love even those dearest to them according to the flesh, more than Jesus Christ, they are, according to the express words of our Divine Lord, undeserving of the glory He has merited for us. "He that loveth father or mother more than me; and he that loveth son or daughter more than me, is not worthy of me" (Matt. x. 37).

There is no greater enemy to the attainment of truth than indifference. If a man will say to himself, "Differences of creed do not concern me. I do not want to be better than my parents. What was good enough for them, is good enough for me. I believe that they served God faithfully according to their lights, and died in peace with Him. I desire no more. Far be it from me to say that they are lost. If I changed my Religion, I would pronounce, by this act, their condemnation."

All such sentiments are directly opposed to the Christian maxim of individual responsibility. "Every one of us shall render account for himself to God" (Rom. xiv. 12). Those whom men most reverence may have erred through no fault of theirs, and so escape blame before God. Their involuntary error will however not excuse others who have found reason to doubt the security of their own position.

Even saints have erred. St. Cyprian maintained an opinion, which was afterwards condemned by the voice of the universal Church. He might have been altogether innocent; but after the decision of the Church, those who, for reverence for his virtues, clung to his error, were justly regarded as heretics. This led the celebrated Vincent of Lerins to say, "*Absolvuntur magistri, condemnantur discipuli*"—"The masters are absolved, and the disciples are condemned" (Vincent Lerin, Commonitor, cap. vi.).

One thing is quite certain, and it should be answer enough to all these miserable subterfuges by which men, careless about "the one thing necessary," seek to justify supreme indifference about their eternal destiny, and at the same time it vindicates from all reproach, the doctrine of the Church on "Exclusive Salvation." "God will render to every one according to his works" (Matt. xvi. 27), and will take account only of our *voluntary* transgressions.

There may be many brought up in false doctrine, and filled with the strongest prejudices against the Catholic Church,—prejudices so inveterate and deep-seated, that they would rather doubt their own existence than call them into question. I have myself spoken with many converts, now earnest and holy priests, and they assured me that, until the light of Faith, through God's infinite mercy, beamed on their troubled souls, they conscientiously believed, that it would have been a crime in them to have looked towards the Roman Catholic Church, for help in their distress; so deeply did they consider her sunk in corruption. They who have read Cardinal Newman's "Apologia" and seen how long even his giant mind was held in bondage by the belief that the Pope was Antichrist, can understand fully the slavery of prejudice.

For a considerable time, it may be, the ignorance of men of this class, who are led astray from the main point by questions of captious criticism, may be, and probably is, invincible : but the moment the great grace came and their eyes were opened, they sacrificed all worldly prospects, and severed the closest ties that bound them to the Church of their fathers, and friends dear as life, to join "the one fold," to which all must be brought who earnestly seek their eternal salvation (John x. 16).

There may be very many earnest Christians, who never receive so great a grace as this, and who live and die in invincible ignorance. They would willingly lay down their lives for Christ's sake. They hate sin, because it displeases God; and they pray fervently for light and strength to do His holy will. Such as these belong, as St. Augustine says, to the soul of the true Church, though not externally united to it. They will be saved, we may believe, even though it required a miracle of Divine mercy to enable them to fulfil the necessary conditions for salvation. They may be saved in this way, and at the same time the proposition be perfectly true, and a dogma of Catholic Faith, that out of the true Church there is no salvation.

It is not invincible ignorance that saves them, for this is only a valid excuse for an involuntary fault; but the grace of Baptism, and the habit of Divine Faith, infused by this sacrament, their firm belief in all the doctrines of Christ, that, humanly speaking, it was possible for them to know, and their earnest desire to do the will of God in all things. Invincible ignorance will not heal the wounds inflicted on their souls by sin; but sorrow for the love of God, a firm purpose of amendment, and hope in the infinite merits of the Redeemer. Such as these are not heretics or schismatics; they are real members of the one true Church.

The eloquent and large-hearted Lacordaire has said of these—" Her children (the Church's) they are, although she knows them not; for they have been born in her womb, and still live in her substance, as they have sprung from her fecundity."

This is the teaching of St. Augustine. "We must not place in the class of heretics," says this great Saint, "even those whose errors are most pernicious, provided they do not defend them obstinately, especially if these errors are not the fruit of their own presumption, and their own rashness; but rather inherited from the misfortune of their fathers, who allowed themselves to be led astray, and who earnestly seek after truth, and are prepared to abandon their errors, as soon as they perceive them" (St. Augustine, Letter xliii. to Galarius).

If I were asked to be more definite, and to point out those who are in good faith, and in a state of invincible ignorance, whether they are numerous, whether such and such persons, who, as far as their friends could see, died in a belief different from the Catholic Church, are lost, I would say, as every well-instructed Catholic must say, I know nothing about the fate of individuals. It is God alone who sees the secret of hearts. No one can tell what passes, at the last moment, between the soul and God. That cry to God for mercy, which He has made the instinctive impulse of suffering human nature, when all other hope has faded away; and which can spring from the heart, when the power of speech is gone, may change the eternal destiny of the expiring creature. It is certain that judgment belongs to God alone; and that we dare not say, of any one, though his whole life may have been polluted with sin, that he is lost for all eternity. "Who art thou that judgest another man's servant? to his own master he standeth or falleth; and he shall stand: for God is able to make him stand" (Rom. xiv. 4).

It is the duty of the Church to proclaim concerning the law of salvation—there is but one true Faith, as there is but one Lord, and one Baptism; and without this true Faith, "it is impossible to please God:" "He that believeth not shall be condemned." If the world regards this as a hard saying, it should remember, that it is not the word of man, but the sovereign decree of Him, through whose Infinite mercy alone, we can hope for eternal life.

In the next chapter, and before I say something about the various "isms," that amuse the fancy of the present generation, I mean to set forth briefly the principles, on which Catholic Christianity combats the objections so flippantly urged by Infidelity against the facts recorded in the Old Testament.

CHAPTER XVI.

Catholic Christianity and the Alleged Errors of the Sacred Scriptures.

IT is obvious that, in one short chapter, little can be said in reply to the numerous objections, which unbelief has at all times urged against the sacred books of the Old and New Testament. Still, I believe, it will not be difficult to point out the principles, on which simple Faith can rest securely, in encountering all these assaults of error.

As I have already said, in the commencement of this book, most of the infidel objections are of very early date in the history of Catholic Christianity; those of the present day differing from the old objections of Julian, Celsus, Porphyry and the Pagan Philosophers, only in this, that they are either decked out in a new dress, likely to catch the fancy, and excite the amusement of this frivolous age; or supported by arguments derived from scientific progress, and unknown to the early Christian apologists.

Ridicule is no doubt a potent weapon against any truth, that is disagreeable to human nature, and which by its solemn and venerable aspect, rather than its solid grounds of persuasion, appeals to our respect. When the Divine wisdom, incarnate in the person of our Redeemer, was dressed in the garb of a fool, even the majesty of His patient silence, and His sublime meekness, produced little effect on the courtiers of the proud monarch, who, out of vain curiosity, asked for a sign of Almighty power, only that he might, in his fancied superior wisdom, deride the folly of the multitudes who believed in "the contemptible Nazarene."

"See," exclaim the leaders of Progress, "how little these Fathers, so long respected for their learning by the ignorant crowds of the dark ages, knew of the true nature of 'signs and wonders,' who would have bowed down and worshipped a steam-engine, and beheld angelic spirits at work in the ordinary operations of our telegraphs and telephones, and the various applications of electricity."

I wonder if these eagles of physical science, who plume themselves on the triumphs of patient, plodding, inventive industry, and soar aloft, in the conceit that they are the rulers of nature, ever think that, when they exultingly point to the material progress of these latter times, and regard themselves as the Gods of creation, that the great master-minds of past ages would only smile in pity, were they to witness the vast importance attached, by men created for eternity, to these trifles. How they would wonder—these giant intellects, who dared to fix their penetrating glance on the bright sun of the Divine nature, and to solve the problems of Eternal life, at the indifference which now prevails for the investigation of these grand subjects which absorbed their own life-long reverence and love!

There is a thought that naturally strikes me here, and it will be a good introduction to my subject. One of the main objections to the first pages of Revelation, a very favorite one too, as it is supposed, in a special manner to elevate "Humanity" to its proper throne, as the Divinity of the cultured races, and the supreme ruler of Nature and her laws, is the short period allowed, by the Mosaic narrative, to the existence of man upon this earth.

If the long days of creation, involving perhaps myriads of years, in the development of the works assigned, by the inspired writer, to each of these periods, passed slowly along, uncontrolled by Humanity, what became of the Idol all this time? The bare notion that man, "The lord and sovereign master," was a mere nothing, not yet even conceived in the womb of time, while his slaves, in the shape of the huge Behemoths and Leviathans, disported their happy lives away, is too humiliating to be endured. Therefore the various ologies, the creations of modern progress, are turned from their legitimate scope—and pressed into the service of the offended "Deity." Theories are heaped on theories, to establish, the much desired, and satisfactory deduction, that man was in his proper sphere, as Lord of the creation, whole ages, perhaps millions of years, before he is introduced into this world by the writer of the Pentateuch.

Suppose we make a great effort to reconcile the numerous conflicting systems of Geologists, each of whom was of course far superior to Moses, and satisfied with the poor amount of evidence, that is evolved from this mill of learning, not excluding even "the fossilized human skeleton," which some Geologists have the unkindness to say was manufactured, by an enterprising American, we admit this great antiquity of the pre-Adamite man, what would follow?

Let us reason on the sound principles of analogical philosophy, whatever we may think of the Geological "facts," for mere theorizing is not reasoning, and what should be our conclusion?

Granted that man did live on this earth, and, from some secure cave, looked out on the gambols of the Ichthyosaurus, and his brother saurians of every degree, a much hardier individual, by the way, than any of the *genus homo* of degenerate historic times, one who could luxuriate in cataracts of boiling water, and exult in the music of those stupendous convulsions, the bare traces of which fill us with terror,—what then? Unless his mind were dwarfed, in proportion to the development of his physical powers, he too must, on all sound principles of reasoning, have progressed marvellously in these almost infinite periods of existence. What is there in human nature that should have so contracted its powers of observation and experience, as absolutely to have rendered progress impossible, in these prehistoric ages? These triumphs of modern civilization, steam, electricity, magnetism, and all these things of which we are so proud, should, in the natural course of things, have been discovered long ago. If half a century can, in these times, change the face of the earth, and the ways and habits of its people, what immense progress should have been made in these thousands, and tens of thousands of years, when men, real men like us, intelligent beings, lived and toiled upon this earth! Yet there is not the smallest vestige of their labors.

I can easily fancy to myself the amusement of some bright philosopher of progress, whose eye may be caught by this argument, as he positively revels in the enjoyment of my ignorance—" Look," he will exclaim, " was there ever such nonsense penned before? Here is one writing something, which he expects will be read by people of ordinary intelligence, and he seems to know absolutely nothing of the grand discovery of the age— Evolution. Evolution explains at once all this difficulty. You know," he continues, addressing himself to some disciple, who has shared his mirth, "the men of these early times were not properly speaking men at all: they were human beings only in the germ, mere animated cells, or later on, shell-fish, or swimming fish, and then fish without tails, whose fins were being gradually developed into arms and legs and feet, as they fed on the slimy shores of lakes and rivers, or in fact were proximately connected with the present species, in the form of apes and baboons, or what not."

The fatal answer however to these extravagant theories, which remind us of the words of St. Paul, applied by the Apostle to the dreamers of his day—"senseless men!" (1 Cor. xv. 36,) is to be found in the fact that, in no stratum of the earth, has there been found, the fossilized remains of a creature marking, in its formation, this transition. Any one possessed of a glowing imagination may easily theorize; but the most attractive theories, unsupported by a single fact, vanish, in the analysis of waking reason, like "the baseless fabric of a Vision."

Here I would lay down one safe principle, in dealing with these fanciful objections, which have no foundation except in the heated brains that conceive them. Until some fact can be *demonstrated*, as against the teaching recorded in the Bible, it is worse than loss of time, to give it the least serious attention.

Even, at their best, the scientific teachers of irreligion can only excite doubts with regard to any portion of the Scripture narrative. This is the confession of their great oracle, whom I remember designated, in the "Old Religion" tract of Theology, as "*Vaferrimus Bayle*,"—one of those, of whom it is written, "I will catch the wise in their own craftiness" (1 Cor. iii. 19). He says—"Those who live in irreligion do nothing but doubt. They never attain to certainty. Even when they are most agreed, they create, in the minds of their disciples, only doubt. It is clear enough," he continues, "that they who affect in company to combat the most common truths of Religion, say much more about it than they think, Vanity— rather than conviction, enters into their disputations. They imagine that the boldness and singularity of the sentiments they maintain, will secure for them the reputation of great minds" (Dict., tom. i. p. 561).

"Harebrained and worthless men," says De Montaigne, "who strive to be worse than they really are"!

Earnest Christians, when they hear language of the kind, indicated by these writers, should remember, that the holy cause, which is thus stupidly assailed, is sustained by dogmas, and morality, and history, against which nothing can be demonstrated. They should consider, that the admirable life and death of the Author of Christianity is sustained by the Divine wisdom and sanctity of its precepts: and that the authority and sublimity of the Holy Scriptures, the testimony of apostolic men, the blood of millions of martyrs, the accomplishment of numerous prophecies, the overwhelming testimony of miracles incontestably established, in the face of the severest criticism, the tradition of all ages, the conversion of the whole world, in spite of the most fearful persecution, the perpetuity of the Faith, notwithstanding so many heresies and schisms, and the immovable stability of the Catholic Church, in defiance of storms, that have shaken thrones to atoms, and conspiracies and assaults, that would have upheaved any human institution, are proofs beyond all doubt, of the supernatural character and constitution of the work of Christ. When we think of these triumphs over all that is great in human estimation, we can but smile in pity at the daring impudence which fancies that, by sorry jests and ridicule and blatant nonsense, it can destroy "the pillar and ground of truth," against which, we are assured, by the promise of the God-man, not even the powers of Hell shall ever prevail.

The fiercest of these assaults are self-destructive. We have only to marshal the sayings of men of the same camp against each other, or to bring forward the contradictions of the leaders; and, as the hosts of Sennacherib, they melt away like snow, "in the glance of the Lord."

Take for example, the well-known objection of Voltaire against the Pentateuch. It might, regalvanized into life, be put as popularly and as plausibly as if it were advanced by Ingersoll, or any of the voluble and ready speakers, who appeal to an unthinking public, in jauntily-got-up lectures.

"Moses," it is said, "wrote the Pentateuch, wrote it in the wilderness, without pens, ink, or paper, at a time when writing was unknown, and when those, who had the means of perpetuating their thoughts, caused them to be inscribed on pyramids of stone, in hieroglyphics, that offer even to the most learned, the bare substance of some scattered ideas; wrote all the five books, which it would take one so long only to transcribe into modern language! But of course it was a miracle! And we must imagine something superior to modern spiritism, no doubt angelic hands, to supply the writing materials, and to act as his amanuenses."

I am not aware that Ingersoll has ever put this objection. But if he did borrow the thought of Voltaire, as he has borrowed so many similar objections, he would have put it in something of this style, but of course much more smartly.

And what is the answer? It is answered by the objector himself. Voltaire never troubles himself, when he is assailing Religion, about palpable contradictions.

In a book, called "*Dieu et les hommes,*" Voltaire says that a Phœnician author, named Sanchoniaton, lived before the time of Moses; and that this writer admits, that he had derived part of his history from the writings of Thot, who flourished eight hundred years before his time; and Voltaire adds naïvely, "This admission proves that, eight hundred years before the time of Sanchoniaton, there were books written by the aid of the alphabet."

So much for this objection, which is a fair specimen of many others of the same kind. "Some forty years ago, it was still deemed possible for critics of the ultra-sceptical school," says a learned writer in the *Dublin Review*, "to call in question the very existence of the art of writing in the Mosaic age. The adventurous Von Bohlen, laid before his readers, what he was pleased to call, the 'latest results,' which the study of Palæography yielded; and with Vater, and Hartmann, to support him, boldly concluded, that the art was unknown to Moses; and turned the allusions to writing, in the Pentateuch, against us, as anachronisms or 'unfortunate slips' of the author. Mr. Norton, in America, made the same assumption one of the grounds of his own attack.

"Yet to an Egyptologist of the present day, acquainted with still 'later results,' such scepticism can appear only ridiculous."

I happen to have in the diocesan library here, in Grahamstown, the celebrated work of Dr. Smith on the Book of Moses, and there, note most interesting particulars, that should cover with shame, any Infidel writer daring to make such unfounded assertions.

Dr. Smith shows that the process of writing is pictorially represented on a rock tomb of the Fourth Dynasty (Moses lived in the Nineteenth Dynasty), accompanied with the constantly recurring hieroglyph for writing, the combination of reed-pen, water vase, and palette. In a papyrus of the time of Moses, Anastasi No. 1, we have the names of nine writers then distinguished in theology, philosophy, history, and poetry. At the same period, we find proofs that there was a writer of books among the Kheta, in Northern Palestine.

"But the most striking proof of the antiquity of writing is found," Dr. Smith tells us, "in the fact that Semetic characters, signifying *write, book, ink*, are common to the Semetic people in prehistoric times, before they broke up into separate nationalities, as Chaldees, Syrians, Hebrews, Phœnicians, Arabs, or Ethiopians."

But how few care, in these business-loving times, to study a subject of this kind! It is a *terra incognita*, even for fairly educated people; and hence there is little fear of being "brought to book," if a popular lecturer is disposed to indulge his playful fancy, in daring attacks, on the Veracity, or Authenticity of the sacred books.

It was argued by Voltaire, that no such person as Moses ever existed, pretty much in the same way, but not with the same ability and cleverness, as, in later times, Archbishop Whately undertook to prove that there never existed the man called Napoleon Bonaparte.

This would be amusing, if it did no mischief; but there is so little taste for serious reading on points of this kind, and so great a rage for any theory that is new and startling, that if a lecturer, even in the presence of a numerous and select audience, prefaces the boldest assertions against the inspiration or truth of the Sacred

Scriptures, with such words as, "It is now well known," or "It is now admitted by all scholars," or "It cannot be denied," few will be found to question, or perhaps doubt, what is so confidently stated.

I will here lay down another principle, which will be a safe guide for all Catholics, and for all Christians who venerate "the Word of God." It is the principle of the great St. Augustine—"*Ego vero Evangelis non crederem nisi me commoveret Ecclesiæ auctoritas.*" " I would not believe in the Gospel itself, unless I was moved thereto by the authority of the Church."

It may seem strange that I should venture to recommend this principle to non-Catholics. But the days are gone by, when "the testimony of the Spirit in the soul of the reader" and " the inner witness of the Spirit," and such like pious expressions, carry conviction to the minds of those who hear or read what Biblical criticism has to say about the authorship, or the authenticity of the sacred Books.

As Mallock puts it—" The Church's primary doctrine is her own perpetual infallibility. She is inspired, she declares, by the same Spirit that inspired the Bible; and her voice is, equally with the Bible, the voice of God." Without the infallible authority of the Church, we cannot know, with certainty, what is true Scripture, and what is not; nor catch the hidden inspired meaning that lies under " the letter that killeth." Those who will not hear the Church, may be assured, that a time will surely come, when the bright and cheering prospects of their fondly cherished Faith, and the darling hopes that cheered the weary paths of life, and the glowing love for a God of infinite goodness and mercy, which they gleaned from the pages of the Bible, will vanish from the minds of the rising generation, like a dream, and leave not a rack behind. Sentimental Religion is too delicate a plant to stand the fierce blasts of cold scepticism. Religion must be built on a logical basis, or, in the wrestle of vigorous minds, it will surely be overturned; and there is no other solid foundation than the Rock, indicated by our Divine Lord.

But whatever non-Catholics may think of this, the true Catholic, will, in every temptation to his faith, raised up it may be, as time goes on, in appalling shapes, by the magic wand of impatient science, look to the Church, and confidently wait her infallible answer to the difficulty or objection, that, hailed by the applause of an unbelieving world, may at first startle his convictions.

There is another principle, which is all-important in the conflict with Infidelity, and it is this, that we must never lose sight of the fact, that the Religion of the Catholic Church to-day, and the Religion of our first parents, and the Patriarchs before the flood, are most intimately united.

The Old and New Testaments form but part of the one great plan, before the Divine intelligence. One explains the other; the New cannot be understood apart from the Old; and the Old receives its perfection and accomplishment in the New.

When Infidels say tauntingly—"Are we to believe that the wonders recorded in Exodus, and the miracles of the Pentateuch were all wrought, for the benefit of a handful of people, inhabiting a mere corner of the world?" they display only narrowness of view, and the blindness of obstinate prejudice.

Judea was not a mere corner of the world, when the Jewish people existed as a compact nation. Viewing its position with regard to the great peoples of early times, the Egyptians, Phœnicians, Arabians, Chaldeans, and Assyrians, it was, considering the means of communication then known, the very theatre on which to exhibit, to the whole world, the grand spectacle of the economy of Divine Providence, for the salvation of mankind. The wonders wrought amongst the Jewish people were not so much for their sakes; but, as the Lord expressly declared to Moses, "that I may show my power in thee, and my name may be spoken of throughout all the earth" (Exod. ix. 16).

This is most strikingly brought out in the prophecies of Moses. He tells the people, in his last discourse to them, that, if they are faithful to their laws, God will perform, in their behalf, miracles like those wrought in Egypt: and this we see verified, in the wonderful things accomplished by Josue, Sampson, Gideon, Ezechias, etc. He warns them of the scourges prepared for them, if they should rebel. They will be reduced to slavery, transported from their country, and scattered over the earth. How signally was this fulfilled in the captivity of Babylon! And is it not even now, manifested to all eyes. He sees with prophetic vision every circumstance in their singular history, connected with the great work for which they were chosen.

All this is shown most distinctly, in the 28th chapter, and concluding chapters of Deuteronomy. He tells them they will have a king to rule over them, an event which came to pass four hundred years after; and in the 18th chapter, 15th verse, he points out the great event, with which their wonderful history, as a people and nation, selected by the Almighty, to be the connecting bond between the promise of a Redeemer to the first of the human race, and its accomplishment in the person of the long-expected of nations. " The Lord thy God will raise up to thee a PROPHET of thy nation and of thy brethren, like unto me, him thou shalt hear" (Deut. xviii. 15).

Moses appears at the very time most suitable to connect, by the history of his people, the obscure beginnings of the human race with the vocation of the Gentiles, and the diffusion of the Gospel " to the uttermost bounds of the earth." He is near enough to the early Patriarchs, and to our first parents, to gather up the traditions of the primeval revelation, and the great events of the earliest history of the human family.

Lamech, father of Noe, had seen Adam. Abraham had lived one hundred and fifty years with Sem, the Son of Noe. At the death of Abraham, Jacob was still young, but he was instructed by his father Isaac, who was still alive, when Jacob returned with his family from Mesopotamia. Moses had lived with his grandfather Caath, who had seen Jacob in Egypt. So that between Adam and Moses, five witnesses—Lamech, Sem, Abraham, Jacob and Caath, bring down, without interruption, the traditions of the first of the human race to Moses.

What Moses received in this way, he briefly narrated. There is nothing in his record, that resembles the misty and shadowy tales which obscure the early histories of other nations. Events are bound together with the ties of family descent, that could not be mistaken. The history of two thousand years, or from the creation of man to the birth of Abraham, is given in eleven chapters : there is no prolixity, no matters of trifling detail, only the great events, which must have stamped themselves indelibly on the memories of the witnesses.

Moses does not attempt to enter upon subjects, that

form the natural study for the exercise and development of the intellectual faculties. He was not called by God, and inspired, to teach us Geology, or natural history, or astronomy. These sciences men could learn by their own observation, and their own reasoning : but, marvellous to say, humanly speaking, there has not been a single fact clearly and unquestionably demonstrated by Geologists, or naturalists, or astronomers, that contradicts one statement recorded in Genesis.

There have been theories almost without number, mostly antagonistic and self-destroying, bold assertions about ignorance of Physical science shown by Moses, on the part of men who seem never to have studied profoundly any science. There have been thousands, who affecting to be savants, have sneered at the expressions of the great Jewish prophet, that seemed to conflict with theories of light, and the growth of plants, and electrical conditions of the atmosphere.

When these affectations of learning have been carefully divested of the pretentious garb of scientific knowledge, and submitted to the patient analysis of real Philosophers, and Experts in every branch of science, they have invariably been found to be stupid mistakes, many of which stood corrected, even by the accurate knowledge of the meaning of words.

When the grand conception of the writer of Genesis comes distinctly before our minds, one can feel only pity for such vain puerilities. It is, as though a smart accountant, acquainted only with figures and balance-sheets, were attempting to ledgerize the conceptions of a profound Philosopher.

As we trace the further history of the Jewish people, as one living at the time when Moses lived, himself the leader and the guide of this people emerging out of tribeship into a nation, could alone write it; as we trace it further still, as he beheld it, by the light of the clear knowledge of the future, vouchsafed to him by God, we understand that the great work before this wonderful man, was to write the history of Religion, and of God's Providence in relation to the whole human race.

He divides his subject into three great epochs, the state of isolated families governed only by the law of nature, and the primeval revelation; then the state of these families united together as a people, and governed by a written law, and the traditions of their forefathers; and, in fine, the future of a mighty nation gathered from every quarter of the globe, and bound together by the closest bonds of religious unity, and in the full light of the first revelation, developed and perfected by the teaching of the Son of God,—the great Prophet not only of the Jewish people, but of its brethren throughout the world.

As the plan so vast, and so sublime, rises before our mental view, we feel that it is a conception too grand for the finite mind of man, and comprehend, that God alone could conceive and effect it. Filled with these thoughts of the mission and work of the Jewish lawgiver, we no longer wonder, that the face of Moses, to whom this splendid vision was vouchsafed, shone even with a ray of the Divine light and majesty; and learn to appreciate more highly the genius of Michael Angelo, who, in his farfamed statue of the Mosè, has stamped on the marble, an air of grandeur that awes the beholder.

Viewed in this way, the history of the Jewish people in their deliverance out of bondage, and in their wanderings through the wilderness; considering them as under the special guidance and government of God for great ends, the connecting bond between the first Revelation, and the last, must, from the very nature of the case, be filled with supernatural manifestations.

The learned Bishop "of facts and figures," who was driven into the wild theories of German unbelief, by the simple reasoning of an untutored savage, could never have realized to himself the exalted mission and trust, confided to the Jewish people, when God Himself guided their steps, through his faithful servant. If he had, his splendid abilities would have spurned with contempt, these petty wranglings about certain facts, that can be explained by so ordinary laws of nature. The deliverance out of Egypt, which was to symbolize the greater deliverance of mankind through Jesus Christ, was effected therefore as one would expect, with "signs and wonders" that would forever stamp it on the memories of the race.

These mighty portents, which indicated the special presence of the most High in their midst, manifested constantly to a whole people, celebrated in their national songs and festivals, as long as they remained a united nation, and even to the present day, treasured in the grateful remembrance of their descendants, scattered over the whole earth, reveal distinctly the supernatural workings of Divine Providence, in the deliverance, preservation, and even punishments of the Hebrews. Admit one great miracle, such as the last plague, which terrified the hardened heart of Pharao, or the passage through the waters, that swallowed up the Egyptian king and his army; and then the mysterious cloud by day, and the pillar of fire by night, and the appalling announcement of the Law on Mount Sinai, and the other marvellous things recorded in Exodus, are only the outcome we might expect from such extraordinary beginnings.

If an ignorant savage could not understand how so many people and their cattle could be fed in the wilderness, because he knew, that the grass round his kraal, would soon be trampled down by his oxen, it was only natural for him to regard the story as something beyond belief.

But a Christian Bishop, who was taught, I suppose, by a pious mother, to trust in God, who feeds the birds of the air, and clothes the wild flowers of the field in all their beauty, and learned, in his early Scripture lessons, that the same God was pleased to rain down bread from Heaven, for his people, whom He was training for a special service in the wilderness, might have told his interesting neophyte, better things than are to be found in the childish absurdities, of the now almost forgotten commentary, of Dr. Paulus.

This is the fourth great principle, which believers in Revelation should remember, when they are disturbed by the sneers of unbelief. The history of the Hebrew people, while they were governed immediately and directly by God, is the history of God's Providence, fitting them, notwithstanding their perversity, for the fulfilment of a most important part, in the Divine plan for the salvation of all mankind.

They were indeed frail " earthen vessels," in which the blessed light was to be carried in the midst of Pagan darkness, that it might, one day, shine forth on a world of iniquity with the life-giving " knowledge of the glory of God in the face of Jesus Christ" (2 Cor. iv. 6, 7). From what Moses tells us, we know that they were prone to all the horrible vices of the Pagan nations around them. They were not probably worse than these peoples, of whose early history we know so little. They rebelled again and again, even when their sensual appetites were enjoying the riches of God's bounty. They fell into the lowest form of idolatry, while their hearts were still quivering within them, at the terrors of His manifestation on the mountain.

They might of course rebel, and plunge, as often as they pleased, into shameful excesses, for they, like other men, had free-will. But, for the sake of others, for the sake of the whole human race, they should be kept mindful of the treasure they were destined to carry, for the benefit of the children of God, in every age, to the consummation of the world.

When gratitude for miraculous favors, rendered more striking in the desolation of the wilderness, could not restrain them from crimes, which threatened the Divine gift with annihilation, they were subjected to severe but salutary punishment. Thousands were suddenly cut off, that the rest might be terrified into obedience. The law was no doubt rigorous, wherever there was danger of devil-worship, and the abominations that accompanied it, for had the whole people sunk into this abyss, no evidence would have been left to future generations, who, in the merciful designs of God, were to enjoy the blessings of Redemption, of the infinite value of this gift. Those who witness, with what facility whole nations slide into unbelief, notwithstanding the irrefragable testimony of Prophecy, preserved by the Hebrew people, in favor of the Divine origin of Christianity, can easily imagine, how wide would be this desolation, if the " Wandering Jew," as Lacordaire so fittingly calls the scattered race, did not continually stand forth, as a witness to the truth, which they detest. Therefore, the Divine arm uplifted, in seeming wrath, fell heavily at times on " the chosen people."

These exhibitions of the Divine anger, as we so wrongly call them, are a favorite theme with the enemies of Revelation. The Almighty is even called "a fiend," because of the apparent severity attributed to Him, in the Old Testament.

Those who reason so, particularly in Free America, should remember what rivers of blood were opened in that country, before Slavery could be abolished, and the blessed gift of liberty secured for themselves and their children.

And if the fatal blight of Mormonism should unhappily break through the barriers, which a people, enthusiastically devoted to free institutions, have been forced, in self-defence, to form round the Territory of Utah, and spreads and pollutes the land with its foul impurities, would there be no stern determined action taken to check its progress? The innocent would suffer with the guilty.

It is always so; even when, as far as human eye can see, God directly punishes those who dishonor Him. The wretched blasphemer, who is suddenly struck down in the moment of his defiance of his Maker, may have a fond wife who deplores his impiety, and little children, and others dependent on his industry and bounty. In the convulsions of nature, when thousands are swept away in an instant, the young, and the weak and helpless, and the innocent, perish with the guilty. Famine, War, and Pestilence make no distinction between their victims.

It was so, no doubt, when the wicked among the Hebrews, threatened, by their perversity, the happiness of a future world with destruction. Had the gift of Faith perished amongst them, and the preparation which a merciful and far-seeing God was making through them, for the benefit of the true freedom of a whole world, been frustrated, how many millions should, by the most grievous fault of this people, have sunk down hopelessly into the dark shadow of everlasting death!

When this view of the subject is calmly entertained, can any man with real grasp of mind, seriously consider as of any weight the petty objections against the truth of the Old Testament, often founded on no other basis than the misspelling of a name, or the substitution of a false date for the correct one, caused most probably through the carelessness of a transcriber? This hypercriticism, and this pettifogging play on mere words, not well understood in the original language, or doubtful figures, and numbers in the old manuscripts, is absolutely contemptible, and would be best met, not by the laborious erudition of a scholar, but with the pungent satire of which Sheridan is so profuse, in the admirable play of the " Critic."

Let these principles be remembered; and one can afford to rank amongst the curiosities of extravagant literature, most of the objections urged against the Pentateuch. I summarize them for the more easy remembrance of my readers.

1st. No objection or difficulty against Sacred Scripture is worth heeding, unless fairly and clearly demonstrated.

2d. In all anxieties of soul, excited by the arguments of unbelief, we are to look to the " everlasting Church," and patiently await her answer.

3d. When we are annoyed by petty, and irritating, and stinging sneers, and ridicule against our Faith, founded on certain things recorded in the Sacred Scriptures, especially in the Old Testament, we should rise to higher and broader conceptions of the ways of Divine

Providence, than are visible to these troublesome admirers of stupid profanity.

4th. We should always keep before our minds as a fixed maxim—that the manifest ways of God are not to be measured and determined by the ways of men; for "His judgments are incomprehensible and His ways are unsearchable" (Rom. xii. 33).

These principles may save unstable Christians from much trouble and anxiety; keep them clear of dangerous society, and still more dangerous reading, and confirm in them, God's most precious gift in this world, an earnest and lively Faith in everything that He has revealed.

In the next chapter, I mean to examine some of these popular questions, which it is the fashion of cultured "Progress," to set up in opposition to Catholic Christianity.

CHAPTER XVII.

Catholic Christianity and some Popular "isms."

WHEN I first set before me the plan of this book, it was my intention to have given brief sketches of the various "isms," that amuse the restless spirit of this age, so fond of trifling with the eternal interests of mankind. It seemed to me then, that it would be well fully to analyze them, and point out, in plain and untechnical language, their glaring defects.

But as I thought the subject out, I felt that this, as far as practical results were concerned, would be a useless task; and that it would be much more profitable to direct the attention of my readers to certain points, in these fantasies of unbelief, that seem most attractive,—points such as can easily be seized by ordinary minds, and which can be briefly demonstrated to be absolutely untenable.

What practical purpose, for instance, could be gained by tracing Pantheism up to Spinoza, and pointing out the metaphysical subtleties, by which this hard-headed Jew, evolved his system from the Cartesian philosophy?

Descartes had, for a while, charmed the thinking world, with a philosophy, that appeared, in its simplicity, to constitute the natural basis of all certitude. "I think, therefore I exist," and "substance is that which has no need of anything else to exist"—are propositions which, at first sight, appear to be almost self-evident.

But any one accustomed to think, in the real sense of

thinking, that is to say, not using the thoughts of others, and merely giving them utterance, but drawing up, calmly and with fixed attention, ideas from the deep well of his individual consciousness, will soon perceive how ambiguous, and consequently how flimsy, are these foundations of certain truth.

It might be interesting to a few, to trace the connection, which Spinoza fancied he saw between individual thought, and the great impersonal thinking principle, which appeared to him to pervade all nature.

This is what is meant by Pantheism in its simplest form; for the object of this philosophy is mainly to establish the principle, that, in the beginning of all things, there existed one original substance, which, gradually developing itself, by its own inherent life and energy, in course of time, absorbed everything into itself.

It would be very easy to fill whole chapters with the speculations of those clever men, who, fascinated by the charm of sharing in a new creation, springing spontaneously from the human mind, go on progressively from the individual self-consciousness of Descartes, to the fully developed Pantheism of to-day. I might show, for example, the point reached by Kant, and the pure idealism of Fichté, and the perfect abstraction of Hegel, till Cousin perfected the theory. The path was tempting; but I could not help saying to myself, *cui bono?* It will be quite enough, for ordinary readers, to know the outcome of all this ingenious thinking, as a species of Religion, which, in its present state of elaborate finish, constitutes the belief of many men of culture.

It amounts to this, that there is but one substance in the world, a great oneness, from which all things emanate, and to which all things return: and, as it is impossible to conceive a simple oneness without multiplying it, this one substance goes on multiplying itself, and exhibiting itself in countless forms of diversity, while unchanged and unchangeable in its essence, it is always in a state of progress. If this one substance, this vital essence, or this Force, which Herbert Spencer, in the *Nineteenth Century*, for March, 1884, calls—"the Infinite and Eternal Energy," were admitted by the Philosophers of this school, to be the Personal God, distinct from created things, and the Sovereign Lord and Master of all that He has made, then it would be easy to reconcile Pantheism with Catholic Christianity.

Admitting the existence of a God, infinite in all His attributes, self-existing, existing of necessity from all eternity, "by whom all things were made," Evolution would then constitute a charming system of unfolding the vast work of creation.

But alas! the "Infinite and Eternal Energy" is, in the minds of Pantheists, only a blind unconscious Force: it cannot know the beings that emanate from its restless energy, and is utterly incapable of caring for them, or loving them. How a thing like this, can be supposed to hold the place of the Christian God, the Supreme Omniscient Being, can scarcely be imagined, as a possible conception, by beings gifted with reason.

Still less can it be accounted for, that a senseless force should seem to any one, an improvement on the God of Revelation, "Our Father, who loves, and sustains even the least things He has made, and knows their wants, and without an effort, only by the very nature of His being, provides for each, according to its necessities; who loves His rational creatures with a love too great to be conceived by our finite minds, and sweetly leads them, when they trust to His guidance, to the enjoyment of His own beatitude."

But there are men, highly gifted men and women, who have brought themselves seriously to entertain this extravagant theory. Perhaps it is the very fact of possessing rare intellectual gifts, that has led them into these errors. We can hardly believe another temptation capable of seducing those, who in their refined tastes, spurn the low attractions of animal pleasures, than the fatal one, which dragged Lucifer and the rebel angels, from the height of Heaven, and led our first parents and their offspring into misery—Pride, the wilful entertainment of the thought—" you shall be as Gods."

If the majority of those, who are thus led away from the true source of their being, would only admit, into their darkened souls, one ray of that heavenly light, which " enlighteneth every man" of good-will " that cometh into this world," what splendid Catholics they would be! They vehemently desire to rise above their fellows, with a sort of passionate enthusiasm, that is constantly aiming at generous self-sacrifices. They are filled with noble aspirations; but then they believe only in their own brave hearts; they will not stoop to ask even Divine help; they trust only in themselves, and in a sort of imaginary self-perfectibility, that seems to satisfy their ardor; and so they are led away, from the very centre of their being, in whose bosom alone there is rest for the weary spirit.

There would have been no counsel of perfection too high for the generous appreciation of such as these, if they only dwelt, for a moment, on the claims of the Savior, to the love of their whole hearts and all their mind. Theirs would necessarily be an earnest Faith. More devoted in their singleness of purpose than "the young man whom Jesus loved," they would gladly have left "all things" to follow Him. Had they only one spark of that humble docility, which makes us "fit for the kingdom of Heaven," how that spark would have glowed with the fire which our Divine Lord came to kindle on earth! It would soon consume in them every atom of earthly dross, and change them into angels of charity.

How different would be their happy lot even in this world from what it is! For, now, blinded by the wild fancies of Pantheism, they are no better than beings without hope, uselessly wasting away their splendid gifts on airy nothings, and ever dashing themselves impetuously against these gloomy barriers of Infidelity, in which they have so foolishly imprisoned their noble aspirations.

One cannot read the fervid eloquence of such as these, as it is poured forth in their writings, without feeling like the slave Syra, in Fabiola, that it would be an act most pleasing to God, to purchase their liberty, and a place for them in His loving bosom, by the sacrifice even of one's own life.

What is this Pantheistic religion to them but the mocking spirit, which, whispering in their ears "Excelsior," is ever luring them to fatal destruction. There are many of these really great souls, who, like the rash penitent of the illustrious Fénélon, aim at greater heights than even Christian perfection, and who deem it selfish to care even for one's own eternal welfare, when they can promote the happiness of others.

If we once bring ourselves to believe, that the eloquent words which have thrilled the hearts of so many who pity them, are the genuine expression of real sentiments, what

I say of the highly cultured of this class of unbelievers, will not appear in the least overstrained or exaggerated. Take for example these verses of George Eliot—quoted by Mallock.

> "Oh may I join the choir invisible
> Of those immortal dead who live again
> In lives made happy by their presence. So
> To live is heaven. . . . .
>
> "May I reach
> That purest heaven, and be to other souls
> That cup of strength in some great agony,
> Enkindle generous ardor, feel pure love,
> Beget the smiles that have no cruelty.
> Be the sweet presence of a good diffused,
> And in diffusion ever more intense;
> So shall I join that choir invisible
> Whose music is the gladness of the world."

"Here," as Mallock says, "is hope, ardor, sympathy, and resolution, enough and to spare." But what is this hope? What is the aim and object of all this ardor? Alas! there is no definite object; all is vague, transitory, unreal, as is that love of the neighbor, which is not founded on the love of the Personal God.

To such as these however, dazzled as they are by the glory of a humanity perfectible in itself,—"a substance," which in the words of Spinoza, "has no need of anything to exist" (not even of God), the words of Uncreated Wisdom—"Unless you become as little children you shall not enter into the kingdom of Heaven" (Matt. xviii. 3)— are simple folly. To be converted from Gods to what is weakest, physically and mentally, in the world, would seem to them utter degradation. But our Divine Lord, in this passage, so dear to every earnest Christian, is not speaking of the deprivation of personal gifts, which the Lady Fabiola imagined might be taken from her, when she became a child of God in Baptism. He is pointing out, in the little child, only that absolute ignorance of worldly greatness, which is the chief characteristic of happy childhood; and that unfeigned humility, which is the real charm, even in the eyes of men, of every human perfection.

As a rule, Pantheists of this cultured class do not despise or abuse Catholic Christianity. They admit that it is very good, as far as it goes. They only complain that it does not go far enough to satisfy their aspirations; and that its claims are opposed to the rights of ennobled Humanity. It is worth remarking that Cousin, the mastermind, who is regarded as the man who gave the last polish to this fashionable creed, flung it from him, towards the close of his life, with loathing and disgust; and endeavored to repair the scandal he had given, in his Pantheistic writings, by attending regularly at daily Mass, and frequently approaching the sacraments.

I pass on to another kind of popular unbelief, much more common than Pantheism. This is what is called Materialism, or Positivism.

Although it might be considered the antithesis of Pantheism, it is, like all the other "isms" of the day, the worship, under another form, of Humanity. The distinctive feature of Materialism is, that it ignores anything like a dual nature in man. While Pantheists exalt the aspirations of mind and thought, to heights beyond the reach of unaided human nature, and scarcely give themselves time to analyze the source whence these exalted sentiments spring, the modern Materialists, like the "hogs" of the school of Epicurus, love to wallow in sensuality. They, unlike the Pagans of this sect, who believed in a sort of immortality, for even the voluptuous Horace says, "*non omnis moriar*," "my whole being shall not perish," maintain, that all that concerns the individual man ends with death.

They will not even believe that death is a sleep, an eternal sleep; for by admitting this, they might be led, like Hamlet in the play, to question the possibility of a troubled dream. They are determined not "to puzzle the will" "with the dread of something after death." This is what I have called, a few times, "the bag of bones theory;" or that belief which tells its votaries, that when they die, and the body returns to dust, there is a complete end of the human being; not simply the loss of individuality, by a reabsorption of the living principle into the one universal substance, but annihilation pure and simple.

It is difficult to believe, that there can be earnest materialists. It is almost as difficult for a serious thinker to realize this to himself, as the existence of a real Atheist. One can understand, that a low, ignorant sensualist, a drunken sottish Kaffir, or Hottentot, might quietly rest in this mud of unbelief; but not a man capable of thinking and reasoning.

I remember, once, on a journey, pointing out to the native driver, a dead ox, that lay by the roadside, and I said to this man, who, I knew was always on the look-out for what he called "a chance,"—that is an opportunity of indulging heavily in Cape brandy, "When you die, will it be all over with you, like that dead beast?" He replied, "Yah, Baas, I think so." And when I spoke to him of the soul, and the spirit, and seat of life within him, he merely laughed, and said that he believed white people spoke of such things; but, for his part, he had never seen anything of the kind.

Stupid as was the reply, it seems to me far more excusable, than the assertion of an educated man, the child perhaps of Christian parents, or it may be once himself a Christian, who would say, " When I die there will be, as surely an end of me, as of the flower that dies in the garden."

According to the Materialist, who to quiet the reproaches of conscience, and to pursue the gratification of his passions, has coached himself up, so far in Infidel reading, as to make himself, "a poor imitation of polished ungodliness," there is no such thing as spirit or soul, distinct from the body. He will say, spouting most probably the words of some fashionable Infidel writer, " The grand discovery of modern times is ' Osmosis.' You know," he will continue, in a dogmatic strain, as if he were about shedding a ray of light on the darkness of your understanding, and dispelling the shadows of unpleasant and disturbing thoughts,—" Osmosis means that man is only an aggregate of cells : the will and all that, is but the succession of cellular vibrations ; and the action of the mind, as it is called, is only the combination of brain waves, as they pass over the delicate nerves, and brain tissue. Of course, you know that ' we are fearfully and wonderfully made,' and in fact, we have not yet reached, in our most delicate instruments, anything like that splendidly assorted combination, which natural development has effected in the organs of sense; but we are so rapidly coming to that point, that by and by, illustrations taken from the most perfect telephone, or even musical instrument, will bring the matter clearly before you. But something in the same way as the sound of the voice, or the most delicate touch will cause these exquisitely fine vibrations, in the same way, sensations excite vibrations on the highly sensitive nerve centres, and thus we come to feel, and think, and reason.

"Of course," he will continue, "You never imagined that animals had what they call souls: yet you see they have reason. What is called instinct is in reality exactly the same in *kind* as reason. And then perhaps, he launches out into proofs and illustrations, commencing with—'I had a dog once;' or 'I knew a man who had a pet monkey' or a 'pet canary,' and these creatures did so and so,—fully and perfectly reasoned just as a human being, not so perfectly of course, because they had not acquired the same perfect organization."

This is generally speaking, the style of philosophizing of the young Materialists, that one meets so frequently nowadays. A little real Philosophy will sweep away at once all this mystified jargon, even though supported by the authority of great names.

There is no use in entering deeply into the question with those, who seem to consider, that they have summed up all that can be said against the existence of spirit, when they argue—whoever saw, or heard, or smelt a spirit, or could tell us anything about its shape, and color, or what it is like?

When they affect to be satisfied with this peculiar sort of metaphysical reasoning, we can only say that, considering their opportunities, they are much lower in the scale of intellectual activity, than the native to whom I have just alluded. The poor fellow argued straightforwardly on the only data he ever had for forming a conclusion. He knew all about a splint, or a spavined horse, when he saw certain indications, or could even feel, in his sensitive bridle-hand, though he saw nothing amiss, that there was something wrong with the reins or harness, but spiritual essence was beyond his comprehension.

Hence, there is not much use in establishing the existence of spirit and soul as distinct from body. It will suffice to give the rudimentary principles of sound philosophy. We say the soul is distinct from the body, not because we rest on the testimony of sense, which can certify nothing on a subject altogether beyond its powers; but on the evidence of reason only, where there is no appeal to Revelation.

The mind has the power of forming abstract ideas, and the power of generalizing: and this is absolutely beyond the reach of matter, however attenuated, and brought towards the confines of spirit. The instinct of a brute animal, whatever instinct may be, can receive a certain impression, and retain it even for a long time, and thus remember it, just as a scene described to us, can be, as it were painted on the memory. The scene had a real existence, and therefore it can, in some way, be received by a material substance, as a picture can be stamped on the sensitive collodion surface of a plate in the camera.

But an abstraction, the putting of mere thoughts together, and the conclusion deduced from them, cannot be so impressed on any material substance; because there is no existing substance that can be copied. Thought is something, that no camera, however delicately constructed, can conceivably seize, and transfer, by any medium, to the sensitive plate. If men gifted with extraordinary powers of observation, like those who profess to distinguish the vowel and consonant sounds in the mewing of a cat, succeed in demonstrating marvellous powers of observation in domestic animals, this only would prove that there is a faculty in these creatures, far beyond anything conceived by Materialists; but the power of generalizing, and combining abstract thoughts, is completely beyond the capabilities of mere matter.

To effect this, matter should be a thing divested of parts, and superior, in its form, to thought itself. Who will attempt to divide a simple thought, as the Copula that unites premises and conclusion, into parts, so as, by any stretch of imagination, to divide into halves and quarters, that which is simplicity itself? Matter is essentially sluggish, and divisible, and cannot therefore adapt itself to receive and combine, what is, in its very nature, more rapid than the lightning, which appears and is gone, before the most perfect articulation can bear testimony to its existence.

Evidently the substance, which can, more quickly than any conceivable motion, arrange the evanescent thoughts, must be a substance perfectly simple in itself, and therefore cannot be anything material.

Contradictions cannot coexist in matter; a bar of iron cannot be red hot and icy cold at the same instant. Yet there is no more common operation, in the mind of even the most uneducated of the human race, than the coexistence of thoughts which are perfectly antagonistic.

Take the case of a perplexed juryman who has simply to say yes or no to a certain proposition, on which life or lives depend. The antagonistic elements are there, face to face, equal, for the time at least, in their opposing power. In any material substance, such forces should, by one of the first laws of nature, destroy each other: yet they subsist together in the mind of the juror; and may subsist even, when, under the pressure of peculiar circumstances, he has delivered his ill-considered verdict.

Take another familiar illustration; the good Templar, or strict Teetotaller, is sorely pressed by thirst; there is nothing to satisfy this almost irresistible longing of nature, but a glass of alcoholic spirit. Yet the mind bravely resists the pressure, because it feels a paramount sense of duty.

Can any Materialist ever imagine, that a day will come, when matter, in any shape or form, will evidence this mental struggle, in the shape of a picture cognizable by sense?

Of course, in a book like this, it would be altogether out of place to pile up metaphysical arguments. He who runs may read, if he have ordinary capacity, in what I have said, that Materialism as a Religion or a comfort to distressed consciences, is a thing not to be dreamt of by beings gifted with intelligence.

If we rise above the nature of man, and his religious wants, in connection with materialistic theories, and consider its speculations about the first cause, in the chance formation of atoms in the protoplasm, the eternal combining, and breaking up of cells, under the influence of an unconscious and unintelligent energy, and all the nonsense that has been formulated under the name of Philosophy, to account for the origin of things, the answer it seems to me, is best found in the well-known lines of the Poet.

"How should matter occupy a charge,
Dull as it is, and satisfy a law,
So vast in its demands, unless impelled
To ceaseless service by a ceaseless force
And under pressure of some conscious cause?
The Lord of all, Himself through all diffused,
Sustains, and is the life of all that lives.
Nature is but a name for an effect,

> Whose cause is God. He feeds the secret fire
> By which the mighty process is maintained.
> Who sleeps not, is not weary; in whose sight
> Slow circling ages are as transient days;
> Whose work is without labor; whose designs
> No flaw deforms, no difficulty thwarts;
> And whose beneficence no charge exhausts."
> COWPER, "The Task."

The late Lord Beaconsfield well summed up, in a few lines, all that common-sense cares to say about the wild dreams of Atheism, and its masked sisters, Pantheism and Materialism, and the other "isms" that affect to ignore the existence of a Personal God—"Nothing can surely be more monstrous, than to represent a Creator as unconscious of creating."

A few words on Agnosticism will fittingly conclude this chapter. I have already, in previous chapters, described it as the great fall-back and bulwark of unbelief. When sorely pressed, unbelievers of our times entrench themselves in this imaginary stronghold.

What does it mean? Simply nothing. It is the absolute "No" of the Seer of Chelsea, the "know-nothing-ism" of rampant infidelity. You press the Agnostics for an answer to some cogent argument, and the reply is—"I know nothing about it." And, lest this confession would be too humiliating, they say, "Nor can you know anything on the subject." It is "the unknown and the unknowable." What an absurdity! What a manifest contradiction in terms! If it be altogether the unknown, how can it be logically predicated of it, that it is the unknowable?

As to the claim of Agnosticism to be anything like a Religion, its creed formulated, as Frederic Harrison says, by the acknowledged head of the Evolution philosophy, "with a definiteness such as it never wore before," the claim has received a death-blow from this clever writer. Harrison has indeed proved beyond doubt, that it is the "Ghost of Religion," "defecated to a pure transparency."

When St. Paul, standing in the Areopagus, would, in a trenchant phrase, dispose of the claims of its great men to anything like Philosophy; and show that they were "too superstitious" to be reasoned with, he pointed to the altar, which they had erected "to the unknown God." What would the great Apostle have said, had he found that they had added to the word unknown, the self-contradiction of "unknowable."

Men must be blinded to their own foolishness, when they commit themselves dogmatically to the stupid assertion, that the thing of which they know nothing whatsoever is so complex in its nature, and so far beyond ordinary things, that no one can possibly know anything about it.

A few passages from Harrison, will show that Agnosticism were better dead and buried forever, than that any one should attempt to utter such nonsense in connection with it.

"If," says Harrison, "Religion is still to be, it cannot be found in this No-man's land, and Know-nothing creed. Better bury Religion at once, than let its Ghost walk uneasy in our dreams"—"Agnosticism is no more a Religion than Differentiation, or the Nebular hypothesis is religion."

And again—" To make a Religion out of the unknowable, is far more extravagant, than to make it out of the Equator; it influences seamen, equatorial people, and Geographers not a little, and we all hesitate, as was once said, to speak disrespectfully of the Equator. But would it be blasphemy to speak disrespectfully of the Unknowable? Our minds are a blank about it. As to acknowledging the unknowable, or trusting in it, or feeling its influence over us, or paying gratitude to it, or conforming our lives to it, or looking to it for help,—the use of such words about it is unmeaning."

And, as if this were not enough to excite contempt for the wretched abomination, which has captivated the religious tastes of so many cultured admirers of the fashionable God of the hour, he caps the climax of its absurdity, by introducing it to us, as the Formula (x^n) x in the nth power, or the Unknown raised to infinity; and represents its worshippers, as appealing to this strange God in the language of emotional piety. "O! x^n, love us, help us, make us one with thee!"

But there is something more than ridicule, there is enough to awaken, not mere contempt for this absurd idol, but the indignation of all, who have ever felt what Religion means, when he draws a vivid picture of those who feel the need of Religion, appealing to its great master, for help in their bitter woe—" A mother wrung with agony for the loss of her child, or the wife crushed by the death of her children's father, or the helpless, and the oppressed, the poor and the needy, men, women, and children, in sorrow, doubt, and want, longing for something to comfort and to guide them, something to believe in, to hope for, to love, and to worship. . . . They come to our Philosopher, and they say—'Your men of science have routed our priests, and have silenced our old teachers, what religious faith do you give us in its place?' And the Philosopher replies (his full heart bleeding for them) and he says—'Think on the Unknowable.'"

If this does not give a quietus to Agnosticism, I know

not what will. If it still survives, even as the transparency of nothingness, its light shade can only be found flitting round the studio of some distracted Philosopher, insensible alike to laughter and to tears, and wholly bent on constructing a system which may yet, through the frivolity of the age, turn some demented beings from the attractions of Catholic Christianity.

If this creed of the "don't knows" is the only fall-back for those who, without serious thought or study, take up every religious paragraph, that may meet their eyes in newspapers, or magazines, or pamphlets, and hurl it spitefully at the "everlasting Church," they ought, in common-sense, to give up their unholy and contemptible warfare, before the feeble barrier, behind which they so ignominiously hide their heads, at the least show of resistance, is blown from the face of the earth, by the expression of public scorn and universal derision.

In the next chapter, I purpose to deal with another foe to Catholicity, deserving of more serious notice than those I have combated here. It is that Realism which is found in the worship of Humanity, and which is so strongly advocated in the paper from which I have taken the above extracts.

CHAPTER XVIII.

Catholic Christianity and Realism.

THE article of Mr. Harrison, in the *Nineteenth Century*, for March, 1884, from which I have taken so many extracts, given in the last chapter, ends with these significant words—" Shall we cling to a Religion of spiritism, when Philosophy is whittling away spirit to nothing? Or shall we accept a Religion of Realism, where all the great traditions and functions of Religion are retained unbroken?"

If by spiritism is here meant ghost stories, and devil worship, and the various superstitions which have, in every age, engaged the attention of men, when they abandoned the true light to grope in darkness, not Philosophy alone, but practical common-sense are indeed divesting these dreams of the charms which once hung around them, and whittling them away to Nothing. Some half-crazed individuals will no doubt cling to the invocation, and worship of the spirits of darkness: but the *sanior pars* of unbelieving mankind, to whom the Epicurean maxim—" *Ipsa utilitas justi prope mater et æqui,*" and " the almighty dollar" form the substitute for a Religion, whose treasure is in Heaven, will have no fellowship with these " tricks" that lead to nothing profitable and substantial.

If the Providence of God allowed the lying spirits to disturb the order of the world, and to reveal to their votaries, the treasures of gold and silver and diamonds and other precious things, that lie hidden in the earth, then the case might be different. If these coveted treasures were to be the rewards, not of honest industry, and that toil and labor which form the allotted task of fallen humanity, but of magical rites, then the case would be much altered, and an excuse would readily be found by the many, for devoting their attention to the occult sciences. But now, that "the game" is found to be "not worth the candle," all this abomination is heartily consigned to where it came from.

Still men, however worldly minded, must have a Religion of some kind; one particularly that has an air of respectability about it, and at least certain functions, which, whether they satisfy the aspirations of the heart or not, will at least maintain public order and decorum, or fall in with their sympathies when they are disposed "to feel good."

In this way, I read the quotation given above, and this meaning, the aptness of which will be more generally felt, than openly acknowledged, leads me to speak of that Religion, which is, according to the Philosophers of the *utile* and *dulce* school, the worship of Humanity.

The article of Herbert Spencer, "the Prophet and guide" of the Agnostics, which provoked the reply of Harrison, is not without considerable merit in the eyes of its critic. "It is," the latter says, "in its final outcome, the most cogent and suggestive, that has yet appeared, in the whole range of modern religious discussion." And why? Because, no doubt, it brings out, clearly and distinctly, the nature and the origin of the worship of Humanity; and not only this, but because it interweaves this charming Religion of the cultured children of unbelief with Evolution,—the popular Philosophy of the day.

A short passage of this remarkable article "Religion, a Retrospect and Prospect" (*Nineteenth Century*, January, 1884), will explain my meaning. "Thus," writes Herbert Spencer, " recognizing the fact that, in the primitive human mind, there exists neither religious idea, nor religious sentiment, we find that, in the course of social evolution, and the evolution of intelligence accompanying it, there are generated both the ideas and sentiments which we distinguish as religious; and that, through a process of causation clearly traceable, they traverse those stages which have brought them, among civilized races, to their present forms."

It was always a favorite theory of unbelief (we can trace it back to the unbelievers in the national religion before Christianity), that man was gradually evolved from a savage state, and led, chiefly by feelings of self-preservation and mutual protection, to society, and civilization, and good government, and order.

The Darwinian theory, as regards the origin of man, is only an exaggeration of this old Pagan notion. And, so the modern Philosophers of Realism trace back religious ideas and religious sentiments, to feelings of admiration and respect for chiefs and heroes distinguished from the crowd by their lofty stature, their physical strength, and their commanding abilities. Men of this stamp were looked up to with veneration by their fellows; and after death, were honored in the memory of those who survived them, as heroes and demi-gods. Their valiant exploits were in time exaggerated; their virtues and transcendent talents described as more than human; and thus in time, their images were set up, and made objects of adoration.

It is easy to construct theories and systems; particularly when facts are not considered necessary to constitute their bases, and they fall in with individual and national prejudices.

No one can doubt but that the Darwinian theory of Evolution is beautiful in its simplicity; and though it somewhat shocks our pride, by connecting our earliest origin with rather discreditable-looking ancestors, and savage propensities, most men however, who admire the creations of original thought, are disposed to forget or ignore these very distant beginnings of the race, in their admiration of the charms of the bold grasp of mind, which conceived so grand a system.

Unfortunately for the Darwinian theory of "natural selection," and "the survival of the fittest," it wants a firm basis on which to rest. There is, as I noticed in a former chapter, the absence of any memorial in the shape of a fossil, or earth-mark indicating the transition state from brute animal to man, the want of "the connecting link," as it is commonly called; and this is fatal to the system, as a science.

There are a number of stark facts, very curious and interesting no doubt, about animal instinct; but they are all beside the question, when the ingenious author completely sets aside, as if he could not see it, the essential difference in *kind* between the highest operations in man and the lowest; between the operations of the animal, and the "human acts" of the reasonable being; and seeks the connecting link between brute and man, only in the lower and sensitive nature of the latter.

Common-sense will see, even without a particle of science, that there is something considerably greater than the difference of *degree*, between the purely sensitive talk of a parrot, and human conversation; between the animal affection of a dog for his master, and the abstract judgment implied in man's worship of God; between a cat fondling with a friendly hound and a man judging between right and wrong.

If Darwin held that the thinking principle in man was the same in kind, though far different in degree, from the seat of instinct in beasts, and therefore, that what we call the soul in man was only a highly delicate nervous organ, then the unanswerable point I touched upon in the last chapter, showing the absolute impossibility of contradictory thoughts in the same material substance, would apply to the theory of Evolution. The evolution of a man from a brute beast would then be as impossible to imagine, as that a man could sit and run, be asleep and awake, be in a fever and quite well, at one and the same moment.

There is nothing in Catholic teaching to prevent us holding the doctrine of evolution up to a certain point. God may have created life germs, at the first instant of creation. This would simplify considerably many of the difficulties urged by Unbelief against the unity of race, and the preservation of animal life from the waters of the Deluge, as recorded in Genesis; but it is certainly contrary to Faith to hold, that the soul of man could be evolved from the seat of instinct in a beast.

It is much the same with the evolution of Religion, as with the theory of animal evolution: it has no basis on which to rest. It starts too on a wrong principle; it begins at the wrong end.

It may be questioned if the theory of Darwin is not subject to the same fundamental error. Artificial selection, and careful breeding will, every one knows, develop a sort of perfection in animals; and the same care with plants, and flowers, and trees, lead to similar results. This is of course the foundation of "natural selection" and "the preservation of the fittest:" but, I say, it may be questioned if animals or plants, left to themselves, will, by any process of nature, go on to perfection. Experience I believe generally testifies to the contrary; that breeds of animals and plants will deteriorate, if not carefully attended to. Peculiarities of structure, if not constantly watched and selected, will, as in nature, whereever the peculiarity is transmitted, become deformities. Even the celebrated ancon sheep, with its long body, and short bow-legs, might, if left to breed like the common flock, have propagated, for a time, a sort of monstrosity. If this be true, the whole theory of Darwin, which supposes natural progress towards perfection to be an ordinary law of nature, is a grand mistake, even in its broadest conception.

But certainly Evolution in Religion is open to this charge. The notion of Religion gradually rising from hero-worship, and eliminating, in its growth, human imperfections from future Gods and Goddesses, and evolving Theism from Polytheism, until its perfection is reached in Catholic Christianity, is a gross mistake; and is palpably contradicted by facts in the early history of nations.

The most certain and universal fact, that can be ascertained from the primitive records of all ancient peoples, is this, that there was a revelation made to man in the very beginning of his existence; and that this tradition gradually degenerated, and became disfigured, and weakened, and corrupted, till it had almost perished before the advent of our Divine Lord.

I was very much struck, some years ago, by becoming

acquainted with a class of works, eagerly devoured by certain cultured readers, professional men with hazy notions about Christianity. These works undertook to prove, that all Religions were one, when they were carefully examined. The gentleman, since dead, who introduced me to this class of reading, gave me something of his own investigations into the Religion of the Buddhists and Parsees, and pointed out to me some notable instances of similarity, in these Eastern Religions, to Catholic doctrine and worship.

The Abbé Huc has given most interesting information bearing on the same subject, discovered during his visit to Lassa, the capital of Thibet.

Of course this was naturally to be expected after the fact of a Revelation made to our first parents. The truths relating to the unseen world, would have been communicated by them to the early patriarchs, and be, in this way, transmitted to the founders of the different nations and peoples of ancient times; and thus gradually brought down, embalmed in the religious rites of many peoples actually existing.

What struck me with surprise was, that this argument, so favorable to revealed Religion, should, by some obliquity of judgment, be supposed by men of reading and intelligence to make against it. They saw the difficulty only in one way. "Here," they say, "is an overpowering argument against Christianity. You imagined that what Christians believe, was first taught by Christ, and lo! here is the self-same doctrine taught by Egyptian priests, and Buddhists, long before the birth of Christ."

The answer is manifest. What more natural than that the elements of Christian revealed religion should have permeated all nations, long before Christ appeared on

CATHOLIC CHRISTIANITY AND REALISM. 361

earth. The Jewish law, and the books of Moses, which contain its substance, were but the written record of the first revelation. And Christ came, not to destroy the law, but, to fulfil it, and perfect it. Christianity, in its essential parts, the Unity and Trinity of God, the necessity of a Redeemer, the restoration of a fallen race, the Resurrection and eternal life, forms a body of doctrine as old as the existence of man upon this world. When we glance at the traditions of some of the earliest peoples, we may well hold up our hands in amazement, that the leaders of progress should be completely ignorant of this key to all their difficulties, and expose themselves to the ridicule of educated Christians, by fantastic theories about hero-worship, and the Evolution of Religion.

From a learned work by L. de Rouën, Baron D'Alvimore, I will quote a few passages, which show, that, not only the knowledge of the Fall, and the promise of a Redeemer, were carefully preserved in the traditions of early nations; but also the remembrance of the great events recorded in the first eleven chapters of Genesis.

1st. We have the Chinese traditions, testifying to the original Revelation. In the book called *Chou-King*, regarded by the Chinese as the immovable basis of their history, we read of the creation of the universe out of nothing by an eternal Being, the Creator of the earth; the whole human race derived from one pair; the deluge, in which all perished except one family. It is stated in this book, that Niu-wa (Noe) was saved in a boat; and that a colony of his descendants settled in Chen-si, and that the chief of this people was the wise Yao. In another of the sacred books, we find still more striking records. There is mentioned the state of innocence in which man was created, the terrestrial paradise, the tree of life, the forbidden fruit, the fall of the woman, the long life of the Patriarchs, and even the promise of a Redeemer. Confucius says expressly, that the holy-one, sent from heaven, will know all things, and that he will have power in heaven and on earth; and in many places, he speaks of the holy man who is to come. M. Abel Rémusat shows that the coming of a holy one was generally believed in China, six hundred years before the Christian era.

Sanchoniathon, who, Voltaire says, lived among the Phœnicians before the time of Moses, writes—"There were in the beginning a dark Chaos and a spirit. The spirit reacting on this Chaos, and warming it, brought forth a sort of fermenting substance, which became the seed of all creatures, and determined the formation of the Universe." He also says, that "the first man and woman were brought forth by a vivifying breath and by Chaos." In the Védas of the Hindoos, we read,—"The universe existed only in an indefinable manner in the Divine thought, so that the understanding could not discern it. Then the self-existing power created the visible world, with the five elements, and the different principles of things. From His thought alone, He created the waters. They were first called *nara*, because they were produced by the nara or spirit of God; and as they were also the matter on which the first *ayana* (movement of the Creator) acted, they received the name of *narayana* (movement over the waters)."

One of the Védas calls the first man *Adima* (the first;) it gives him for his companion a woman, whom it names *Pracriti*, a word which among the Hindoos signifies the same as *Heva*, or life, among the Hebrews. They are first in a state of innocence and happiness; but this happy state lasts but for a short time. The first parents are corrupted, and the children become still worse than their fathers. God is angry, he covers the heavens with clouds, separates the poles with thunder and lightning, raises the waves of the sea, till they cover the earth, and buries the human race beneath the waters. Brâhmah escaping the general ruin, repeoples the Universe.

Amongst the Persians, we find the following traditions in their sacred books. Ormuzd (principle of all beings) created the world in six times. He made first the Heaven, then the water, earth, trees, animals. Man and woman were the last works of creation. Placed in a garden, both were destined to be happy; but both allowed themselves to be seduced by Ahriman, the great serpent, the knowing one, the liar, and they became unhappy by their disobedience. Death is introduced into the world by Ahriman. Ormuzd will send a Saviour, the prophet Sraosha, to prepare them for the general Resurrection.

It is not only among Oriental nations, that these traditions are found, but among the early inhabitants of the new world. We read, in the early history of the Mexicans, that before the great deluge, the country of Anahuac was inhabited by Giants. All those who did not perish were converted into fish, with the exception of seven, who took refuge in caverns. When the waters had subsided, one of the giants constructed an artificial hill, in the shape of a pyramid. The Gods were angry, and launched down fire on the monument, and killed many of the workmen. Among five of the peoples, who originally inhabited Mexico, were found paintings, in one group of which were represented the woman with the serpent *Quilaztli* (woman of our flesh). The Mexicans regarded her as the mother of the human race. Another group represented the deluge of *Coxcox*, the Noe of these people, saved from the waters, with his wife in a raft of *Anahuete*. Another tradition described Tezpi in a large vessel, with his wife, children, many animals, and all sorts of grain necessary for the preservation of the human race. Tezpi, on the retiring of the waters, sends forth a vulture, and afterwards other birds, amongst them the humming bird, which returned with a branch covered with leaves; and then Tezpi left the vessel near the mountain of Colhuacan.

The learned author, from whose book "*Recueil de Réfutations*," I have taken these extracts, fittingly observes —" Must we not recognize in these traditions, of people so separated from each other, clearly the traces of a common origin?"

Even the longevity of the early Patriarchs is attested by the history of early India, and Persia, of China, and Egypt, and of the new world. Amongst the Indians, the records of *Menou* speak of the age of gold, when the *Satya*, young men free from sickness, lived for four hundred years.

Vulcan reigns one thousand years in Egypt. *Caioumarath* (the first man), first king of Persia, lived one thousand years. In China, *Ching-Nong* reigns one hundred and forty-five years. Among the early Americans, *Behica* lives two thousand years. The same longevity is attested in the histories of ancient Chaldea, Phœnicia and Greece. Chance could not have produced this uniformity of tradition in countries so far remote from each other. The ideas of peoples, who had nothing common in their laws, language and religion could not agree so remarkably, if there was not truth at the bottom of these early traditions.

I have dwelt on these interesting details, because they seem to me completely to upset the theory of Religion by Evolution from hero-worship, the only speculation that seems at first sight, apart from the account given in Genesis, to satisfy diligent inquiry into the origin of Religion. If such is the fate of what is called Realism, to distinguish it from transparent crudities, it is not too much to say, that all this farrago of unbelief will soon be consigned, by all thinking men, to "the tomb of all the Capulets."

It is remarkable that every sustained attack on Revelation, that is to say, every attack that was backed by a show of learning, and thus provoked careful inquiry and study, has resulted in new triumphs for the truth of Revelation. What the inscriptions on the stone monuments of early Egypt and Assyria are doing every year, as they are deciphered by learned experts, corroborating the history of the sacred books even in minute detail, has been the constant result of calm and dispassionate investigation of all such objections.

The modern German school of Bible criticism has, in this way, strikingly confirmed the truths recorded in the Old and New Testament. The truth of the Resurrection of our Divine Lord, for example, which is, according to St. Paul, the sum and substance of the proofs of the Divine origin of Christianity—" If Christ be not risen again, then is our preaching vain, and your faith is also vain" (1 Cor. xv. 14) is, if possible, more clearly demonstrated than ever, by the sustained attempt of many German infidels to prove that Christ was not dead, when laid in the sepulchre.

They said He was only in a trance from loss of blood, and that, when laid in the cool vault, and refreshed by the smell of the aromatic spices, placed about His head, He recovered and quietly walked away. Christian writers easily proved the absurdity of this hypothesis.

They showed that the great quantity of myrrh and aloes, " about a hundred pounds" (John xix. 39) wrapped round the head of our Divine Lord, would effectually have smothered Him, if He had not been already dead. They pointed to the weight of the stone that closed the sepulchre ; to the presence of the soldiers ; and cited the testimony of the Roman officer to Pilate, and many other arguments bearing on the subject.

But when the objection was still pressed, and medical evidence was brought forward to support it, some eminent German physicians (the two Gruners and Richter, and more satisfactorily Doctor William Stroude) took up the matter ; and not only proved the absolute certainty of death from the wound of the lance, and the flow of blood and water from the pericardium, but demonstrated the fact, which makes a deeper impression on every Christian mind than any circumstance of the dolorous Passion, that our Divine Saviour had died of a broken heart, the heart having literally burst from the excess of His mental and corporal agony.

In the same way, when constant efforts continued to be made to disprove the unity of the human race, notwithstanding the accumulation of facts to show that various causes lead to change of color, and peculiarities of formation, the attention thus directed to this subject, tended to promote the comparative study of languages, which, as far as it has yet been pursued, establishes conclusively and evidently, from the strong affinity between them, the common origin of all these creatures of God, who enjoy the holy power of speech ; and demonstrates that the members of the human race, however widely scattered, and differing however much in many important characteristics, yet belong to the same original family.

The Philosophers who cling to the Evolution theory of Religion, will also, I have no doubt, if they are persistent in their view, secure another triumph for Catholic Christianity, by concentrating the minds of men of extensive learning on the original habits of the human race, till evidence beyond reply is brought forward to show, that such a theory is directly in conflict with the earliest historical records of the primeval Revelation.

In the next chapter, I mean to say a few words on the *bête noire* of all systems of Religion—the accursed thing called Spiritism.

CHAPTER XIX.

Catholic Christianity and Spiritism.

THE spirit of this age is unquestionably a spirit of progress. Whether this progress be real or only apparent, it does not so much matter in connection with the subject of this chapter. The main idea of thinking and active men is, that we must go forward somehow: it would be the worst error conceivable, not simply to halt in the onward march of intellectual and material development, but to take a step backwards. As Charles Dickens has said somewhere, he would be a mere obstructive, who would attempt to induce the surging and ever-hurrying crowd to join with him, in putting back the hands on the great dial of time. We may not even pause to think seriously over what was once believed to be the wisdom of past ages; "*nous avons changé tout cela.*"

This is, I believe the irresistible prejudice which prevents non-Catholic Christians, as well as Free-thinkers, from considering patiently what Catholic Christianity has to say about Spiritism. When our theologians raise a cry of warning, and point to the proofs of its diabolical character, they are at once met by the counter-cry, that the dark ages of witchcraft, and magic, and the occult sciences, with their goblins and demons, have vanished in these enlightened times. The men of progress, the bright-eyed eagles, who exult in the noontide splendor of the sun of progress, cannot consort with the blinking owls that affect only gloom and its shadowy horrors.

I feel therefore, that anything I can say about the dangers of this mischievous delusion, will serve only to warn Catholics against it.

Luckily however, as I noticed in the last chapter, the teaching of the spirits is not found to pay. Its most ardent votaries derive neither wealth, nor honor, nor glory of any kind, from their devotion. Its high-priests are not looked up to by the multitude, as Prophets, or inspired sages; and so it leads a sort of spasmodic existence. Occasionally when trade is dull, and active minds grow tired of reading and ordinary recreation, they catch the ardor of a languid excitement, from some wandering spark, who professes to know the secrets of this mysterious belief, and to be able to initiate disciples into an acquaintance with its wonders. If any of these latter are developed into promising mediums, vanity, the love of notice, and the sense of possessing a power not given to others of their friends, fan the smouldering fire into something like a light, that attracts curiosity; and so it blazes up for a while, and then dies out, leaving behind it however a noxious effluvium in some morbid natures, that may, for a long time, poison the freshness of healthful pleasures, or, it may be, blight the happiness of a life. This is the ordinary story of Spiritism, as far as careful inquiry has shown it to me in South Africa.

It may be, and I believe it is, far different in parts of America, where it is the accepted and acknowledged belief of hundreds of thousands. In England, it has not made much way; in France, and Germany, for a while, it promised to have a successful career: but it is dying out in the countries of Europe, where it is now regarded as something less than "the ghost of a Religion."

Why it should have established itself permanently in

the new world, is, I think, easily explained on the Catholic principles concerning it. In America, unfortunately Agnosticism, has long prevailed among certain classes. These have, even for generations, broken with the traditions of the past: they have almost forgotten God and His Christ, and through that want of something supernatural, which exists in human nature, they have taken this superstition to their bosoms, and cherished it.

It seems, among such as these, to reward the affection and earnestness of its worshippers by extraordinary manifestations. I have read descriptions of these wonders, that were startling even to those, who learn, from the teaching of the Church, their true cause. Voices, shadowy shapes, the power of speaking unknown tongues, and throwing off impromptu verses by the hour, in the person of uneducated mediums, aerial music of an enchanting character, brilliant waving lights, etc., keep alive the faith of enthusiastic spiritists in America.

Europe, even in those countries where Protestantism and Infidelity have so long waged war against the Church, is too deeply leavened with the old Faith, to desire, or to place confidence in such manifestations. They might too awaken a slumbering faith; and as our Divine Lord tells us, Beelzebub is too wise to fight against himself—"And if Satan is divided against himself, how shall his kingdom stand" (Matt. xii. 26), the arch-enemy of mankind puts forth, amongst those who have a remnant of Christian faith, only just enough of his "lying signs and wonders," to satisfy curiosity and gradually lure his victims into the toils.

It is, I am convinced, their total ignorance of this principle, and of the true source of spiritual manifestations, that has led many remarkable American mediums into serious difficulties, when they tried their powers before large audiences in the old world. Hard-headed Englishmen congratulated themselves, when these individuals were convicted before the magistrates of palpable trickery and fraud, that their practical good sense had exposed the wretched swindle. They seem to forget that their cousins beyond the Atlantic, are quite equal to any people on the face of the earth, in shrewdness and sagacity, and that a smart Yankee would see through the performance of the cleverest trick that was ever manipulated, before a cautious Englishman would have got over his first impressions of wonder, at the marvellous skill of the conjurer.

There is manifestly another explanation than that offered by the convictions of fraud, or the performances in the Egyptian Hall, London, to account for the progress of Spiritism in America, and its discomfiture and failure in England.

The only rational explanation is this, that as the manifestations of the spirits could not be depended on, wherever they were likely to encounter the disturbing influence of Faith, Slade, and others of his class, were bound to supply the failing power, by practising the tricks of an ordinary conjurer. It would never do, to come forward, on the stage of a crowded theatre or Hall, and tell the audience that the circumstances were unfavorable, and the spirits had "struck work." Any one can tell what would be the immediate consequences of such an announcement, even though it were accompanied by the assurance that the money would be returned at the door. Thus they tried some clumsy tricks, and did them so badly, that a smart child could have detected the attempted deception in a moment. How the confirmed spiritists in America must have been amused, at the comments in the English newspapers on the exposures of their pet Religion!

I have seen the exhibitions of Maskelyne and Cook, and wondered how people of ordinary intelligence, who have been taught to reason from effect to cause, could possibly run away with the notion, that the cleverly arranged mechanism of these performers, or their confident assurance, or anything of the kind, which might excite the wonder of children, could be reasonably assigned as the cause of that fascination, which, in America, has confirmed so many thousands in their self-sacrificing support of Spiritism. As well might they maintain that mere tricks performed by the priests and augurs of Paganism, had enslaved minds greater than this present world of petty business concerns, and inordinate conceit and vanity, ever beheld. When we look on the ruins of the works of "the great days of old," and mark the steady progress, and perseverance, and giant resolve devoted to the accomplishment of works that in their mere conception would take away the breath of the great engineers and master-builders of our time, we cannot but feel astounded that the men of these old times should be imagined capable of such puerile credulity.

Do I therefore mean to say, that I actually believe that there is anything but sleight-of-hand and trickery in Spiritism? I no more doubt the presence of deviltry in the manifestations, that have led away so many from Christianity, than I doubt my own existence.

The most profound theologian of modern times, Perrone, has, in his work "*De Virtute Religionis*," so powerfully and conclusively argued the whole question, that it is impossible for any one who studies this work, to entertain a doubt about the agency of diabolical influence in Spiritism properly so called. This book of Perrone, which received the special approval of the late Pope Pius the Ninth, has accumulated such a mass of evidence, and has so minutely and clearly answered every objection against the doctrine of the Catholic Church on the point, that the keenest perception cannot discover a flaw in the reasoning. He does not trouble himself with an examination of the higher manifestations, which, although founded on grave and respectable evidence, might, by their very extraordinary character, excite amazement, and cause the serious-minded reader to question if the Providence of God could give so great power to His infernal enemies.

He takes up the ordinary phenomena, with which many in this colony are unfortunately too familiar,—the banging about of heavy articles of furniture, the life-like movements and intelligence with which these things appear endowed, at the bare touch of a medium; the rapping out of answers, so connected with questions proposed in the interior consciousness of the curious, and manifested by no outward sign, that they have caused swooning, and really dangerous excitement in the nervous system of many who had been tempted to make trial of these unholy experiments; and has demonstrated that, neither Divine influence, nor that of good angels, nor the souls of deceased friends, but veritable demons, are at the bottom of these hateful exhibitions.

About seven years ago, I felt it my duty, hearing from creditable sources that *séances* were becoming a fashionable recreation in certain towns of the colony to give a lecture on modern Spiritism and thus sound a note of warning. As I fully expected, I drew on myself much censure in the newspapers. I was accused of giving importance to ridiculous ephemeral wonders, and encouraging superstition, and attempting to bring out stupid exaggerations of long-forgotten stories of the dark ages. My only hope was, that my carefully measured words might check the evil. I think what I said had some good effect; and that it deterred a few good people, not Catholics, from meddling with matters, about which they knew very little, and the familiarity with which might have been followed by serious consequences to themselves and others.

The line taken by those who seem to hope that they can put down Spiritism by boldly denying that there are, or ever were, any manifestations, except those which Dr. Carpenter has attempted to account for, under the theory of "unconscious cerebration," or "involuntary muscular action," on the part of those who in a circle touch the table, or other article of furniture that is expected to spin or twirl, is simply ridiculous, in the judgment of those who have witnessed anything beyond the first attempts of amateurs in this direction.

A writer in the *Times*, when these learned explanations made their appearance, very justly observed, that if scientific men had no better reasons to offer except these and similar theories, wrapped up in technical phraseology, they had much better be silent altogether. Such puerile attempts at mystification, which were overstrained beyond the limits of common-sense, and did not take into account the actual phenomena, as attested by credible witnesses, only served to establish more firmly, what they were meant to destroy. He was quite right.

I have heard young men describe what they had witnessed at certain seances, and after expressing their amazement at the extraordinary evolutions of pieces of heavy furniture, which seemed to be animated, to move hither and thither of their own accord, and even climb up walls, invariably wound up with some remark upon the singular effects of electricity and magnetism. I could not help saying, on one occasion, to a young friend, "As you have never studied these sciences, you should be careful in giving dogmatic opinions about them, in the presence of those who have; you may make serious blunders."

Electricity and its cognate science are indeed doing very wonderful things; and the storing of this subtle something, which we call a fluid, and the other "imponderables"—light and heat, may yet, in this age of invention, revolutionize the ways of the present generation. But no conceivable development of these powers can, without a cunningly prepared and costly apparatus, give apparent life to the furniture of an ordinary room, which happens by mere chance to be selected as the scene of these mysterious operations.

There is scarcely a limit to the surprising things which can be done on a prepared stage, and with suitable apparatus. It is almost beyond credibility what apparently intelligent acts will be gone through by mere seeming automata, such as those exhibited in the Egyptian Hall; but every one knows that inanimate dolls do not play whist, and execute neat drawings, and life-like portraits, unless they are worked by the movements of an intelligent and well-trained human being, who, screened from sight, deftly manipulates the carefully prepared mechanism.

When we see inanimate things rap out, by indicating the letters of the alphabet, a long and well-connected answer to a question, whether uttered aloud, or written privately on a piece of paper, and carefully sealed and held in the hand of a reliable witness, and that this process is carried on in a well-known room, where there is no place for concealed wires or apparatus of any kind, and where the trial is attempted without any previous arrangement, a sensible man, superior to vulgar prejudice, will conclude that an intelligent being has communicated its power, in some mysterious way, to the lifeless wood, or brass, or whatever else it may be that appears to give the answer.

When I was in Germany, a few years ago, I asked a venerable ecclesiastic, who had been for many years a distinguished professor of theology, and was at the time filling one of the highest offices in the Church, if he had ever met with a case of Spiritism. He told me he had met with one very remarkable case, and that it had left no doubt on his mind that the person affected was under the influence of the devil. Before he had this experience, he said, that he had scouted the whole thing, as too contemptible for serious examination; he believed that everything extraordinary attributed to it was the effect of trickery and deceit. He was visiting, one day, in the lunatic asylum of the city where he lived, a young person, whose mind had given way, through addiction to table-turning and the like. She had lucid intervals; and it was on one of these occasions, when the patient was perfectly sane and tranquil, that he visited her. He spoke to her of the folly of trifling with things, which had so seriously affected her health. But she told him, that whenever she touched the table, it became animated, and that she could not help believing what she had seen so constantly. "See," she said, rising and touching a table in the room, "it will follow me like a pet animal." To his surprise it did so; and then, for the first time, it flashed upon his mind, that there was something diabolical connected with this movement. His visit had been unexpected, there was only a touch given to the table: she did not keep her hand upon it, and it seemed to obey her directions. There was no possibility of wires, or any communication between her and the piece of furniture. Under the impulse of the strong impression made upon his mind, he prayed interiorly that God might have pity on the unfortunate victim of diabolical illusion, and break the chain that bound her to the enemy of her salvation. He had scarcely completed his short prayer, when she exclaimed, that the table was dead or insensible to her command. She saw that her visitor had in some mysterious way controlled its movement, and earnestly begged for an explanation. It was given, and led to her prompt conversion, and the permanent restoration of her reason.

It seems to me that a case like this is beyond cavil and that it should be quite enough in itself, to deter all right-minded people from meddling with this dangerous folly. Some will say what harm can there possibly be in amusing one's self with one's companions over the erratic movements of a piece of furniture, which is in all probability set going by the act voluntary or involuntary of some one in the company, or in watching the absurd jerking of the pencil of *Planchette*, particularly when all notion of dealing with the powers of darkness is never for a moment entertained?

Yet I have been assured by persons, who I know were

not deceiving me, that even in these seemingly harmless diversions, impressions have been received, that seriously affected the nerves of some one or other of those engaged in them.

A medium, said to possess a remarkable power, told me, when I remonstrated with him, on amusing himself and others with exhibitions of his influence, that he never began without saying the Lord's Prayer. The very fact of doing so, I said, indicated a suspicion that there was something wrong in the practice; and that the effect of the prayer was vitiated by the positive act. I see that the same view is taken of similar cases given by Perrone.

But it will be said, that there may be some subtle law in nature which produces these effects. "Who can know all the laws of nature," says the experimenter, "and therefore, who can say there is not?" "Perhaps," he may add, "I may be the lucky one to stumble on some principle of science hitherto unknown."

A chance discovery of this kind is most unlikely, seeing that scientific men of the greatest abilities have given their attention to these phenomena. As to not understanding all the laws of nature, every one knows, that it is directly contrary to one of the fundamental laws of nature that an inert body will move itself; and that these movements are opposed to other well-known laws that form the very basis of true science.

"But how can an immaterial spirit act on matter?" It might as well be said, how can this soul of ours act on the material body? If one will read the opening chapter of the book of Job, he will see reason to bless God, that the physical power of the evil one is held in check by the Providence of God. We might otherwise have something to deplore in His appointments, far beyond the evils which ordinarily afflict mankind.

There is one great principle which forms the basis of all sound reasoning, and this is, that the effect cannot exceed the cause which produces it, or, in other words, that the cause includes the effect. If a mere touch can communicate life and intelligence to an inert piece of furniture, this axiom of reason would be overturned.

But the fact is, wherever there is question of the supernatural, non-Catholics, as a rule, will not reason at all. Men have brought themselves to believe that there is no Devil, and they are doing all they can to get rid of the troublesome idea of a Hell. Eternity of punishment, and the sanction of the Divine law, must, with the disintegration of Catholic dogma, which is the natural and logical consequence of Free-thought, be somehow cast away with other revealed truths.

If human reason is free to reject one mystery, why should it not have the power of repudiating another, that is most disagreeable to natural feeling? And, if there be no Eternity of punishment hereafter, there is then no essential difference between good and evil. The end of both being the same, they are essentially the same. And if this difference is not real, what is the use of troubling ourselves about sin or temptation or the devil? Why in this case, we might say, should God have given up His only Son to deliver us from an unreal evil. *Facilis decensus*, all melt away in the presence of unbelief, just as snow before the rays of the sun.

Men should think of this, and that there is no halting, once they have begun to doubt and deride revealed truths. If they ridicule the idea of the existence of a devil, and persist in disregarding all supernatural phenomena, and acting in direct opposition to the principles which guide them in the ordinary affairs of life that demand investigation, they will, of course, succeed in keeping far from them the disquieting thoughts that—"our adversary the devil, as a roaring lion, goeth about, seeking whom he may devour" (1 Pet. v. 8).

But I would ask Christians, that is to say, men who really believe in the Divine mission of the Saviour, but who have been brought to deride the existence of the Devil, what is meant by these words of the Apostle, "He that committeth sin is of the Devil; for the Devil sinneth from the beginning. For this purpose the Son of God appeared that He might destroy the works of the Devil" (1 John iii. 8). The meaning of the passage evidently is, not that our Divine Lord has put an end to the existence of the Devil; for those who sin belong to this great enemy of mankind; but that He might destroy this work of the Devil in the souls of men of Good will.

I have heard some advocates of Spiritism say,—men who had been familiar with supernatural manifestations, and fancied that good spirits, angels, or the souls of deceased friends, might have caused them, "How can the Devil be the cause of so much good? Many, by means of Spiritism, seeing the wonders it effects, have been converted from Materialism; and the messages we receive are generally pious exhortations, and perfectly conformable with the most exalted morality."

The answer, that at once suggests itself, is found in the words of St. Paul, where he is speaking of false Apostles, and deceitful laborers, transforming themselves into the Apostles of Christ. "No wonder," says the Apostle, "for Satan himself transformeth himself into an angel of light" (2 Cor. xi. 14).

These apparently holy messages are only in perfect keeping with the artifices of him, who was "a liar from the beginning." He promised fine things to our first parents; and attempted to seduce even our Divine Lord, by a show of kindness and sympathy for His hunger, when he tried the temptation in the wilderness. If Materialists are brought, by these unholy means, to recognize the existence of spirits, they will not be brought nearer to God by this means; but rather attracted to the eternal enemy of God and man.

Perrone, quoting from many distinguished writers on the subject, shows, by many examples, that once the unfortunate victims of this superstition are caught in the toils, they receive messages of a very different character, absolutely shocking in their open rebellion against God, and their revolting suggestions. When the Devil assailed our Divine Lord, it was not long before he threw aside the mask, and said—"all these will I give thee, if falling down, thou wilt adore me" (Matt. iv. 9).

Those mediums who eschew the society of turbulent spirits, that at once reveal their true character by blasphemous and obscene language, and affect the company of the more gentle kind, who indicate their presence by soft taps, and sweet words of comfort and pity, will, if they persevere in these communications, be, some day or other, as startled as was the witch of Endor, when the ghost of a just man suddenly appeared in the midst of her "familiars."

But may not these spirits be the souls of dear friends, who are dead? This is the greatest delusion of all. Catholics, of course, see at once that this could not be. The souls enjoying the beatific vision, cannot be torn from their bliss, by the incantations of a medium.

Those who are expiating the punishment due to sin forgiven, or venial faults, cleansing away "the wood and hay and stubble," or imperfections from the "gold, silver and precious stones" of their good works, " shall not go out from their prison till they have paid the last farthing" (Matt. v. 26). What power on earth shall release from their bondage those who are lost beyond redemption?

Men, who are not Catholics, and have the least self-respect, loathe and detest the very name of the accursed thing, which pretends to the power of calling up their souls after death, for the amusement of an ignorant crowd, who hang on the words of a stupid medium by whose ungrammatical or slangy language, their sentiments are supposed to be expressed.

This notion, that the spirits who speak through mediums, are the souls of departed friends, shows that the delusion, gross as it is, is not altogether modern; for we find St. Thomas quoting St. Augustine, and St. John Chrysostom in denunciation of it. "Demons frequently pretend that they are the souls of the dead, to confirm in their error, the Gentiles who entertained this belief" (St. Thomas, Part I., Q. 117, Art. 4). But the revolting belief goes back much farther, even to the earliest days of Paganism; for amongst the abominations mentioned in Deuteronomy, as abhorred by God, is the very one of seeking knowledge and truth from the dead. " Let not there be found among you one that consulteth pythonic spirits, or fortune-tellers, or that seeketh truth from the dead, for the Lord abhorreth all these things" (Deuteronomy xviii. 11, 12).

I say this is the greatest delusion of anything connected with Spiritism, and the most fatal, because it is the most

CATHOLIC CHRISTIANITY AND SPIRITISM. 383

attractive. When the clever demons, who by their fall have not lost their superior intelligence, and other gifts essential to their nature, counterfeit the ways and manner of a deceased friend or relative of those who invoke the spirits, they bind the unfortunate victim of their deceit to their service by bonds, that it seems almost hopeless, by any instruction or argument, ever to loosen.

Learned priests in Europe have told me, that, when Catholics have been thus seduced, and afterwards touched with remorse expose this plague-spot of their souls, it seems by their constant relapse, to be absolutely incurable. Well may we say of such deplorable evils, with the great dramatist in Macbeth—

>   Unnatural deeds
> Do breed unnatural troubles,
> God, God, forgive us all!

CHAPTER XX.

Conclusion.

IF what I have, with much labor and careful study and consideration, put together in the preceding pages, prove, through the Divine blessing, a help to earnest souls, who are seeking a knowledge of the truth "as it is in Jesus," it will be the happiest work of my life. If it is not blessed with this desirable fruit, I hope that He, who sees the secrets of the heart, will be mindful of my intention, and for Christ's sake, whose blessed will it is that none should perish, pardon my manifold sins.

I have endeavored, all through, to set Catholic Christianity before my readers, as a whole body of doctrine and practice; and carefully to distinguish both, from ordinary misapprehension and misrepresentation. It seemed to me, that a book, in which this simple view would be steadily kept before the mind of those who may care to read it, and in which the sense would not be obscured by heaps of learned arguments, and attempts at fine language, is a real want at the present time.

The desire to do this so effectually, that it might catch the attention, even of those who would cursorily turn over its pages, has I see, now that I look back upon what I have written, led me occasionally to repeat in another form, what had been already previously written; to apply, for example, a certain train of thought, laid down in a general way, to individual sentiments and perceptions. I kept before me steadily the Horatian maxim, to avoid obscurity in attempting over-brevity; and found it difficult at times to escape the other extreme of prosiness, in the bringing out of what seemed to me a matter of peculiar importance. If this will not prove wearisome to those who follow the argument, and help to develop more distinctly my meaning, I will cheerfully bear the castigation of critics on this redundancy of style.

We have a great number of admirable books in English, which expound Catholic doctrine in the clearest and most forcible manner; but they generally take up a doctrine by itself, just as it probably would be taken up by a non-Catholic or Infidel, define it accurately, and support it by sound and logical argument, and then answer the objections which are urged against it, as it stands. This is scarcely fair to the body of revealed doctrine, as taught by the Catholic Church.

The Real Presence, for example, however clearly proved, as a distinct dogma of Faith, cannot strike the mind of a stranger to our Religion, as it will, when it is brought out as the complement of the Incarnation. It is the same with the other sacraments: each may, and does rest on distinct proofs; but the whole sacramental system strikes, even a non-Catholic, with its majestic beauty and perfect consistency, when the system is seen to grow up, almost by a natural unity, from the "Word made flesh" —the great abiding sacrament of the new law.

I have therefore endeavored, as much as possible, to blend together all the mysteries and doctrines of Catholicity in one great centre of religious truth, whence emanate, as so many rays of light, the various devotions and practices, and the entire life and spirit of the Church.

How far the study of Catholic belief regarded *seriatim* has caused misapprehension, I cannot say: but I feel certain, that considerable difficulty has been experienced by intelligent Protestants, when they have tried to master the real teaching of the Church, by taking up her doctrines in detail.

Let them study for example, the worship of the Sacred Heart; what more natural than that this devotion should be considered, by diligent inquirers, a sort of materialistic object of superstition, when viewed by itself. It seems absolutely repulsive to Protestant notions, that a mere combination of flesh, and blood, and muscle, could, by any process of reasoning, be set up as an object of worship: and it is not surprising therefore, that many intelligent journalists, and writers in Reviews and Magazines, have adopted the Jansenistic idea of this devotion, and denounced it as gross materialism.

But let it be considered in its intimate connection with the Incarnation, and all these difficulties vanish; nay more they seem to bring forth, into the clearest light, the true doctrine of the Incarnation. I would even go so far as to maintain, that the mystery of the "Word made flesh" cannot be received by Faith, in all its plenitude, unless the doctrine of the Sacred Heart is accepted as explained by the Church.

Those who speak and write of the materialistic worship of the Sacred Heart, show, by their misunderstanding of the very elements of this devotion, that they do not comprehend Catholic teaching in reference to the perfect union of the Divine and human natures in one person. I think I have shown conclusively, in what I have written on the subject, that even the Catholic belief proclaimed in the General Council of Ephesus, that Mary is the mother of God, does not develop the truth so plainly and unmistakably, as it is brought home to the mind of every Catholic by this devotion.

We may believe that the soul and body, or the entire human nature of the man-God, is inseparably united with the second Divine Person of the Blessed Trinity; and yet falter at the inevitable conclusions of the doctrine, as it is plainly expressed in the devotion of the Sacred Heart, and determined by orthodox teaching. When the soul of our Divine Lord was really separated from the body by death, and the lifeless corpse lay on the lap of the Virgin Mother, or was placed in the sepulchre, we might imagine that, in the period after His death, that preceded the Resurrection, there was a change in the relations, that had been established between the union of the two natures. We might be tempted to suppose, that the Divinity clung to the active and living principle, and leaving the inanimate body, for a time at least, had accompanied the soul of our Divine Lord to the lower regions, where the spirits of the saints and Patriarchs of the old dispensation awaited their deliverance.

But it is not so; such a separation would, as all theologians believe, have broken, in its very essence, the bond which makes us children of God, brothers of Jesus Christ, and heirs to His kingdom. God the Son allied Himself to our nature perfectly; not to the soul only, but to the body also, to every part of the human nature, which He had made His own; not alone to the head, or heart, or limbs, that were pierced for our sakes, but to every drop of the Precious blood shed for our salvation. The whole human nature was so intimately united to the Divine person, that not one particle of the Flesh and Blood derived from the Virgin Mother could, as long as they remained flesh and blood, for an instant be absolutely severed from it.

This is a marvellous truth, which requires the entire

subjection of our reason to the word of God. The unregenerate reason startles at the proposition, questions it, rebels against it, cannot possibly receive it without Faith. It is only this supernatural gift of God, that enables us to receive the astounding mystery.

Once duly instructed, by the infallible living voice, which even scepticism perceives is absolutely necessary to the full acceptance of Revelation, we then perceive the true nature of these bonds, by which the Son of God has allied Himself to a fallen race. Then, with the sense of Faith, looking as it were through the eyes of the mother of sorrows, we behold the angels worshipping the inanimate Body, and see them clustering round each drop of the Precious Blood, that flowed for our sakes, in the garden of Gethsemani, and bespattered the hall of Pilate, or was trodden under foot by the crowd that thronged to Calvary.

What a wondrous help is this to realize all that is given us in the Blessed Sacrament—"*Sumunt boni, sumunt mali*," desecrated by diabolical passion, cast out into the muddy streets, pierced by daggers in honor of the demon, blended with poison for purposes of murder, to what indignities has not the most Holy Eucharist been subjected!

When we picture to ourselves these marvels of Divine patience, as they stand out distinctly before us in the doctrine of the Sacred Heart, as in no other, we can exclaim with St. Thomas—"*O res mirabilis! manducat Dominum, pauper, servus et humilis*," and bowing to the earth, in humble adoration, thank the good God, as best we may, for such prodigies of mercy.

If I have said anything, in my remarks on sentimental Religion, that will cause pain to earnest Christians, who are not Catholics, I can only express my regret that they should be offended, by what I felt it my duty to say in the interests of truth.

I have often felt, I feel it now acutely while I write, that their earnest attachment to the mere traditions of the Faith " once delivered to the saints," their heartfelt reverence for the crumbs of Holy Doctrine, that have, in spite of sectarian rage, been saved and piously guarded by so many devout souls, shame the languid faith of too many, who, through the gratuitous mercy of God, have without any merit on their part, been called to sit as guests at the bountiful table which He has spread for Catholics. What shall we plead in our defence, at the awful tribunal of judgment, when these shall rise up against us, and say, had they only heard of the good things, so plentifully set before us, they would have rivalled the saints, in the fervor of their unbounded love for so good a Saviour.

But I cannot help repeating what I have stated already, that there is no greater enemy to the true Church, than those false teachers, who undertake to feed the hungry with the husks of this piety of mere feeling, and by this means, satisfy their urgent wants, and prevent them from throwing themselves, sorrowing and repenting, at the feet of their loving Father.

When I picture to myself with what anxious care such as these prepare themselves for the Lord's Supper, how they strive to repair their faults, to forgive those who trespass against them, to excite in their souls the reverence and tender affection to our Lord, which animated the Apostles, as they ate the last Pasch with their Divine Master; and how fervently they ponder on His sufferings, while they eat and drink mere bread and wine in remembrance of Him, I feel humbled and abashed at my want of a lively faith, as often as I partake of the true Body and Blood of Jesus Christ in the Holy Communion.

How different would be the aspect of this weary world, if Christians of all denominations were made one, in the participation of the Blessed Sacrament! Thus animating one another by mutual prayer, and good-will, Christians would exhibit to an unbelieving world, the most striking proof of the Divine origin and character of the Religion Christ has left us.

Our Divine Lord prayed, at his last supper, that not only they who were present, but those who would believe in their teaching, might, notwithstanding the perversity of our free-will, be thus united, made one as He and the adorable Persons of the Blessed Trinity are one. Could this have been accomplished, even by the marvels of Divine Grace given sufficiently to every one, we should hear nothing of the outcries of unbelief. Alas! they who deride the Blessed name of the Saviour, can well say, in mockery and scorn, what the Pagans were forced to say, in admiration of the first followers of the Crucified,—"See how those Christians love one another."

But we are free to do as we please. Though the charity of Christ "presseth us," when we behold the excess of His love, as it is exhibited in the teaching of Catholic Christianity, it does not constrain or compel us, in spite of our prejudices, to be "of one mind," and to confess, as it were "with one mouth" all things which He and His Apostles have announced to the world. We can only pray with all our hearts, that good men may be brought somehow to see the beauty of Catholic doctrine; and thus, if separated from our brethren in Christ, to be really united to Him in His desire that there should be "one fold and one Shepherd."

I have not entered deeply into the consideration of the Phases of modern Unbelief. I felt it would do no good to let my fellow-Christians know the full extent of these aberrations from revealed truth, which are exhibited in every new theory of Religion. It might perhaps shake the faith of weak brethren in the Providence of God.

No doubt when the blasphemies of the great Revolution were echoed through the world, believers in Christ could hardly restrain their indignation. They must have cried out, in horror and amazement, as they heard that a worthless woman was set up on the altar of the true God, and worshipped, amid the acclamations of an excited people,—" How long, O Lord, how long wilt Thou endure this profanation?"

But because God is patient and long-suffering, men hold their peace now, when Agnosticism or black hideous Materialism, or Pantheism, or even the worship of the Devil, invite the adoration or the homage of the unbelieving masses. But if God is patient, "He is not mocked" with impunity.

There are sins that cry aloud to Heaven for vengeance; and surely, above all other sins, is the great "Revolt," for which the coldness and indifference of these latter days seems preparing us. I never hear that beautiful prayer of the Church—"Spare, O Lord, spare Thy people, and be not angry with us forever," that I do not feel it should be the constant cry of all Christendom. God is terrible in His anger; but He is most terrible, as the Prophet declared, when "His indignation seemed to rest above the head of His people," and no great tribulation fell upon them, to remind them of His wrath.

There were great nations in the world before now, which experienced the fatal consequences of forsaking

God, for the service of His enemies. As we read the vivid pictures which able hands have sketched, in recent years, of the chastisements of Imperial Rome, and mark the fulfilment of the woes pronounced against this Babylon of the Apocalypse, we see as clearly the hand of an avenging God, as it was manifested in the destruction of the cities of the plain. When Goth, and Vandal, and Hun, burst down upon the great mistress of the nations, like successive ocean waves, and swept before them her mighty palaces and temples, no wonder the most distant provinces of the vast empire, beheld, in these rude shocks, the marks of the "terrible scourge of God."

Standing, as I stood some years ago, on the Palatine, and picturing to one's self the splendor and magnificence of a Roman triumph in the palmy days of the Empire; watching in imagination the interminable throng of captives of all countries, toiling along the route under the weight of the gold, and silver, and precious things, carried away by the spoiler, and the flashing armor, and the banners of the proud legionaries, hearing the deafening clang of trumpets, and the martial music, one can realize what is meant by "the pride of life," and not wonder, that the victorious Cæsar or General should need one beside him to remind him constantly that he was not yet a God. With such a scene extending amid the miles and miles of stately buildings, and glorious monuments of that vast wealth and wonderful civilization, away over the seven hills, and farther than eye can reach on the Campagna, and then looking down on the ruin and desolation in the Forum beneath his feet, the lesson is brought home of the perishable nature of man's grandest achievements. Under such circumstances, the traveller from distant lands feels so sensibly that "this world passeth away," that another vision, sketched by a masterhand, naturally suggests itself. Men filled with the spirit of the world, proud of their country's progress, and worshippers of its wealth, may smile at the often-quoted extract of Macaulay.

But there are already signs in the North, and South, and East, and West, which might chill their ardor, and even the ghost of a vision, like that of the "battle of Dorking," might cause a numbing of the heart to steal upon them, of startling significance. Mighty cities of the past, that once seemed, to their inhabitants, durable as the everlasting hills, are now a mass of shapeless ruins, melting away year after year into utter desolation. History repeats itself; and future generations, not far remote, may realize to their dismay that the accumulated wealth and power of nations is not the property of the idol called "Humanity;" but that "the earth is the Lord's and the fulness thereof." It would be well to have these words of wisdom, not merely engraved on the marble that at present marks the centre of worldly aspirations, in the great metropolis, but in the hearts of a mighty people, who seem already spoiled by continuous and unchecked prosperity.

There is however one great kingdom, and because it has been set up by the God of Heaven, "it shall," as the Prophet Daniel writes, "never be destroyed," and "it shall stand forever" (Daniel ii. 44). This kingdom, which is called by Macaulay "The everlasting Church," the Church built by our Divine Lord on Peter, will resist even the worst assaults of Hell itself.

Even when Satan shall, by the worse than Pagan irreligion and impiety, that prevails, and is every day spreading with fearful rapidity, resume his empire in this world; and its laws shall be delivered into his hands "for a time," the rock, "cut out of the mountain, without hands," shall defy his efforts to upheave it. The successor of St. Peter may be driven out, and become a wanderer on the face of the earth; but wherever he rests his feet, there shall the rock be found beneath them, —"*Ubi Petrus, ibi Ecclesia*" (St. Ambrose in Psalm xl.,— n. 30). Weapons, more potent even than that product of diabolical ingenuity which, while it saps all human rights, is applauded by those who profit by it, as one of the bright discoveries of modern progress,—" the logic of accomplished facts," may be hurled at this rock, but they will strike in vain. The " word that shall never pass away,"—the promise of perpetual stability, will be fulfilled till time shall be no more, and when this kingdom is transferred to Heaven, there, shall the Church Triumphant reign in glory, as long as God exists.

How vain and silly it is for men who have read history, to be ever on the look-out for the telegram, that shall announce the tidings, so joyful to the enemies of Christ that the Holy Father, the successor of St. Peter, is about to fly from Rome, or better still, has actually abandoned the holy city! Why they, who so confidently proclaim that the Papacy is no more, should give themselves so much concern about the movements of an old man, weak and helpless in all worldly power, is more than they can themselves well account for.

They who regard the complete spoliation of Leo XIII., as a vital question for Catholic Christianity, should remember, that his predecessors, for three hundred years of the most sanguinary persecution, ruled the Church " to the uttermost parts of the earth," from the tombs of the Catacombs. They should also bear in mind, that, in those evil days of Pagan supremacy, the kingdom of God on earth grew so luxuriantly, fertilized as it was by the blood of nearly twelve millions of martyrs, that Christians crowded even the palace of the Cæsars.

And why is this? Because Persecution is the chief means, adopted by Divine Providence, to develop its ever-youthful strength and vigor. Never, during its whole history, were its powers so knit together in healthy activity, as in these very days, in which the existence of Christianity, outside its fold, is threatened by the ravening wolves of a wide-spread and ever-growing Infidelity. The last definition of the Vatican Council marks the utmost extreme of spoliation and bondage that is possible for daring impiety. Though the last refuge of the Holy Father in Rome may be closed against him, and his brethren, "placed to rule the Church of God which He hath purchased with His own blood" (Acts xx. 28), his infallible voice shall go forth, with an influence, more touching to every Catholic heart from the fact that he is suffering for justice sake, and guide the flock, spread throughout the world, in all its perplexities and difficulties.

There is yet another point worth remembering, it is clearly brought out by Cardinal Manning, in his work, "The Independence of the Holy See." "The head of the Christian world can never be disturbed from his rightful seat without causing perturbation throughout the Christian world." "Never," says his Eminence, "in the history of Christian Europe, since the year eight hundred" (when Charlemagne was crowned Emperor of the West by Pope Leo III., and secured the Holy Father in his temporal power), "has the Sovereignty of Rome been violated by force, but, throughout the whole of Christian

Europe, there has been spread a perturbation, which has only been redressed through sanguinary wars" (p. 39).

It must be a sore affliction to the children of unbelief, who are exulting over the proximate annihilation of Catholic Christianity, to learn, that, in free America, as I see by the Directory of this year, the Church is making the most wonderful progress. There are now in the United States, 13 Archbishops, 57 Bishops, 6835 priests, 1651 ecclesiastical students, 6613 churches, 1150 chapels, 1476 stations, 22 ecclesiastical seminaries, 87 colleges, 599 academies, 2532 parochial schools, 481,834 pupils attending the parochial schools, 294 asylums, and 139 hospitals. The total Catholic population of the States is set down at 6,623,176: many Catholic writers say that this estimate is too low, and that it is nearer ten millions. I do not find the number of convents and monasteries, given either in this Directory, or that of 1883; but referring to Bishop Spalding's "Essays and Reviews," published in 1877, I found that the number of convents for women in that year was 350, and for men 130.

Considering that in 1790, there was not one convent in the United States; and that a hundred years ago, there was no Bishop, only 25 priests and about 40,000 Catholics, this vast increase certainly does not look like decay. I will say nothing about the growth of the Church in Australia and throughout the Colonies. It will be quite enough to note the growth of Catholicity in the United States, where it was once confidently stated, by men of much learning and authority, that the old religion could never prosper.

Who can say what the future of the Christian Religion, outside the Catholic Church, will be, fifty years hence?

Lacordaire, who died in 1861, one of the most gifted men of his generation in France, and who had given considerable attention to the nature of Protestantism, expressed his conviction, that, before the opening of the next century, it would, as a Religion, cease to have any hold on the minds of the cultured classes.

In the face of the spreading Infidelity, its entirely negative character is becoming every day more apparent. Now that it has other work on its hands than to abuse the old Church, and is obliged to make every effort to rally its supporters against the vigorous assaults of the "isms," I have described in the concluding chapters of this book, it is brought to feel and acknowledge its inherent weakness.

If the force of popular opinion carries disestablishment, and there ceases to be a National religion in England, it is not easy to see, what can stop the rapid progress of disintegration. Certainly mere sentimentalism and emotional piety will not do it. This sort of unnatural excitement suffers, more than any other sentiment, by reaction; and with the spread of Godless education, mere pious words, and phrases, and unctuous appeals to feeling, will not satisfy the irreverent spirit of Free-thought, which is the natural outcome of education without God.

Most thinking men, and they are so few in these busy times that one can easily collect their views, agree that, soon, even before fifty years are past, there will be in the world that once was Christian, only two camps. Infidelity on the one side, and Catholic Christianity on the other.

Then shall come the decisive test, which will try every human being able to form a judgment. Christ and His entire message of Peace to men of good-will on the one hand, and Anti-Christian theories on the other will set themselves plainly and unmistakably before each individual, and he shall realize to himself the meaning of these words of our Divine Lord—"He that is not with me is against me" (Matt. xii. 30).

In view of those evil days, when Faith will be sorely tried in all who will not hear the Church, Christians of every denomination should say from their hearts—"Come, Holy Ghost, fill the hearts of Thy faithful, and enkindle in them the fire of Thy love, send forth Thy spirit, and they shall be created, and Thou shalt renew the face of the earth." It is only this Heavenly grace that can dissipate the darkness of error, and bring all, who really desire it, to the knowledge and love of Truth. This is "a consummation devoutly to be wished for" beyond all other blessings:—"For this is good and acceptable in the sight of God our Saviour, who will have all men to be saved, and to come to the knowledge of the truth" (1 Tim. ii. 3, 4).

INDEX.

ACCOMPLISHED facts, 48.
Adler, Dr., his sermons, 28.
Agnosticism, its tactics, 350; absurdity of the "unknowable," 350; St. Paul and unknown God, 351; refuted by Frederic Harrison, 351.
Agnus Dei, 127.
Alice, and her childish dreams, 55.
Allenstein, Von, testimony on undenominational schools, 197.
Alvimore, Baron d', extracts from old traditions, Chinese, Hindoo, Persian, Mexican, 361, 362.
America, freedom favorable to Catholic Church, 190; common-schools in, 199–202; almighty dollar, 277, 354; newspaper testimony on common-schools, 202; sacrifices for preservation of liberty, 334; extraordinary growth of Catholic Church in, 396.
Antichrist and scarlet woman not applied by Infidels to Catholic Church, 172.
Apocalypse, and Christian worship, 155.
Appenzell, canton of Inner and Ausser Rhoden, 286.
Après nous le déluge, 71.
Assaults of Infidelity self-destructive, Voltaire, 322.
Assurance of salvation, danger of, 217; no positive in Catholic Church, 220.
Athanasian Creed dissolving, 33; on Incarnation, 84, 269.
Athens, Rome, Alexandria, schools of thought, 178.

Atonement, Ingersoll's "infamy" of, 238.
Augustine, St., the altar, 128; quotation from "City of God," 290; principle of belief in Scripture, 325; on Spiritism, 382.

BAG of bones theory, 181, 302, 344.
Baptism, water essential in, 109; necessary for salvation, 307; Church of, true meaning, 307; fate of unbaptized children, 309; unbaptized Pagans, 309.
Battle of Dorking, 393.
Bayle, on doubts of Infidels, 320.
Benediction of Blessed Sacrament, 97.
Belief in Christ includes all His doctrine, 303.
Beaconsfield, Lord, on Atheism, 350.
Bible, its wide propagation useless, 23; as rule of Faith, 39; Christianity, Infidel assaults against, 44.
Bingham on worship, 155.
Blessed Eucharist, objection from irreverence of Catholics, 135; connection with Incarnation, 165; worship of, not Idolatry, 165.
Blind man, in relation to mysteries, 42.
Bohlen, Von, Vater, Hartmann, Norton, on antiquity of writing, 323.
Boldetti, Bosio, Bottari, Aringhi, D'Agincourt, on Catacombs, 156.

Bonjean, President, and Mgr. Darboy, their death at La Roquette, 114.
Bourdaloue on salvation of Pagans, 310.
Bradlaugh, sentiments of his class, 18.
Brutum fulmen, strong arm of law, 18.
Buddha, resemblance to Christ; objection answered by Bentley, 180.

CAIPHAS and Exponents of Prophecy, 147.
Calvin, his teaching on Predestination, 254-256.
Canada, its colonization, 291; Champlain, 291; Hochelaga, 292.
Callan, Dr., Maynooth, 176.
Cant and Hypocrisy hated, 53.
Capital, and its possessors, 23.
Carpenter, Dr., on Spiritism, 374.
Castracani, Abbé, count de, 175.
Catacombs, martyrs of, 113; successors of St. Peter in the, 128; worship in, 156.
Catholics, bad lives of some, 93; Catholic countries always cheery, 252; always poor, 279.
Catholic Church, said to be enemy of Progress, 44; Intemperate arguments against, 45; contradictory charges against, 46; old-fashioned, 47; never persecuted, 49; her right to teach, 51; how to be attacked, 51; secret of her vigorous life, 124; sublime grandeur of, 127; a society of men, 138; and material progress, 187; doctrine on Original sin, 267; Catholic truth how sustained, 321; Catholic doctrine expounded as a whole, advantages of, 385; Catholic want of devotion, 389; extraordinary growth in America, 396; her future in the world, 396; everlasting kingdom, 373; grew luxuriantly in persecution, 394; Catholic countries poor, objection, 279.
Celsus and Porphyry, caricature of Christianity, 28.
Charles II. and his problem, 67.
Christmas devotions, 104.
Children dear to Christ, 55.
Chinese traditions, 361.
Christ in garden of Gethsemani, 137.
Chrysostom, St. John, adoration of angels, 149; Spiritism, 382.
Clement, St., Church of, in Rome, 128.
Colenzo and Polygamy, 226; and Zulu convert, 331.
Colonial youth, irreverence in churches, 161; their notions of Religion, 211; travellers in Europe, their impressions, 288; explanations of Spiritism, 374;
Communion, Holy, makes us individually sharers in atonement, 125.
Comparative study of languages proves unity of human race, 366.
Concupiscence, 237.
Convents, why people shut themselves up in, 225; folly of, 247.
Converts, false ideas in reference to sanctity of Catholics, 140; not much study required of them, 166; conversions singular, 213.
Cook and Maskelyne in Egyptian Hall, 371.
Cousin, Pantheist, 338; his conversion, 343.
Cowper, Poet, on Materialism, 349.
Cromwell, a saying of his, 254; his war-cry, 285.
Cyril, St., and Christ-bearers, 130.

DARWIN, his facts, 67; his theory and Evolution of Religion, 358.
Deceased friends, spirits of, 381.

INDEX. 401

Demonstrations Évangéliques, celebrated work of Abbé Migne, 68.
Descartes, his Philosophy, 337.
Devereux, Bishop, 96.
Devil not believed to exist, 379; still exists, 380.
Dickens, Charles, his sympathy for the fallen, 53; David Copperfield, Heep, and Littimer, 223, 224; Mrs. Clenham's religion, 253, 368. .
Deists intolerant, 304.
Divorce courts, 207.
Divine right, 187.
Donatists, false ideas of perfection, 143,
Duty of parents, 193, 195.

EASTERN Religions and Catholic Christianity, 360; peoples, traditions of, 361.
Education without God, 19; its main object, 191; denominational and undenominational, 192; Compulsory, 196; "Godless," 196; in American "common-schools," 199, 202; in Prussia, 196; in France, 198; effects in America, newspaper testimony, 201.
Egyptian Hall, Cook and Maskelyne, 371.
Eliot, George, poetry, 342; Mallock's view of, 342.
Emotional Christianity, 215; dangerous illusion, 220; extempore prayer, 244; Revivals, 242, 245; weakness of, 396.
End never justifies the means, 37.
England "workshop of the world," 287; poverty in, 290; frauds of spiritists detected in, 371.
Epicurus, 348.
Eternity of torments, belief in, not incompatible with enjoyments of life, 94, 132; decree of God, 182.
Evolution, 318; on hypothesis of Personal God, 339; possible to certain extent, meets certain scriptural difficulties, 358; Evolution of Religion, 359; both begin at wrong end, 358.
Exclusive Salvation, dogmas of Catholic Church upon, 306; exclusiveness, 302.
Extreme Unction, its consolations, 98.

FABIOLA, loss of natural gifts, 343; the slave Syra, 341.
Faith, wilful rejection of, 139; misery of renunciation, 169; in Lord's supper, 390; Catholics live in atmosphere of, 172.
Family, without God, 21.
Fawcett, his testimony on state of working-classes, 71.
Fichte, 338.
Fire of Hell explained, 133; decree of God, 182.
Formulary of concord, 235.
France, theology in, 17; Education in, 198; degeneracy in, 18; not poor because Catholic, 293.
Free-thinkers not abusive of Catholic Church, 172.
Frescos in St. Clement's, testimony of, 128.
Frothingham, his essays, 28.
Froude, his testimony about protection of trade in Ireland, 284.

GLORIA in excelsis, 127,
God of the Bible according to Ingersoll, 52; our Father, 339; Indignation terrible, 391; "Scourge of God," 392; hardening hearts, 259.
Gospel, parables of, in reference to Church, 142.
Gordon riots, 19.
Grace, divine, interior compared with natural gifts, 264; common, 265; power of co-operating with, 266; Moehler's teaching on, 267; main difficulty, 271; Pelagian heresy on, 271;

beauty of Catholic doctrine on, 275; Newman on power of, 147.

HALLAM, his views of persecution, 49.
Hamlet, dread of something after death, 344.
Harmony of Revealed truths, 76.
Harrison, Frederic, Religion of Humanity, 277; a few passages from *Nineteenth Century*, 354.
Haulleville Baron de, Catholic and Protestant progress, 286.
Heart, Sacred, 386; strengthens other mysteries, 388.
Hegel, 338.
Heretics and Schismatics, fate of, 310.
Humanity, worship of, 355.
Human liberty and intolerance, 306.
Hock, Doctor, 146.
Hurter, Frederic, 146.
Hypocrisy and cant, hated, 53.

IDLENESS, not encouraged by Catholic Church, 250.
Idolatry, no, in worship of Blessed Sacrament, 165.
Imagination developed by Catholic teaching, 104.
Immaculate Conception, 35; definition of, 86.
Incarnation, Newman on, 80; errors about, 81; Belief in, makes Blessed Eucharist easy, 129; connection with Blessed Eucharist, 165.
Incomprehensible, God necessarily, 58; can God require us to b e l i e v e incomprehensible truths? 60.
Indian traditions, 363.
Indifference, enemy of truth, 38; danger of, 311.
Individualism another name for Rationalism, 29.
Inductive Philosophy, 67.
Infallibility, a necessary claim, 40; different from impeccability, 147; guide necessary, Mallock's view of, 325.
Infants unbaptized, fate of, 309.
Infidelity of present time, its characteristics, 14; "poor imitations of polished ungodliness," 325.
Ingersoll, Colonel, his lectures, 28; name applied to God of Bible, 52; on Trinity, 57; large audiences he commands, 57; his vision of judgment; 222; atonement, his ideas of, 238; hatred of God of Bible, 255; objection to Pentateuch, 326; consequences determine nature of acts, 261.
Inquisition, 183.
Instinct and Reason, 346.
Interior life of Priests and Religious, 148.
Intolerance of truth, 48; true meaning, 299; of error, 181; of civil law, 305.
Invincible ignorance, 312; not save souls, but excuse wilful fault, 313; is it extensive, 314.
Invocation of saints, argument against, 43.
Ireland, name applied to Blessed Virgin in, 80; weird traditions of, 78; progress of religion in, 123; causes of poverty, 282; Ulster and Connaught, 283.
Irish, their deep seated religion, 79; and Scotch compared, 284.

JANSENISTS, their doctrine of what is becoming in God, 100; pernicious influence, 105.
Japan, Buddhism and the prosperity of, 293.
Jehovah, name of awe, 88.
Jerome, St., and judgment, 135.
Jesuit Fathers of Zambesi, 115; earnestness of their faith, 116; College rue des Postes, Paris, 176; Stoneyhurst, 176.
Jew, a learned one at Bethlehem, 92; Jewish people, history of Providence, 333.

Julian the Apostate, his objections, 28. 316.
Justice and Reason, 340.
Justification, 229; definition of, 231; Moehler's symbolism on, 232.

KANT, 338.
Kaye, political economist, 70.
Kyrie eleison, 127.

LACORDAIRE, his view of degeneracy in France, 31; on salvation of heretics, 313; "Wandering Jew," 333; decline of Protestantism, 397.
Land of the nation in the hands of a few, 70.
La Roquette and its martyrs, 115.
Lavaleye, M. de, on Catholic and Protestant progress, 282; Catholic countries do not colonize, 291.
Lectures, Wiseman's, Gospel parables, 142; on science and revelation, 179; Lectures on spiritism, 373.
Leyden school of theology, 302.
Liberal Protestants intolerant, 304.
Liberty, human, and intolerance, 305.
Lie, never lawful, 38.
Life, rule of, in fashionable London, 22.
Light, too much, 179.
Liturgies, 156.
Longevity of patriarchs, 362.
Louise Lateau, 136.
Louisiana, its colonization, 292.
Louis XV., his courtiers on eve of Revolution, 70.
Louvre, picture in, of decadence of Imperial Rome, 69.
Luther, his strong language, 25; his centenary, 26; on intimate conviction, 220.

MAHOMEDANS, their notions of Heaven, 73.
Mammon, worship of, 277.

Mallock on necessity of infallible guide, 325; his views of Catholic Church, 38, 51; views of George Eliot, 342.
Manhood of Christ to be adored, 102; His body in death object of adoration, 103.
Manning, Cardinal, on love of neighbor, 225; sanctification according to, 235; notion of true liberty, 306; temporal sovereignty never disturbed but with confusion of all Christendom, 395.
Maria Monk and scandalous stories, 117.
Mary, "Mother of God," 85.
Maskelyne and Cook in Egyptian Hall, 371, 375.
Master of ceremonies, 167.
Materialism and positivism, 343; contradiction not possible in matter, 348.
McCarthy, Abbé, on mysteries, 60, 66.
Melancthon, curious testimony of, 236.
Mexican traditions, 363.
Microscope, its revelations, 62.
Midas, Sir Gorgius, 290.
Miracle of loaves and fishes, 91; Christ walking on waters, entering closed room, 92.
Moehler, symbolism, 232; testimony about good pagans, 267; doctrine on Grace, 267; Freewill, 268.
Morality of Catholic and Protestant countries compared, 292; same for all classes, 296.
Mormonism, 334.
Moses, writing known to, 322; remarkable history, 327; grand conception of, 328; his division of history, 330.
Müller, Von, testimony to Catholic Church, 207; Rev. Michael, 204, 207.
Mundella, France worthy of imitation in godless education, 32.

Mungo, St., cathedral of, in Glasgow, 153.
Mysteries, belief in, honors God, 41; has Religion a right to teach them, 58; their use, 72; how consoling, 72; not contradictory, 74; Protestants afraid to analyze, 99.

NATIVE driver on immortality, 344.
Nature, a hard mistress, 260; knowledge of laws in spiritism, 378.
Nestorius, his denial of divinity of Christ, 101.
Newman, Cardinal, on power of God's grace and supernatural life, 147; Apologia, 312.
Nicodemus and Baptism, 109.
No-popery cry not used by Infidels, 174.
Novitiate of Religious orders, 116.
Nuns, how they build their schools, 121.

OAKLEY, Rev. Frederic, contradictory charges v. Catholic Church, 45; on Sacraments, 111; on Vocation to Religious life, 119.
Object of adoration something sensible, 96.
Offertory of the Mass, 97.
Omousios and Omoiousios, 269.
"Osmosis," its meaning, 345.
Original sin, effects of, 239; Calvin on, 238; Catholic doctrine on, 239.
Outward means of Grace taught by Christ, 107.

PAGANISM, wonders of, why believed, 372.
Pantheism, 337; its meaning, 338; what it amounts to, 338; what splendid Catholics they might be, 340; their eloquence, 341.
Pauperism, 194; a curse, 290; efforts of Catholic Church to relieve it, 291; objection on this, 290.
Papists believe anything, 163.
Parables of Gospel in reference to Church, 142.
Pelagians, zeal of Reformers against, 53, 232; their errors on grace, 271, 274.
Pentateuch, objections against, Exodus and, 326.
Period short for man's existence on earth, objection, 112.
Pérraud, Father's, sermon on Mgr. Darboy, 113.
Perrone, on Spiritism, 372.
Persecution, Catholic Church never persecuted, 49, 183.
Persian traditions, 363.
Pharisees, their cry, 27; piety of, 221, 234.
Philippine Islands colonized by Catholics, 292; Sir John Bowring's testimony, 292.
Physiology, little known to the many, 63.
Pilgrimages, use of, 186.
Planchette, 377.
Polemical disputation avoided in this book, 213.
Popery, in the notions of colonists, 160; denunciations of, 164; no-popery, 174.
Popes, said in some cases to be wicked, 145.
Pre-Adamite man, 318.
Preacher, what expected of him, 21.
Predestination, 246; Calvin's notions of, 254-256.
Preface of Christmas Day, 97.
Pride, temptation of, 30.
Priests and Religious not swayed by Pharisaical pride, 119.
Processions, 97.
Protestantism, Schleiermacher's view of it, 33; decline of, 396; - Lacordaire, 397.
Providence, Voltaire on, 261; check on Spiritism, 354.
Prussia, one third Catholic, 292; education in, 196.

Public penances and "experiences," 230.

"Quod nimis probat, nihil probat," 75.

RATIONALISTIC conceptions of Catholic Church, 173; Rationalism, its latest outcome, 30.
Realism, Harrison, 354; its latest view, 28.
Real presence, connection with Incarnation, 88; its difficulties, 89; not appreciated, 93; once the Faith of Christendom, 127, 389.
Reason and Instinct, 346.
Reign of terror, recent in Paris, 114.
Religion, common origin of, objection, 180; one as good as another, 302, 303.
Resurrection of Christ more clearly proved by sustained attacks, 365.
Revelation, has God spoken, 66.
Reverend teachers of error, 28.
Revivals, 245.
Ridicule, its influence, 316.
Rigor of Catholic doctrine no discouragement, 265.
Ritualism, 153.
Rock, Dr., 155.
Rock of Church, its perpetuity, 23, 326, 394.
Romans languid, insensible to danger, 70; Roman triumph and contrast, 392.
Roscoe, 146.

SACRAMENT, of penance, 95; definition of, 108; sacramental system, errors of Reformers, 110.
Saint Augustine, 290, 325, 382.
Saint Chrysostom, 149, 382.
Saint Clement, 128.
Saint Cyril, 130.
Saint Jerome, 135.
Saint Thomas, 382, 388.

Sacred Heart, can we worship it? 100, 386.
Salvation exclusive, 297.
Sanchoniathon, 323, 362.
Sanctification and justification, 228.
Schleiermacher, his view of Protestantism, 33.
Scientific research not opposed by Catholic Church, 175.
Scripture, summary of objections to, and principles of reply, 335.
"Scourge of God" in ruin of ancient Rome, 392.
Secchi, Father, 175.
Sentimental religion, objection to, not meant to be offensive, 388.
Sidgreaves and Perry, Fathers, 175.
Simon, M. Jules, his eloquent words on national decay, 32, 294.
Simplicity of Catholic worship, 151.
Smith, Dr., on Pentateuch, antiquity of writing, 323.
Society without God, 47.
Soul of the Church, 305; soul not material, 343.
Spalding, Bishop, on wealth and poverty, 287; unbelievers make common cause with Protestants, 293.
Spencer, Herbert, God hardening hearts, 259; worship of Humanity, 238.
Spinoza and Pantheism, 337.
Spiritism, 185, 187, 369; objection—belongs to dark ages, 369; temptations to, 369; why succeeds in America, 372; wonders of, 370; frauds detected, 371; explanations of young colonists, 375; lecture on, 373; Egyptian Hall and Slade, 372; proof of diabolical agency, 376; Planchette, 377; knowledge of laws of nature, 378; who can know them all, 378; produces good, 380; souls

of deceased, 381; not modern, 382; in Deuteronomy, 382.
Success, in Catholic sense, 122.
Switzerland, rich and poor Cantons, 286.

TABERNACLE and meeting-house, 152.
Temptation of Pride, 340.
Testament, old and new united, 326.
The Holy Ghost sensibly indicating His presence, a delusion, 171.
Thought not divisible, 347.
Traveller in Ireland, 247; colonial in Europe, 291.
Trinity, mystery explained to children, 56; Ingersoll on, 57; true doctrine of, 57.
Truth intolerant, 299.

VEDAS of Hindoos, 362.
Vincent of Lérins, on salvation of heretics, 311.
Vocation, Religious, 117; Father Oakley on, 119.

Voight, Professor, 146.
Voltaire, his disciples and their labors, 14; on Providence, 261, 323.

WHATELY, Archbishop, on Napoleon's existence, 324.
Wickliffe and Huss, false ideas of perfection, 143.
Wiseman, Cardinal, Exposition of Parables, 142; Lectures on Science and Revelation, 179.
Worldly-minded notions of Religious life, 249.
Worship, regulated by Divine ordinance, 154; Catholic, objections to, 157; attractive in Catholic Church, 158; unfolds sacramental system, 168; in early Christian times, 155; Apocalypse and Christian worship, 155; simplicity of, 150; Bingham on, 155; mode in Catacombs, 156; of Blessed Sacrament, 165; upholds the Sacraments, 168.

MEDITATIONS
FOR
EVERY DAY IN THE YEAR,

COLLECTED FROM DIFFERENT SPIRITUAL WRITERS

And Suited for the Practice Called

"𝕼𝖚𝖆𝖗𝖙𝖊𝖗 𝖔𝖋 𝖆𝖓 𝕳𝖔𝖚𝖗'𝖘 𝕾𝖔𝖑𝖎𝖙𝖚𝖉𝖊."

EDITED BY
REV. ROGER BAXTER, S. J.,
OF GEORGETOWN COLLEGE.

This book was first written in Latin, in 1639, by N. B. (an English religious), and handed around in manuscript for years, during the times of persecution in England, where it was used by many holy persons. It was translated into English in 1669 by Rev. E. Mico, and revised and modernized in 1822 by Rev. Roger Baxter, S. J., of Georgetown College. It is now republished and revised in the 251st year of Jesuit labor in the United States by REV. P. NEALE, S. J., of St. Inigo's, Md.

"*Recte novit vivere qui recte novis orare.*" "*He knows how to live well who knows how to pray well.*"—ST. AUGUSTINE.

"*Every day will I bless Thee: and I will praise Thy name forever, yea, for ever and ever.*"—Ps. cxlv. 2.

With a Letter of Approbation from
His Grace, Most Rev. JAMES GIBBONS, Archbishop of Baltimore.

12mo, Cloth, 512 Pages, - - $2.00.

BENZIGER BROTHERS, NEW YORK, CINCINNATI, AND ST. LOUIS.

A Great Success! Over 40,000 sold!

The Right Rev. Bishop of Erie writes: "These books must and should receive the name of

"The Catholic Family Library."

The Christian Father;
What he should be, and what he should do. With Prayers suitable to his condition. From the German by Rev. L. A. Lambert, Waterloo, N. Y. With an Introduction, by Rt. Rev. S. V. RYAN, D.D., C.M., Bishop of Buffalo.

Paper,.................25 cents | Cloth,........................50 cents
Maroquette,.........35 " | French Mor., flex., red edges, $1.00

The Christian Mother;
The Education of her Children and her Prayer. Translated by a Father of the Society of Jesus. With an Introduction by the Most Rev. JAMES GIBBONS, D.D., Archbishop of Baltimore.

Paper,.................25 cents | Cloth,........................50 cents
Maroquette,.........35 " | French Mor., flex., red edges, $1.00

A Sure Way to a Happy Marriage.
A Book of Instructions for those Betrothed and for Married People. Translated by Rev. Edward I. Taylor.

Paper,............ 30 cents | Maroquette, ...40 cents
Cloth,................................60 cents.

In token of my appreciation, I request you to forward me **A thousand (1000) copies** of each of the two former books, and **five hundred (500)** of the third for distribution among my people.
Yours faithfully in Christ,
✠ JAMES VINCENT CLEARY, *Bishop of Kingston.*

From the Pastoral Letters of Rt. Rev. M. J. O'FARRELL, D.D., Bishop of Trenton.

"For Parents we recommend 'THE CHRISTIAN FATHER' and 'THE CHRISTIAN MOTHER,' in which they will fully learn all their duties to their children." —*Pastoral,* 1883.

"We **strongly recommend for your perusal and serious consideration** two little books lately published; one is entitled 'A SURE WAY TO A HAPPY MARRIAGE,' and the other 'An Instruction on Mixed Marriages,' by the Rt. Rev. Dr. Ullathorne.—*Pastoral,* 1882.

Warmly recommended and approved by **Five (5) Archbishops** and **Twenty-one (21) Bishops,** as follows:

The Most Rev. Archbishops of
BALTIMORE, CINCINNATI, OREGON, TORONTO, Can., TUAM, Ireland.

The Right Rev. Bishops of
ALTON, GRASS VALLEY, LONDON, Can., NEWARK, ST. PAUL,
BUFFALO, KINGSTON, Can., MARQUETTE, OGDENSBURG, SAVANNAH,
COVINGTON, LA CROSSE, NATCHEZ, ST. CLOUD, TRENTON,
ERIE, LITTLE ROCK, N SQUALLY, ST. JOHN, N.B. VINCENNES,
WILMINGTON.

A Most Liberal Discount to those who order in Quantities.

BENZIGER BROTHERS, NEW YORK, CINCINNATI, AND ST. LOUIS.

www.ingramcontent.com/pod-product-compliance
Lightning Source LLC
Chambersburg PA
CBHW022117290426
44112CB00008B/710